A FAMILY IN EGYPT

A FAMILY
IN EGYPT

BY
MARY ROWLATT

ILLUSTRATED

The Hornbill Press
New York
2004

Revised Edition: September 2004
Copyright © 2004 Estate of Mary Rowlatt

Published by
The Hornbill Press
560 Riverside Drive
Suite 20-F
New York NY 10027

email: thehornbillpress@cs.com
web site: www.hornbillpress.com

Originally published: London, Robert Hale Ltd., 1956

Design and layout by Blair Cummock
Wester Press
St Boswells, Scotland

Text set in 11 pt Sabon
Printed on acid free paper

Cover painting by Elizabeth L. Brown
Cover photo: the author with Nurse Edith Mathews, Giza Pyramids, Egypt,
1910.

Library of Congress Control Number: 2003116693
ISBN 0-9706407-1-4

Printed in the United States of America

CONTENTS

ILLUSTRATIONS

AUTHOR'S NOTE

It is usual for authors of books which include transliterations of Arabic words, to make some comment on the method they employ. I have followed the well-known Ala Baballa System. By stating this plainly I hope to limit the field of scholarly criticism. Critics could, of course, condemn the whole system as bad. Perhaps they would be right. But then again . . . and on the other hand . . . It is a barren argument however and I will say no more on the subject.

I would like to record my thanks to Miss Marjorie Procter and to my uncle, Mr. J. E. Cornish, who have painstakingly corrected errors in the manuscript, and to the staff of the Alexandria Municipal Library for their whole-hearted help in searching their records of the past.

The following have kindly given me permission to quote: The Clarendon Press, Oxford, from *Egypt and the Army* by Lt-Col P. G. Elgood; Ivor Nicholson & Watson, Ltd., from *A Hundred Years' History of the P & O*, by Boyd Cable; J. M. Dent & Sons, Ltd., from *The Little Flowers of St. Francis*; and John Farquharson from *The Glory of the Pharaohs*, by Arthur Weigall. I am also grateful to the BBC, the editors of the *Contemporary Review*, *Everybody's*, and the *Asian Review* for permission to use some matter from articles of mine which they originally published; and finally to the Secretary of the Anglo-Egyptian Society for the re-use of part of a lecture given to members of that Society.

FOREWORD TO THE NEW EDITION BY
PENELOPE LIVELY

A FAMILY IN EGYPT is a fascinating reflection of life in Egypt over a period of a hundred and thirty years—culminating in the nineteen fifties and so, from the viewpoint of the early twenty-first century, a period piece. Episodic and idiosyncratic, it is also an oblique portrait of a woman—a person of humour, warmth, and infinite curiosity. Mary Rowlatt did not set out to write about herself—far from it—but the text is infused with that bracing personality, so that she lifts from the pages quite as vividly as the Egyptians of whom she writes and the place that she conjures up.

It is a vanished place, for the most part. Cairo and Alexandria of the early twentieth century are barely discernable beneath the concrete and the roaring traffic of today; all the more valuable, then, this testimony of another age. And of the preceding ages; the account of the Rowlatt family's five generation association with Egypt serves up some sharp and telling insights into the changing fortunes of the country, and also the role of foreigners. The book was of course written at a point when the relationship between Britain and Egypt was at a disastrously low point, in the time of the Suez crisis; it is all the more poignant to read of Mary Rowlatt's father's presence at the opening of the Suez Canal in 1869, as a little boy of four.

Frederick Rowlatt went on to become Governor of the National Bank of Egypt. Here, I should declare an interest; in 1930, my father, Roger Low, went to Cairo as a very young man to work as assistant to Sir Frederick Rowlatt's successor, Sir Edward Cook. I was born in Cairo three years later, and spent my childhood there until going to England at the end of the second World War. I too was a child who grew up to the sounds and smells of Cairo, whose family home had a garden in which there was a banyan tree with those aerial roots on which you could swing. I knew the name Rowlatt well; in Alexandria there was rue Arthur Rowlatt, along which I walked to the beach when my mother rented a villa there for the summer. And I have a vestigial memory of being taken to a children's tea-party in a beautiful garden, where the hostess was Lady Rowlatt—undoubtedly Zohria, the Rowlatt family home in Gezira.

The Rowlatt house in Alexandria was in Ramleh, a residential suburb of the city when I knew it as a child during the war —a place of elegant villas and of gardens filled with bougainvillea and poinsettias and zinnias and canna lilies and plumbago. When Arthur and Amelia Rowlatt were in Alexandria in the 1860's they used to move out to Ramleh in the summer, then five miles from the city, to pitch a tent among Bedouin neighbours. I was last in Alexandria in 1990. By then, the villas and gardens had been obliterated by a sea of low-rise apartment blocks. A hundred and fifty years, during which two successive landscapes have disappeared.

Egypt itself is another country. Rowlatt reminds us of a place in which bilharzia and trachoma were endemic, in which life expectancy for the *fellahin* stood at around forty. Her book is neither history nor sociology, but one of those intriguing unclassifiable works that often do more to illuminate a time and a place than any calculated enterprise. She simply wrote down what she knew, and what she remembered. The result is a very individual vision of a country and its people, and of what they meant to one family. It is excellent to see it given a new lease of life.

Penelope Lively

FOREWORD TO THE 1956 EDITION BY
SIR RALPH STEVENSON*

FEW people in England are so well qualified as is Miss Rowlatt to write the kind of book about Egypt that she has now produced. The close connection of her family with the country, stretching over five generations, has given her a background not only of knowledge but of feeling against which she has developed her own appreciation of Egypt and the Egyptians. Moreover she has obviously made excellent use of her periods of absence from the country to view it from a wider angle and thus to preserve a proper perspective. Her evident love of Egypt and its people has not blinded her to their human shortcomings nor has it caused her to exaggerate their achievements.

It is clearly a very different kind of feeling from the paternal—not to say patronising—affection for the "natives" which has too often been the basis of the attitude of our countrymen and women in the past, not excluding many honourable and upright people who have spent themselves without stint in the service of the Egyptian people. This affection was real and very deeply felt, I do not deny that for a moment, but it was hardly less galling to the patriotic young Egyptian of this century than the veiled, or scarcely veiled, contempt of the majority of Britons whose lot it was to serve in Egypt in two World Wars.

The long period of British tutelage and its piecemeal termination produced a relationship between the two countries of a curious kind, not wholly bad but far from good, in which it was, and still remains, difficult for either side to acknowledge its own defects and mistakes or to appreciate the other's qualities and achievements. A kindly and clear-sighted delineator of the Egyptian scene, as is Miss Rowlatt, can thus play a vital role, particularly at the present moment when more heat than light is being engendered in and about the Middle East in general, and when for the sake of our future relations with Egypt it is important for the people of Britain to understand not only the aims of the Egyptian Revolution but also the psychological and historical factors underlying it.

In writing of social welfare in Egypt, Miss Rowlatt says, " . . . the right ideas seem to be gaining ground even if it is uphill work; and in which country is it all on the level?" This applies, in my view, to much more than social welfare in Egypt at the present moment; and the gallant efforts of the young men who now govern the destinies of the country, to raise the moral and material standards of the people are worthy of our support, even though we may not always agree with their foreign policy.

RALPH SKRINE STEVENSON

* 1895-1977. British diplomat, former ambassador to Egypt.

INTRODUCTION

EGYPT is a much reported land. From Herodotus, via the great Arab historians and Napoleon's savants, to the present day, those who really know their subject have written in particular and in general on countless aspects of Egypt and her people. And behind the giants have trotted a light-hearted, light-headed company who, knowing little of Egypt, have committed much to paper. But, *mirabile dictu*, there is one aspect which, to my knowledge, has never been written by either category of authors.

It is Egypt as she appears to one of an English family whose lot has been cast in that land for a hundred and thirty years, to one born and brought up there as a child with the sense of four generations behind, and in constant and close touch as an adult.

The number of people to whom circumstances have given that outlook is limited, and in the just nature of things it is improbable that such circumstances will recur. For that reason I have recorded this tale.

The present is virtually non-existent for the writer. The moment just experienced is the past and that to come, the future; so the backward glance gives straight on to the forward look. Though the memories of my Egyptian childhood and youth are dear to me, there is nothing nostalgic about this account, for Egypt's future is alive with interest and possibilities. The dangers which threaten are variously seen by herself, her friends and her enemies, but a growing number of people is agreeing in what direction lie hope and a new life. This, too, I have portrayed as it appears to me.

1

SARAH AND AMELIA

WHEN approaching Egypt by ship, almost the first sign of her is the clouded water of the sea through which the vessel passes—"the riches rolled from the hundredfold mouth of the far-off Nile streaming beneath the waves. . . ."* Euripides knew of it, but according to him these milliard particles of Nile silt were swept out to sea as far as the island of Cyprus. Be that as it may, this phenomenon is still noticeable at some times of the year when one is nearing Port Said, almost before land is sighted.

The north coast of Egypt is so flat, that Port Said or Alexandria are nearly reached before it shows itself. Curious distorted shapes of miraged buildings and palms are first seen; then slowly the landscape heaves itself out of the sea and the outline of a harbour falls into shape.

The noise of the ship's engines slackens. Along the outer breakwater the sailing vessels of the Mediterranean ride at ease. They have changed little in form or function through the ages. The sponge fishers are there from the Greek islands, the melon boats which ply these waters with their beautiful green global freight, and the smaller fishing boats, whose crews hang up the nets to dry on the rigging, are there too. By day it is a gay, living scene; but pass along this breakwater by moonlight and they seem like mythical ships. Silently they dip and bow with the movement of the deep green water. One

* *The Bacchae of Euripides.* Translated by Gilbert Murray

17

rocks behind the other until, at the end of the line of moon-tipped masts, there gently floats the very ghost of a brigantine.

The approach to Egypt by air takes the traveller soaring high above the coast line, above the sea, its white frill and the yellow desert. Soon the crops and rich soil appear, offspring of the river. The Nile itself, broad and brown, is crossed, and Cairo lies ahead looking strangely fairy-like with its minarets just visible through a dove-coloured mist.

Flying this way by night, only one thing can be seen. Where the dark of the sea joins the dark of the desert and delta, there below, laid out on the black velvet, is a diamond necklace, a fitting adornment for Cleopatra herself. That necklace is her capital, the city of Alexandria, strung along the coast, beautiful and shapely.

In the early nineteenth century my great-great-grandparents, John and Sarah Friend, sailed into Alexandria harbour with their two daughters, Sarah and Mercy. This country was to be a second home to them and a number of their descendants for the next five generations.

The Alexandria they saw was the city so well described by early 19th century travellers. It was a fraction the size of the present one. All Europeans lived in a special quarter and the gates were shut at night. The narrow streets were filled with animals and humanity. Wealthy merchants in resplendent ancient dress rode horses with velvet trappings. Before them went servants belabouring the backs of all who blocked the way. Turkish women of position, wholly encased in veils, rode donkeys with such high and cushioned saddles that their feet rested on the donkeys' withers.

Mingled with this, slaves could be seen being led along by a purchaser or seller, and in those days the Bedwins in from the desert were armed with knives and pistols. The plague was still a regular visitor to Egypt of the eighteen-twenties.

Alexandria is now a city of a million people, with large squares, fine streets, and for miles along the coast runs a Corniche road which is certainly the finest of its sort on the

Mediterranean. Yet here and there in the midst of the modernity there are links with the past. The last view I had of Alexandria was in the summer of 1955—some hundred and thirty years after my great-great-grandparents first rode through the streets. It was an everyday summer evening.

When the sundown breeze floats in from the sea, the populace leave their workshops and homes. They stream into the open squares, and wherever a patch of grass can be found they sit themselves upon it and prepare to enjoy the cool of the evening in family manner.

There is a wonderful mixture of Oriental and European dress (American would be more accurate as far as the men are concerned). Many small boys and their elders sport highly-coloured shirts of the square pattern made to hang outside the trousers. Though some fifty per cent of the older men present still wear the comfortable galabia, the percentage of younger men in native dress is less. None of the ladies of the party is veiled but many wear the black drapery over the top of the head hanging down almost to the ground behind.

Whole family circles sit cross-legged in a ring gaily chattering as they eat roasted monkey nuts, salted almonds and dried melon seeds. In and out of this thick parterre of population the vendors of such edibles pick their way. Some sell biscuit rings covered with sesame seeds which are threaded hoop-la fashion on sticks protruding from the rim of a round basket. Nearby is a smart handcart for selling ices, with its name painted thereon in Arabic and French, "Le Nouveau Régime." Did the owner consciously argue that no matter who rose and fell from power, his conveyance need not alter its name?

Other drinks are sold by a perambulating salesman who carries the whole paraphernalia on his person. A huge, long-spouted jug containing a form of sherbert is strapped round his shoulder and waist, often topped by a lump of ice and decorated with jingling brass. On the other side of his belt are the glasses neatly fitted in a case. He announces his approach by using two brass saucers as castanets most deftly with his free hand. The seller of such drinks has a bright coloured cloth from hip to knees wound over his other clothes. He was certainly selling the same drinks in the same fashion when Mohamed Ali was the Nouveau Régime and possibly so when the great Saladin filled that role.

Just as one is indulging in such reflections, on go the neon lights, trams clatter to the left, buses rattle to the right, and the twentieth-century crowds in upon the scene. It is a gay sight and noisy. Yet, in the middle of the hubbub, on a lawn as thickly beset with people as Brighton beach on holiday, a space is cleared, clean matting is now spread, and the leader of the evening prayer stands forth. Some sixty men of all sorts stroll over from among the crowds and take their place behind him in solemn and reverent prayer according to the Prophet Mohamed's instructions thirteen hundred years ago. The prayer leader is not a greybeard in flowing robes. He wears a yellow shirt (possibly nylon) and grey flannel trousers.

At the same time and round about run the small girls and boys, including that group known in England as "mixed infants". They career round in a high state of animation and enjoyment. In one popular square the old Nationalist leader, Saad Zaghloul, high on his granite plinth, presides over the scene. The sculptor has shown him complete in tarboush and overcoat ready for a winter day, one foot forward and one fist clenched as if about to emphasise a point to the crowds of Egyptians who during his lifetime so hung on his every word. What power he had to rouse emotion, and how he fought for what, rightly or wrongly, he considered to be the dues of Egypt!

My great-great-grandfather, John Friend, was a member of a merchant shipping firm which had had the concession for transporting Egyptian corn across to Wellington's troops in the Peninsula. His laden ships cut through the Mediterranean blue with the stiff south-east wind in their sails, while his family spent a happy, simple life, living during the summer in

tents along the seashore between Alexandria and Aboukir
Bay. Here the masts of the French warships still stood silently
out of the sea, with their timber hulls on the sand below the
shimmering water, where Nelson's men had laid them to rest
on 1st August, 1798. The *Guerrier,* the *Aquilon,* the
Souverain Peuple.

Sarah the daughter tells, too, of the relics she used to find
scattered in the sand from General Abercromby's brave offen-
sive in 1801, which finally dispossessed the French of Egypt
but which cost him his life, for he was mortally wounded.
Cannon-balls lay around the family's tents, and buttons off
uniforms were often found. There was one gravestone. "The
piece of granite on which the name of Captain Dutton was cut
out very roughly," Sarah wrote, "I missed for some time, but
afterwards found it about half a mile off on the top of a high
mound placed over the grave of a Bedwin with the name
downwards. Of course we did not offend them by removing
the stone."

The Friend family had a young African servant of slave
origin who regretfully had to leave them and return to the
town, because he was so much disturbed nightly by the ghosts
of French and English soldiers continuing their battle right up
to daybreak, he affirmed.

All that battle-ground, and the semi-desert area over which
the young Sarah wandered shooting quail (for she was a
sportswoman) is now covered with the thickly populated
suburb of Ramleh, with its villas and flats, tramways and
cafés.

In 1830 the daughter Sarah married Sidney Terry of the old
Levant trading firm of Briggs and Company, who were known
as "Agents to H.H. the Pasha", Mohamed Ali the Great, with
whom Sidney Terry often had interviews. So her early married
life was spent happily in and around Alexandria, and there
her four surviving children were born and three babies buried.

At least one broken heart appears to have been left behind
in England when Sarah married, for a certain Mr. W.

Courthope of Camberwell Grove was moved to write these verses on May 17, 1830:

> Has thick Egyptian darkness then enclosed
> The Star of beauty that was wont to shine
> With sweetest beam diffusing health and light,
> And softened radiance on the admiring world?
> Yet though to us the World be wrapped in gloom
> Dark and portentious as when Moses stretched
> His powerful rod o'er impious Pharaoh's realm;
> Still midst the desolation is preserved
> A land of Goshen where concentred all
> Its dazzling rays, by "Love's own burning glass"
> It shines on more than earthly Paradise;
> And Sidney Terry, of this spot possessed,
> If here below man can be, he is blest.

In different vein were the feelings of the following gentleman:

"Thos. Gale presents his best wishes and congratulations to his old friend Mrs. Sidney Terry on her marriage. . . . It has occurred to T.G. that as religious works may be difficult to procure in Alexandria, the writings of Newton who was an eminent Christian may not be unacceptable, he therefore hopes Mrs. Terry will do him the favour to accept the above-named book as a slight token of his esteem and regard. Religion certainly is a subject that deserves the serious consideration of every reasonable creature, as it is connected with our brightest pleasure and satisfaction now, as well as our happiness in a future state. T.G. assures himself that this is Mrs. Terry's opinion as well as his own."

Sarah's sister, Mercy, also settled in Egypt where she married Peter Taylor of Taylor & Co., a business firm whose headquarters were in Alexandria. In 1857 he appears as one of the founder-members of the Egyptian Society, a fore-runner, in a sense, of the present well known Anglo-Egyptian Society, now presided over by the Egyptian Ambassador in London. The list of members of the Egyptian Society in 1845 contains such names as the Marquess of Northampton, the Earl of Aberdeen, E. W. Lane author of *Manners and Customs of the Modern Egyptians*, Robert Hay, the artist, le Marquis de la Valette, Doctor Clot Bey after whom a quarter of Cairo is still named, and Soliman Pasha originally a French soldier of fortune who settled in Egypt, became a Moslem and married into the late Royal Family of Egypt. His statue in Midan Soliman Pasha is well known today to all who visit Cairo.

Both Sarah and Mercy inherited from their parents a deep love and understanding of the Egyptians among whom they made their home. The wife of a Bedwin sheikh whose tents were close to theirs became very ill one year. Sarah went day after day till she had nursed the sick woman back to health. As I write I wear a six-stranded seed pearl necklace which the Bedwin sheikh insisted on Sarah accepting to show his grati-tude for her care. The necklace has a pearl-studded clasp containing a lock of hair—whose, and how the sheikh came by it, we shall never know, which perhaps is just as well. It was quite likely loot from the French at Aboukir Bay.

Although Sarah was obviously most genuinely fond of the ordinary people of the land, she had no sentimental blindness where they were concerned, as is shown by a remark in her letters: "Fatima's son is not dead, though she asked me for money to bury him."

She used to write down little incidents and tales she learnt from the country people. "One day being out walking by the side of a Bedwin Arab," she recounted, "I picked up the tobe or skin of a snake (tobe is the name of the outer garment worn by the Arab male and female). He told me, 'If you wish to get the skins of the very large ones, come out and search on Thursday afternoons or Fridays before twelve, as snakes are obliged to wander during that time and if attacked are easily killed, as the Shaittan, or Evil One, has no power to assist them during the hours of the Crucifixion of Saidna Issa our Lord Jesus).'

"They always speak of our Saviour with the greatest respect, and many bow when mentioning Him or Sitti Miriam, the Virgin Mary," Sarah continues. "They make pilgrimages to Jerusalem when they have been first to Mecca, and can afford to do so. One Thursday, when riding in a narrow path, my donkey started back and would not proceed. I saw a Cobra Capella before me and the Sais told me the same story." I often wonder if my great-grandmother stood quietly by in the presence of the hooded cobra to listen to the groom's story, or whether, Thursday or no Thursday, they fled first.

Sarah also wrote poems about the various traditions she heard speak of in conversation with the neighbouring people. One tells of how the spirits of the dead return to their graves on Thursdays and Fridays leaving the abode of the blest in Jerusalem to meet their living families in the cemeteries. Another recounts the Arab saying that when it rains the angels are weeping for the sins of men. And a longer epic effort tells of the tradition that the fifty days khamseen season of hot winds in Egypt, is the anniversary of the fifty days during which Cain carried the body of his murdered brother Abel from place to place seeking where he might bury it.

Sarah and Sidney Terry's elder daughter Amelia was left behind in England at boarding school in 1842. Extracts from her mother's letters to her show what a love of Egypt the mother and her eight-year-old child both had. "All the donkey boys and people ask, 'Fen Sitti Amina?' ['Where is our lady Amelia?'] and the servants send you many salaams." "Amina" is a well-known girl's name in Arabic and "Amelia" was too near a version of it for them to differentiate between the two. "The servants all send 'salaams keteer,' especially Abdullah and even old Miriam. Atab kisses your hand."

Her mother lost no opportunity of sending Amelia little things to remind her of her Egyptian home, usually in charge of P & O captains—dates, pistachio nuts, shells—and once a ring for her finger, of which she writes: "The latter is of very little value, but you will like it for being of Egyptian manufacture."

Obviously the mistress in charge of the Young Ladies' Establishment, where Amelia resided in London, had rather an Anglo-Saxon suspicion of foreign food, for Sarah writes, "Tell Miss Farenden the dates and pistachio nuts are both very wholesome. I wish I had something better to send you. Whenever I go to Cairo I will endeavour to find some little trifle." Many are the messages that are sent from Mahboubah, their Egyptian nurse. The children were not only looked after but fed as babies by Egyptian women.

Amelia sadly missed her home in Egypt, her parents and sister and brothers, but her mother assured her that it was for her own good that they had consented to part with her. "Believe me, my dear Amelia," she wrote, "it was a very great trial both to Papa and myself to leave you behind us, and it was only our great love for you that made us decide upon doing so, that we may, please God, have the happiness in a short time of having you back a well-informed and genteel girl."

But in the meantime the would-be genteel little girl must have longed to return and play with her younger sister, Mary, and two small brothers. "Mary after saying her lessons runs wild for the rest of the day," writes her mother, "since I have allowed her to be always in the yard or the terrace, she has had no return of fever, but is sadly sunburnt. The children ride on donkeys and as there is no plague at present, they can do so every day!" In spite of this the letters often bear the stamp "Purifié au Lazaret. Malta." "Your pony never goes out except with the Sais. I am afraid to ride him."

Sarah urges her little girl not to forget the wider experiences she had gained from living in Egypt: "I think you may refresh your memory and amuse your young friends these long evenings by telling them what you have seen, for there are few little girls of nine years of age who have seen Cairo, Alexandria, Malta, Naples, the ruins of Pompeii, St. Paul's Cave at Malta, the Pyramids, Pompey's Pillar, the church (Coptic church) where the Virgin Mary hid herself with our Saviour as an infant, or have dined in the desert with a Bedwin sheikh, have been at Greek, Jewish and Coptic weddings and christenings. You must not forget these things as they will interest you and assist you when reading to remember what you study.

"Next Easter I hope to find poor little Mary getting on well with yourself [a threat which never materialised], under the kind care of your dear friends the Misses Farenden to whom you ought to feel very grateful for having the patience and kindness to take charge of such little ignorant girls. . . . Anatasio having just appeared with the eggs and cakes, the children have both run off to distribute some amongst the servants as you were accustomed to do. Dear little Frederick is growing very fast, he has cut six teeth without suffering and is always with the Sais, donkeys and sheep. Your Papa has just gone down to see the Pasha [Mohamed Ali the Great] so I must close this without his part. I have sent the children over to the seaside to collect shells for you which I will send to you one of these days for shell work. There is a Mr. White here from Waghorn's 'house,' in London, who will take charge of anything for you."

Another time Sarah writes, "Your Papa started for Cairo on Thursday by steamer and although he was twenty-four hours in Cairo was home Sunday evening, a very quick passage. He took Sidney with him [then three years old], who was extremely good and contented, but on arriving there he looked about at the hotel and bursting into tears exclaimed, 'I came to see Amelia. Where is Amelia?' When your Papa said she was in England he said, 'Let me go to England, I want to kiss her.'" They were probably staying at Mr. Shepheard's hotel which he had founded the year before, in 1841, and which was then called the New British Hotel. This name however soon fell away and it became known as Shepheard's.

A letter to Amelia in 1843 contains this comic small picture. "Mrs. Lyons [the wife of a P & O captain] has lost her little dog and they had it put in a box and buried it in Mr. Larking's garden. The Janissary walked behind with his silver stick and the servants, Williams and Fanny, walked behind, both crying." It was in an outhouse of this same garden ten years later that Richard Burton, the traveller, lodged in disguise, at the start of his famous journey to Mecca and Medina. "Having been invited to start from the house of a kind friend, John Wingfield Larking . . . the better to blind inquisitive eyes of servants and visitors, my friend Larking lodged me in an outhouse."*

In later years my grandmother told Burton that she would recognise him in disguise anywhere. One day, when he was not expected in the neighbourhood, Amelia came to her husband and said that there was a beggar at the back door who, for once, she was failing to get rid of, and she needed help. Burton had won his point.

* R. F. Burton, *Personal Narrative of a Pilgrimage to El Medinah and Meccah.* Longmans, Brown, Green & Longmans; 1855.

Pyramids: Pencil sketch by Miss Fraser

2

AMELIA AND ARTHUR

IN the year 1843, Sidney Terry, a man of sudden impulses, decided to leave Egypt and join a trading firm in Bombay— "to my great surprise," commented his long-suffering but devoted wife. "Many tears were shed by all the old servants," she writes to Amelia. "Indeed I could not but feel grateful to see the regard with which all our old friends parted with us. I was the oldest established Englishwoman in Alexandria and certainly felt it a painful task to leave. . . . The clerks have lost a kind friend in your father and they will feel his loss—as will many a poor Bedwin. I feel a strong presentiment that I shall once more drink of the waters of the Nile."

Sarah and the children waited in Malta while Sidney went ahead to Bombay. "Freddy is a very sweet fellow," writes Sarah, "and feels so much that his father is away. He crawls to his picture and offers it bread and says 'Taala, Taala, Papa!'" [the Arabic word for "Come"]. Back in Alexandria there were many who missed them sadly. "Our dear old bouab goes after the arrival of every steamer . . . and asks after us. He cries very much when he talks of Sidney, as does Mahboubah."

Sidney wrote thus to his wife, as he journeyed from Malta to India via the overland route, "Briggs' bouab, Hassanein, our last Sais and Hassan all came to salaam me. I have not seen Abdullah but hear that he is somewhere in Cairo. Mr. Briggs is at Cairo but I have not seen him nor any other acquaintances excepting some poor Arabs who seemed glad to see me again. ... I start this evening for Suez in good health but not in good spirits." A few days later: "My thoughts are never away from you and at night when I turn my eyes to the Heavens and look upon my favourite Constellation, Orion, I fancy that you are at the same time regarding it and thinking of me. I left Cairo at a quarter before nine on the evening of the 21st, and arrived at Suez at half past six the following evening in one of the Transit Carriages. [A journey of some eighty miles.] . . . The Governor of Hong Kong [a fellow passenger on the ship from Suez] has drawn out a complaint signed by himself and part of the passengers on board for insertion in *The Times* against the Egyptian Transit Company. I have not signed it though I heartily concur in its statement. All the Bombay passengers were sent off from Alexandria without the least attention paid to their comfort and were huddled on board the steamer like cattle or slaves without even sitting room. We were therefore obliged to sit up two nights." This being twenty-five years before Port Said existed, the journey to Suez started with the lap from Alexandria to Cairo by Nile ship. "Bad provisions. Wine also of the commonest description. For a bottle of common wine which they dignified by the name of Claret they charged me fr.30."

This was just after Waghorn had given up organising the transit arrangements and before the P & O had made big improvements.

"The number of stations for the changing of horses and refreshment of travellers had been increased with changes of horses every five or six miles. . . . The horse-drawn carriage held six passengers who sat three a side on narrow knife-board seats, knees touching knees, backs bowed to fit the curve of the arched canvas cover. The horses were high-spirited Arab steeds hardly broken to harness. The normal procedure was for the snorting restless beasts to be held by the head with a groom to each. . . . Then at the word 'Go' the horses made a frantic leap forward and tried to race each other over the desert. Leaving towns like Cairo and Suez, a footman or two hung onto the back of the omnibus ready to come into action if the frantic horses ditched the vehicle. . . . Some of the passengers thoroughly enjoyed this circus act, others did not and wrote the Company accordingly." (*A Hundred Years' History of the P & O* by Boyd Cable.)

In 1845 Mohamed Ali took over the transit arrangements as a government concern. But uncomfortable conditions still prevailed when Sarah with Mary, her two little sons, and an Egyptian nurse set forth on the same journey to India.

After the freer and more natural life of Alexandria, some aspects of Bombay society grated on the Terrys' spirits. "I do admire Bombay," writes Sarah, " all but the people—that is the lazy, cold, proud English. No wonder they get sick when they lounge about all day with about twenty servants to wait on them." Her husband shared her view. "I cannot fancy the idea of having a lot of idle servants about me and am therefore thinking of writing to Alexandria to inquire if Abdullah would come to me. His passage would only cost five pounds and he would do the work of three of these idle servants. . . . The system of keeping so many servants is very ridiculous ... it has all originated from the indolence of the English residents, some of whom have servants to put on their stockings. I am only surprised that they do not keep servants to masticate their food for them."

Through these Bombay years, the Terrys' touch with Egypt was never broken, for Amelia was taken away from school in London, through ill-health, and went to live in Alexandria with her Aunt Mercy Taylor, who, having no children of her own, had offered to bring her up.

As an old lady, Amelia used to tell how she recovered her health and her spirits when, as a child of twelve, she returned to Egypt. Her uncle and aunt often travelled up to Cairo on their Nile boat or dahabiya. It was anchored off the island of Roda and here she used to wander about all day among the fields, talking to the peasants and amusing herself by making

little clay models of the shaduf and the saqia, old Egyptian
irrigation devices still seen today and dating from ages long
past. There, among the berseem crops, the buffaloes, and the
kindly Egyptians, Miss Farenden's establishment with its lady-
like accomplishments seemed to her happily far away.

Sarah and Amelia kept up a steady correspondence, and the
mother frequently requested Amelia to send her homely Egyptian vegetable seeds to grow in the Bombay garden—
mulukhia, durra, and so on. Nor did Sarah forget her Arabic,
for she had taken with her Bedawia, the Egyptian nurse, and
of course spoke to her always in Arabic; in fact, her letters to
her daughter often include Arabic expressions. When it was
decided in Egypt that Bedawia should accompany them, she
was told to go and buy herself something suitable into which
to pack her belongings. She returned with a vast coffer of solid
wood which must have been most inconvenient on the
journey, especially the overland route from Cairo to Suez
across the eighty miles of desert in a little open carriage, or on
camel back. But it was presumably too late to exchange it for
a more reasonable piece of luggage, the proof being that
Bedawia's box still exists in our family and is useful for
storing blankets.

Sarah also mentions during this time in Bombay that she
started studying the Kuran and found it most interesting. But
she sorely missed the friendly, human life of Egypt in touch
with the land and the inhabitants. "People here are so dread-
fully formal," she tells her sister, "it is a pain to ask or to be
asked out to dinner. ... I am sick of the sight of the carriage, a
walk would be a treat, I shall forget the use of my legs."

However, not being in Government service there were a few
formalities they could avoid. "We take a drive at railroad
speed every evening, sometimes going eight or nine miles
round. Our coachman will not be passed, and he says he
would rather have his ten rupees from us than fifteen from
anyone in Government pay, as he now can *drive past the
Governor* and then turn round and look at him, while all the

officers in their fine red jackets must creep behind his carriage."

Sarah's hope that she would once more visit Egypt was soon to come true, though under sad circumstances. Her erratic but charming husband, to whom she was deeply devoted, died of cholera at the age of forty-six in December, 1847. Sarah left Bombay immediately with her three small children, stopping in Egypt just long enough to pick up Amelia, and continued her journey to settle near her brother and others of the family in Kent. From there she wrote nostalgically:

> "That camel bell, that camel bell,
>   In memory I hear it well,
>   From Alexandria to the Bay
>   Where gallant Nelson's 'Vanguard' lay.
>   And so it is though we are gone
>   That camel bell still tinkles on,
>   Yet still in dreams we haunt the scene,
>   The tents, the trees, where we have been.
>   Those who have trodden on Egypt's ground
>   And tasted the waters of the Nile,
>   By some latent spell are always found
>   To return to its shores awhile.
>   There's a charm that hangs o'er that ancient land,
>   What it is I cannot tell,
>   With its wavy date tree and glittering sand,
>   That binds with a mystic spell."

She herself never returned, but died in Kent, still in her early forties.

The link with Egypt was not broken, however, for after a year or two in England Amelia returned to live again with her Uncle and Aunt Taylor in Alexandria. So letters went backward and forward as frequently as ever, with requests for members of the family now in England for this, that and the other of Egyptian odds and ends, from vegetable seeds and a kind of fibre called leefa with which to wash dishes, to ancient Egyptian mummies and a piece of the Virgin's tree from Mataria, which duly arrived. "If you go to any interesting spots, get a bit of something for the Egyptian Drawer," one of them writes.

Amelia's diary of this time contains some allusions to the ruling Turkish families of the day, but they are not exactly intimate on either side. "Intended to go to Hareem after dinner but . . . advised not to go as Zenab Hanem was there and she is very stiff. . . . We drove to Shoubra but we could not enter the gardens as Halim Pasha's Hareem there."

"After dinner went to Citadel to see the Princess. Chief black wished to send us back, saying Princess was out. Hassan Pasha's wife there and another Turkish lady." They were taken over the al Maka Palace, "a great mixture of beauty and costliness, dirt and untidyness."

With some of the entourage of the palaces, however, they were very friendly. They took outings with young Mr. Basset who was tutor to the seven-year-old Toussoun; "and the Hekekyans we much visited." Hekekyan Bey had been one of the children chosen by Mohamed Ali to be educated in England and who were then placed in positions of responsibility in Egypt where their learning could be used to advantage. Mohamed Ali himself could not read or write till he was over forty, but he had the foresight to demand a high standard of instruction for those whom he chose to be thus educated. Hekekyan as a boy had to master an immense range of subjects.

Many are the touches in letters and papers from Sarah in England, showing how part of her heart was ever in Egypt. Her old blind Uncle Matthew Friend wrote a long elegiac poem on her death:

> " . . . Nor can my busy thought forget the time,
>   When we would converse hold on Egypt's classic land,

And pleased, compare the tongue
Of swarthy Ishmael's race
With that of Sarah's favoured progeny . . ."

They would sit together by the hour talking of Egypt, comparing Arabic and Hebrew. Matthew Friend and his brother, William, had been young Royal Naval officers serving in Nelson's Mediterranean fleet against the French. William was a midshipman in the *Bellerophon* the year before she made her historic voyage with Bonaparte aboard as a prisoner.

Sarah had not been unhappy in England, however, for two reasons. One was her faith in God. She believed in divine guidance and went where she felt she was meant to be; and the presence of God was very real to her.

The other reason was that, like her parents before her and the three generations which followed her, simultaneously with a deep feeling for Egypt and the Egyptians, there existed in her heart a true and sincere love for England. Even in those days Egypt was so placed that a vital touch could reasonably be kept with both countries. Now, Cairo to London is a matter of hours. Sarah Terry jokingly foresaw this, and in a spirited rhyme, written in 1853, she says:

" In another ten years such wonders will there be,
We shall go and dine in Egypt and then come home for
tea",

wherein she was a bit over-optimistic. But though, to modern ideas, the journey was complicated over a hundred years ago, yet it never deterred my forbears. They made it frequently.

It is quite healthy to remind oneself sometimes just how uncomfortable it was, and with what little concern they attacked it. Here is Sarah writing to Amelia in 1842.

"We left at six o'clock Tuesday and arrived at Havre at six o'clock Wednesday morning. We had a most awful night, wind, rain and a very heavy sea which knocked the steamer about sadly. Your Papa was obliged to be with the gentlemen in one cabin and as the waves washed over the deck I was obliged to go below. The ladies' cabin was hot and the ladies sick so that at last I became exceedingly ill, and for the first time in my life was as seasick as I have seen others. We went to several Inns but all were very dirty. We took the best and at twelve we got some soup and slept for an hour or two. It poured hard with rain but we took a walk through Havre. At six in the evening we started in the only place we could get, the Cabriolet of the Diligence (Miss Farenden will describe it to you). We had had enough of steamers and travelled eighteen hours, that was till twelve next day. The only refreshment we could get were some pears and a piece of bread I had in my basket.

"We arrived at Rouen at midnight. We are at a very comfortable Inn here (Paris), and make the best of our time as we must leave Tuesday to enable us to meet the Mail on the 9th."

Continued later, from Marseilles: "At last, my dear child, we are so far towards home, we unfortunately arrived just too late for the steamer that has taken the Mail on to meet the *Great Liverpool*, so that we must go by French steamer tomorrow and shall be as long getting to Egypt as we were from thence to England. However we shall pass an hour or two at Leghorn, Genoa, Naples, Malta and Syra, which will in some degree repay us for the dirt and misery of a French vessel. We went from Paris by the Diligence and were riding thirty-six hours and arrived at Chalons at five o'clock in the morning, went immediately on board the steamer and down the Saône to Lyons where we slept. The next morning we arose at three o'clock and went on board the steamer and arrived at Avignon in the evening. Tomorrow we leave at five in the evening in the *Danté*, the same boat you went over to Naples in, I hope we may have better weather."

They arrived safely in Alexandria on October 23 and on November 16 Sarah Terry's fourth baby was born; however, the whole trip was apparently enjoyed.

A journey the following year was considered rather inconvenient in parts:

"There being a very heavy swell, the children and nurse were all seasick before the pilot had left us. The next day both children, baby and myself were all attacked with violent inflammation of the eyes. At Syra there was some new regulation in the Maritime Department, and we were landed in the evening in a leaky boat at the lazaretto, all wet through up to our waists. I could not see at all. We passed a wretched night, all sleeping on the floor in one small room.

"They wished to keep us fourteen days, but your Papa insisted upon our going on, and obliged them to take us."

Modern passport queues, altercations with authorities and inconvenient inoculations take on a less grim aspect when viewed in comparison to a night on the floor of a Levantine lazaretto, most of the party having ophthalmia.

The last relics of the lazaretto scheme hung on in some places into my lifetime, but mercifully much simplified. At Marseilles a crabbed individual used to come round the ship carrying the forebear of a flit gun with which he was supposed thoroughly to disinfect the cabins before people and luggage were allowed on shore. An Englishman busy packing in his cabin refused entry to this gentleman who stood outside protesting that the law must be fulfilled, public health protected, modern methods upheld, etc. "Oh, all right," said the Englishman, "fumigate that." He stuck an arm out of the cabin door dangling a single sock at Hippocrates without, who aimed a drop or two of liquid at it and, quite satisfied, moved on.

Each piece of heavy luggage had the label stuck on it, "Pestifère," an ominous word, but the tension did not last long. It was trundled down the gangway where an old Frenchman squirted some disinfectant on to the trunk. A few yards further on a still older Frenchman triumphantly slapped a label on it inscribed, "Purifié a Marseilles." We were pariahs no longer.

After Sarah Terry's death in Kent, her mother, old Sarah Friend, was amongst those who kept the close link between England and Egypt by writing lively letters to her grandchild, Amelia, in Alexandria, now a young woman of twenty-one. "I have always forgotten to thank you for the Arab basket, I really longed for one. I hope you will go to the Ball but do not lose your heart to one of the dashing officers of the Tenth as they are going to the Crimea—suppose you know *Mr. Bruce* has left for Corfu, something *may* bring *him* to Alexandria. What is to be, shall be. With my love, believe me, my dear Amelia, ever your affectionate Grandmother."

But Amelia's grandmother was backing the wrong horse. Even as she was penning these lines to her granddaughter, a widower of thirty-five was contemplating leaving England to take up a post in the Bank of Egypt in Alexandria, where England already had considerable financial interests. He had held a responsible position in the Bank of England and had lately suffered the death of both his wife and his only child.

The Bank of England directors offered him this appointment abroad, thinking that he would competently fill the post and that it would also help him to forget his sorrows. His name was Arthur Rowlatt.

It was not until five years after his arrival in Egypt that Arthur Rowlatt finally married Amelia Terry. He came slowly to the point. The wags of Alexandria had been saying for some time that he obviously wished to Ameliarate his position, but was Terryfied to do so. Anyhow on May 9, 1860, they were married quietly in the English church of St. Mark's in Alexandria.

For their honeymoon they were lent a Nile boat in which they drifted and sailed down the Mahmoudiah Canal and the branch of the Nile leading to Rosetta. Often they stopped and walked in fields by the banks, among the corn and rice. The evening scent of Egyptian fields must have made Amelia's heart pound with joy as it had her mother's and grandmother's before her and would her son's and granddaughter's after her. The lightest of mists rises and the smoke from the evening meal goes straight up from the little homes in the still air. The peasant children lead home the cattle at this hour. On the high dykes between the fields they make a moving fresco against the evening sky, which can be any colour from a burnished silvery green to a volcanic rust red. But silver, green or red, all fade imperceptibly into the blue-black of night, with stars scattered like sequins on its surface.

The smallest Egyptian child in these evening processions seems often to be in charge of the largest animal, usually a huge water buffalo. If obstreperous, the animal is addressed in the tones of an infant sergeant-major and in terms which would startle most sergeant-majors. A small fist is thumped into the beast's leg as high up as a four-year-old can reach, and great oaths directed at it. The buffalo usually obeys, laboriously returning on to the path out of the field where it has strayed for an illegitimate bite. If the buffalo, or gamousa as it is called, is in an easy-going mood, its small guardian is often to be seen asleep on the animal's hind quarters. An old and skinny gamousa has almost a cradle between its backbone and the large thigh bones which stick up on the outer sides. These gamousas sometimes have an irregular patch of white hair on their pates which give them the look of decrepit barristers with wigs awry.

In the spring and summer, the very young animals gallivant freely to left and right of the homeward procession. The small white camels with spindle legs are the best behaved and rarely leave their mother's sides, but the little donkeys, which in Egypt for some reason have their ears tied together at the top, dart off all over the neighbouring fields, looking like large white moths in the gathering dusk.

Some young man or child in the party will usually be singing a reed-like love song or an epic of the doings of a mythical hero such as Antar. The scene has great peace and beauty and there is happiness there in spite of poverty.

Arthur and Amelia wrote of throwing little coins to the

children on the banks who helped to tow the boat. They wrote, too, about visiting gardens en route and picking flowers, probably bunches of jasmine, whose white blossoms can scent an Egyptian scene far and wide. The specially Egyptian briar rose grows there too, in great thick hedges besides the dusty paths. It is rather larger than our dog-rose and is white with a bunch of long golden stamens in the centre. What charm there is in the old gardens of date palms and orange trees! Down alleyways of soft warm dust the citrus fruit hangs peacefully on the trees like Andrew Marvell's "golden lamps in a green night." Or, in the spring, the heavy orange blossom scent drenches everything around as actually, it almost seems, as the silver moonlight bathes the whole scene. For it is at night that the scent is strongest.

Amelia notes in her diary how amusing was the men's song as they rowed and sang all night. The river sailors probably invented words to their song with a direct bearing on the young couple of whom they were in charge. The Egyptian workman is a past-master at doing that sort of thing with humour and affection, if he is in the mood and feels that it will be appreciated.

They sometimes use these impromptu songs for other reasons. A certain Egyptologist, when in charge of excavations, used to get stray tourists poking about while his men were at work excavating. Though the most patient and hospitable of men, there were times when he felt that over-inquisitive and unheralded tourists interfered with the gang at work. If he was at another part of the dig and his workmen saw one of these individuals getting suspiciously near, they would start a chant as they worked, and with impromptu rhythmic words inform their master of what was happening. "He's coming too near—he looks suspicious—three ladies are in the party—they are poking with their sticks—you had better come quickly—" such phrases as these would float across the desert air, all woven into song, while the subjects of the running commentary would stand by, smiling delightedly at the music and quite unaware of its meaning.

The Rowlatts lived over the Bank in Alexandria during the winter and in the summer moved into tents on the seashore eastwards, as Amelia had done when a child, and her mother before her. A little railway now ran out to Ramleh where they pitched their tents. The conveyance was sometimes a small steam train and sometimes nothing more than a tram drawn by horses or mules. (When this line was first installed, some mules were imported for their strength, all the way from Abyssinia.) The rest of the journey was done on donkeys, to the sea's edge.

It must have been a pleasant life, though rather lonely sometimes for the wife when her husband was at work all day. But Amelia obviously enjoyed it and felt quite at home and safe with her two Egyptian servants and the neighbouring Bedwin tents. There were other English families in tents, too, at no great distance for visits on donkey or horseback.

Her diary is full of short sentences. "Saddled the pony and rode to Flemings' tents." (Fleming is now the name of a tram station on this spot.) "Pony escaped, much annoyed at it, however, he was found afterwards by Bedwins far away. I read some of Hamlet. Took a long walk by the seaside—idle all day, very pleasant. Worked at Arthur's flannel jacket—bathed—read Shakespeare—went down to the sea by moonlight.

"Read Hebrews . . . bathed in the morning. Caught thirty-seven shrimps for Arthur's tea. Enjoyed the dabbling very much. In the morning we found a very large black scorpion under dear Arthur's bed—put it in a bottle. Very warm—read and ate grapes by seashore. Tent blew down—bathed for more than two hours. Emily and Louisa called, had lemonade and figs. Bathed before breakfast at sunrise. Read newspapers—fished unsuccessfully. Abdullah came out with charcoal fire. Went fishing again alone at sunset, but bait not good. Lent Hossein two dollars."

Francs, napoleons, dollars and piastres were all current in

Egypt during the sixties, but even so the situation was simpler than in Amelia's childhood. The French historian Marcel, writing in the early forties in *Histoire d'Egypte* says: "Les Monnaies estrangères ayant cours en Egypte sont les quadruples d'Espagne, le sequin de Venise, le ducat de Hollande, le sequin d'Hongrie, le piastre d'Espagne et le talari d'Allemagne." Of these, the word "talari" alone remains, being the name for a twenty piastre piece.

Amelia's Ramleh diary continues: "Took a black woman named Pekita at eight dollars a month. Took a black man at seven dollars the month." But a few weeks later: "Very unpleasant night, strange noises which we attributed to owls or jackals but which were accounted for in the morning when poor Pekita was found lying half outside her tent in epileptic fits which continued. . . . Dr. Mellis said there was no hope for her. Arthur came at half past one with another woman servant, carriage and Abdullah. Pekita gradually getting better and conscious and was able to be taken into town on her mattress—so thankful she was better, and her recovery so unexpected."

Pekita must have been quite a character, for a generation later in a family letter comes the statement that Pekita had just been let out to grass and galloped forth, kicking up her heels most gaily. Ponies of one generation are not called after servitors of a past generation unless the latter have made a decisive impression on family life.

"We wrote and invited the Yules to tea also Helen Ranking who is staying with them, but she was not well enough for them to come. I felt cross at no one coming after my preparations. Terrified dear Arthur by a speech. . . . We saw the comet just over Mr. Ross' house." [He was the husband of Lucie Duff Gordon's daughter, Janet]. ". . . After tea we went to see a catacomb—Greek, with a perfect painting. . . . I promised Mahmoud to speak to Mr. Lancing about getting him into the school. . . . I bathed again, having bathed in the morning. Great fun with Miss F. who came down and ran away with my clothes. Owing myself seventeen piastres. Saw a black eel with golden spots.

"Zenab to town conveyed by two women—did not return at night. ... Busy all day making inquiries about poor Zenab. Busy stewing peaches when I was surprised by Miss Saunders who rode out of her own accord to spend the day. We bathed and Miss S. fell in the water when half dressed. Heard of the death of al Hami Pasha, his body arrived from Constantinople to be buried by his father [Abbas I].

" . . . Rose at daylight and we walked over to Flemings' tents. Very jolly day, Louisa full of mischief put my thimble in the rice milk. Had a delightful ride and canter on the pony as far as high hill. Went down to seaside for limpets and in getting them got entirely wet all over. Caught some shrimps and a *fish* in a *towel*.

"Mr. Haselden had a quarrel with Oppenheim in the open square, and struck him twice in the face, bringing blood. King of Naples fled to Spain.

"Very pleased with my drawing, it being a sketch of Sheikh Gaber mosque!" It was here that Abercromby was carried when fatally wounded while fighting the French in 1801. The railway station of Sidi Gaber now stands on the site.

" . . . found Mr. Anketell and Mr. Sinnot had come to tea—had to get quails in a great hurry. . . . Went to Thurburns, found Lord Haddo and Hekekyan Bey—the former a misery but pleasant. . . . Arthur did not come out so Mahboubah slept in my tent.

"Saida and Pekita came and dined . . . Mahboubah preserving the dates which turned out well. Arthur came home worried—horrified at the price of things. Taught Mahboubah to make a meat pudding.

"Walked to Kom el Dik. Found Selina Harris out but sat on terrace with Mr. Harris."

Mr. Harris and Miss Selina were well known and remarkable figures in nineteenth-century Egypt. Another friend of the Rowlatts, Miss Chennells, gives a spirited account in her book of an incident in connection with this Miss Selina Harris.

"Miss Harris' father was a famous Egyptologist and also a great favourite of Mohamed Ali's. She lost her mother (a native woman) at a very early age. Miss Harris was an accomplished musician and the house in which she resided was near the palace of Nazli Hanem, the notorious daughter of Mohamed Ali. . . . One morning while dressing, not dreaming intrusion, three eunuchs unceremoniously entered her room and told her that 'Nazli Hanem wanted her.' The latter did not enjoy a very good repute, so that being 'wanted by Nazli Hanem' was not a pleasant prospect. Miss Harris, however, was of a fearless character . . . and routed them out into her drawing-room until her toilet was finished. When she went into them there, she found they had ordered pipes and coffee and the room was full of tobacco smoke; all her books were turned over and her photographs handled. She reprimanded them sharply on their behaviour and they reiterated their first speech, that their mistress 'wanted her.' Miss Harris positively refused to go. The next day they came again with the same message. This time they remained below and Miss Harris ordered pipes and coffee for them, but the message being of the same peremptory order, she persisted in declining to go. After a third message, and a consultation with her father, it was agreed between them that she should pay the required visit and a lady was asked to accompany her. What Miss Harris was 'wanted' for was a perfect mystery to them both, and they could not divest themselves of the unpleasant idea that Miss Harris had somehow offended Nazli Hanem. They went and were introduced into a room where several slaves were standing, and one person was seated on cushions. This was Nazli Hanem but as no introduction took place, and the person seated never even looked at them, Miss Harris and her friend remained immovable.

"Soon Nazli Hanem made a slight movement of the head to tell them to be seated. Now Miss Harris' companion was a very stout lady, and to sit on a cushion on the floor and afterwards to have to get up again, was a feat to which she was not equal. So she looked about her as though for a chair, and not seeing one, kept in the same position. Nazli Hanem ordered chairs to be brought and after a little while said to Miss Harris, 'I hear you play very well—there is a piano.' 'No, I cannot,' said Miss Harris. 'Why not?' 'Because I am not accustomed to be ordered.' 'Oh, please play.' 'That is a different thing. When I am asked politely I always do what I am asked.' Miss Harris sat down and played for some time. Presently a number of women seated on the ground began, at a signal from their mistress, to play a native air. Turning to Miss Harris, Nazli Hanem asked if she could play that. She had an excellent ear and she played it. Nazli Hanem then said, 'I want you to come every day for three or four hours and teach these girls to play as well as you do.'

"'Oh, I cannot,' said Miss Harris, 'I have my father and my house to attend to, there's the master who taught me—send for him!' After this Nazli Hanem often sent for Miss Harris to come to her and appeared to take quite a fancy to her, the more so no doubt, from her independent behaviour, to which this lady was little accustomed, everybody around her being in the greatest awe and terror of her."*

*Miss Chennells, *Recollections of an Egyptian Princess by her English Governess*. William Blackwood; 1893.

3

THE FAMILY SPREADS

WHEN Arthur and Amelia's children began to arrive in fairly regular succession they built a house in about the year 1868 five miles out of Alexandria, not far from where their tents had been. This district is now wholly built over and thickly populated, but the Rowlatts' house was one of the first buildings in Ramleh. They still had encampments of Bedwin for immediate neighbours and the water supply came out daily on camel-back from Alexandria. When my father was a small boy of nine, in 1874, he remembered his mother calling him to the garden gate of this house one day, saying: "Come and see Colonel Gordon ride by. He is on his way to the Sudan." It was then that the control of the districts of South Gondokoro were given to Gordon by the Khedive Ismail with orders to eradicate the flourishing slave trade. It was on his way to take up this post that he passed the Ramleh house.

It still stands there today, though added to and cheek-by-jowl with modern buildings of every description. The road, which runs past the door, bears the official name of Rue Arthur Rowlatt, though the house is no longer ours.

It was a fairly primitive life still in some ways, during the sixties and seventies, lacking many amenities we now take for granted, and with little protection against infection of any sort. Cholera raged through the land at frequent intervals.

But the children loved the life. They raced over the desert, chasing lizards; they swam and dived like fishes in the blue

45

sea; they played with the Bedwin children and rode donkeys, the large, strong, Egyptian donkey which goes like the freshest pony.

One of the Rowlatts' constant companions was an Arab dog without a tail, which they rescued from a pit as a puppy and immediately christened Joseph Chance. Chance went everywhere with them, including England and Switzerland, where he adapted himself to snow and even to walks over glaciers. The local breed of Egyptian dog is an animal of character. He is often the usual gingery white, heavily garrisoned with fleas; but sometimes he is a fine black creature, with upright pointed ears and a pointed nose—Anubis to a hair. The likeness to Anubis, the god of the dead, is presumably fortuitous, but it is none the less striking.

These dogs have a strong sense of territory, each one lording it within his own defined boundaries. I once saw one of them standing on the edge of a desert escarpment which looks over the valley and fields below. He was barking furiously, apparently only at the view. I looked in that direction for some time and eventually saw another dog, just discernible far away in the cultivation. It hesitated in its advance along the country path, and plainly listened to the distant barking. Picking up courage it continued on its way. At this point, Anubis on the desert cliff renewed the violent protests until the enemy below lost its nerve entirely and, turning tail, scampered home over its own frontier. The attempted trespass had been stopped by some very rude canine words hurled across half a mile.

For the Rowlatts, journeys back and forth to England took place most years. The English months were thoroughly enjoyed, but there was always great rejoicing on the return to Egypt. In one of Amelia's diaries she comments on the fact that as they landed at Alexandria the baby, then a year old, screamed at all Europeans and English, and would not let himself be carried by anyone except Egyptian men.

As the boys grew bigger, they were sent home to preparatory and public schools and, for the first years, returned from time to time for the holidays. My father told me how, the first time he came back as a small boy, he flung himself on the Ramleh sand, and taking up handfuls he kissed it passionately. They often took things to treasure back to school with them from Egypt. An uncle, who met one of the boys at Victoria Station on his return to school, records how amused he was to see his eleven-year-old nephew stagger up the platform with two immense Egyptian water melons suspended from his shoulders in a kind of home-made yoke which he had built for the purpose. "That boy will go far," he commented in a letter to his parents; and he did, ending on the Judicial Committee of the Privy Council.

In the boys' letters home, things of a derogatory nature about the school, simple schoolboy statements about always being hungry and the quality of the food, were often written in Arabic (though in English script), which must have amused their parents, and effectively circumvented any school censorship.

Arthur Rowlatt frequently went to Cairo on bank business: "I came back having seen the Khedive about our £160,000. I had to wait two and a half hours in an antechamber before seeing him. I would not be a courtier for £5,000 a year." But the parties frequently given by the Khedive Ismail were at any rate enjoyed by Amelia. She tells of one at the Mex Palace. "Such a nice party, had great fun. Did not get to bed till 5.0 a.m. Found

Dance card for party in Alexandria

no 'buses' waiting [whatever they were]. Had to sit in a café and watch a donkey eat its beans while a man went for the buses."

Small references in letters here and there indicate the unsettled state of the country's administration, the lavish spending of the Khedive and the curious type of Europeans frequenting the place as a result. "They say the Viceroy is going to give lots of balls this winter and therefore dissipation and gaiety of all kinds I suppose will be rampant in Cairo. . . . Do you remember the 'Countess' and her husband we met one evening? Well it seems that they are regular swindlers. Another proof of the necessity of avoiding all countesses," writes Arthur.

Places with still familiar names are often mentioned in these letters. "The new gardens are open in Cairo and every evening there is music, and plays are acted in a small theatre. I went twice and was much amused." This alludes to the newly planned Ezbekia gardens laid out in the year 1870 by Monsieur Barilet the chief gardener to the city of Paris. They were lit by 2,500 jets of gas in tulip-shaped glasses.

They were invited to a Khedival ball at the Gezira Palace. This had been built to lodge the Empress Eugénie when she opened the Suez Canal in 1869, her special apartments being an exact replica of her own at the Tuilleries. This building was well known in the heyday of Edwardian tourists as the Gezira Palace Hotel. It is now the home of the Lotfallah family near the entrance to the Sporting Club. Its dimensions are wholly dwarfed by immense blocks of flats.

"The Nile has risen well this year (1872) and the Khalig was cut on the 10th." This refers to the old canal which ran right through Cairo. Its waters were entirely dependent on the Nile rising and falling. It is now filled up and contains tram-lines for much of its length, but is still called Sharia al Khalig. My father well remembered the aroma of rotted rubbish which rose yearly round the neighbourhood as the waters fell, revealing an indescribable collection of filth. As an old man, when crossing Sharia al Khalig, he would sometimes exclaim

in mock surprise, "Good Lord, they've filled up the Khalig!"
It had been done some sixty years previously. When the Nile
reached the required height, the damned-up entrance to the
Khalig was cut amid scenes of great rejoicing, for a good high
Nile symbolised a fertile year for the crops.

Edward Lane, author of the famous *Manners and Customs
of the Modern Egyptians* who wrote his book in 1835,
describes the scene thus:–

"Before sunrise a great number of workmen begin cutting
the dam. This labour devolves in alternate years upon the
Moslem gravediggers and upon the Jews, both of whom are
paid by the Government. . . . With a kind of hoe the dam is
cut thinner and thinner from the back (the earth being
removed in baskets and thrown upon the bank) until at the
top it remains about a foot thick; this is accomplished about
an hour after sunrise. Shortly before this time when dense
crowds have assembled in the neighbourhood of the dam, on
each bank of the Canal, the Governor of the Metropolis
arrives and alights at the large tent before mentioned, by the
dam: some other great officers are also present and the Kadee
attends, and writes a document to attest the fact of the river's
having risen to the height sufficient for the opening of the
Canal, and of this operation having been performed, which
important document is despatched with speed to
Constantinople. . . .

"When the dam has been cut away to the degree above
mentioned, and all the great officers whose presence is
required have arrived, the Governor of the Metropolis throws
a purse of small gold coins to the labourers. A boat . . . is then
propelled against the narrow ridge of earth, and breaking the
slight barrier, passes through it and descends with the cataract
thus formed.

"The Government supplies a great number of fireworks,
chiefly rockets, to honour the festival and to amuse the populace during the night preceding the day when the dam is cut
and during the operation itself. . . . Many small tents for the

sale of sweetmeats, fruits and other eatables and coffee, etc., are likewise pitched along the banks of el Roda, opposite the entrance of the Canal. . . .

"Some [boats] all the night are constantly sailing up or rowing down the river. In many boats the crew amuse themselves and their passengers by singing, often accompanied by the durabukkah and zummarrah; and some private parties hire professional musicians to add to their diversion on the river. The festival is highly enjoyed by the crowds who attend it, though there is little that a stranger would think could administer to their amusement."

The Rowlatts had a Nile boat called the *Ablah* which was often moored against Gezira Island between the present Fouad al Awal and Kasr al Nil bridges. Lucie Duff Gordon's boat had been moored close by when she died on board in 1869. It is interesting to note in passing that the old firm of Briggs & Co., with whom Sidney Terry had worked, was still in being then, for Lady Duff Gordon had written to her husband, "Pray direct me to Briggs & Co. at Cairo; if I am gone the letters will follow me up the river." The *Ablah* made a delightful floating home when the Rowlatts visited Cairo, though if it was but for a night or two on business, the *Ablah* was not always used. "I had a visit from Reis Ahmed [captain of the boat] who had heard that I was in Cairo. I think the Arabs excel everyone in finding out the news, so on Sunday morning Mr. Holt and I have arranged to drive down to the river and pass the morning on board the *Ablah* reflecting on the vanity of all human affairs and that we are bubbles on the stream of time—this no doubt will give us good appetites and we shall return to the hotel and enjoy our luncheon and cigar afterwards."

When the family were hard up the *Ablah* was let. "I hear Reis Ahmed has let the *Ablah* to a Bey for six dollars a day, *non c'e male*." "The Emperor of Brazil, under the name of Don Pedro de Alcantara, is coming here from Brindisi by this next mail, he is travelling incognito. Perhaps he will take the

Ablah." He did not. "I have taken six large knives, six pudding spoons and six teaspoons, the very old scrubby ones with an ' R' on them, for the *Ablah*—I expect some opposition from Suleyman who is very careful about everything belonging to the house."

Later on: "I have been tremendously busy getting the *Ablah* ready. She starts this afternoon and her passengers, consisting of two gentlemen and their two sisters, very nice Americans, and all of them cousins, seem very much pleased with her, and although I say it who should not say it, she is an ornament to the river. She has five new beds, new divan covers in the saloon, green and gold colour, damask not chintz to match the painting and two new lounging chairs for the deck, etc., etc. They are doing the trip to Assouan and back for £140 which they hope to do in forty-five days." After this financial outlay on the *Ablah* to be enjoyed by others, the following letter from Arthur to Amelia on her informing him that she had had the pump painted at Ramleh, seems a little hard. "Allow me to remark in the most delicate manner possible that painting the pump may perhaps with some justice be pronounced by anyone who desired to be very hypercritical, as a lamentable instance of the weakness of the human mind in yielding to the desire (in these days too common amongst those who are raised above the reach of actual want and to whom a few pounds more or less of expenditure in the course of the year is a matter of no consequence) of *squandering* money!"

The children appear to have enjoyed their stays in the hotel as much as the times on the boat. An eleven-year-old daughter writes to her brother at school, from Shepheard's Hotel: "We are staying in Cairo and have enjoyed ourselves very much indeed. Day before yesterday we went up the Pyramids by ourselves as Mama did not. We have had awful fun. The first night we slept here was awfully hot and Gertrude and I slept in one bed. You may imagine the heat. So after having thrown away pillows, sheets and everything else, in despair we jumped out of bed and tore about the room . . . and danced

Sir Roger de Coverley." I hope this cooled them.

Amelia and the smaller children went to England most summers now. English servants were here recruited to join the household at Ramleh with the Mahmouds, Abdous and Fatimas already installed. Such was the custom of the time. "As Selina West has such a good character," writes Arthur in advice, "I think you would do well to engage her. With regard to Lewis I think it would be a fair thing to pay her £28 a year and provide her with Bordeaux wine and water such as we drink ourselves at dinner—threepence a day for beer money comes to £4 11s. 3d. per annum, but drinking the Bordeaux wine would hardly amount to that sum, so that an additional £3 to her wages would certainly more than compensate her for this difference. You must make her understand that beer in this country is not at all good and very dear and by no means wholesome and that no drink is so healthy as what is called black (Bordeaux) wine and water."

Another of Arthur's letters reads thus: "I have just had a small adventure. I went down to the open space on the sea side close to the Prussian Church at twelve o'clock to breathe a little fresh air, and as I was standing there I heard a great splash in the water, and turning to see what it was I saw a Tarboush bobbing about in the waves, and then saw it was on the head of a poor little Arab boy, who was evidently in a fair way of being drowned. So I got down on to some old wood-work which I daresay Sidney remembers, close to the sea wall there, and standing in the sea, and then tried to fish him out with the hook at the end of my umbrella, and managed somehow or other to get one arm round him, and with the other to hold on to the woodwork, and then got the poor little chap out of the water. He was about as big as Freddy and was very frightened, poor little chap. He was flying his kite and walking backwards with the string in his hand, and thus fell over the wall into the sea—in the struggle I have lost my umbrella which I was obliged to throw into the sea, and got wet up to my waist, for which I am no worse. He was a very well dressed boy and would certainly have been drowned in a few minutes, as he was sinking when I caught hold of him."

In 1882 the Rowlatt family had temporarily uprooted themselves from Egypt. Arthur Rowlatt had retired, and the boys were at school and university. This was the year that the Egyptian Arabi Pasha rebelled against his Turkish overlord, the Sultan, and against foreign influence in general. England, espousing the cause of Turkey and to protect European interests and lives, bombarded Alexandria and quelled the rebellion.

Among the boatloads of refugees who left Alexandria hurriedly just before Arabi Pasha's men broke into open revolt, was a small English girl of five years old. She and her brother just remember playing a delightful game which consisted of tearing round the deck, hurdling over all the prostrate forms of their fellow refugees, the boat being so loaded that many had but the deck to lie on. This little girl's family lived in Alexandria where her father was manager of the Alexandria Water Company. They were great friends of the Rowlatts and when she grew up she married Frederick Rowlatt, and was my mother*.

When the refugee boat arrived at Beirut, its destination, no place could be found in the overcrowded town to accommodate this English mother and her five small children. Eventually the British Consul said that he had had a stable cleaned out for them. There they took up their abode and the children slept in the manger.

When they eventually returned, my mother remembers how the bodies of those condemned to die for robbery and murder, during the revolt, hung round the main square.

This small girl, my mother, with her brothers and sister, had as happy an Egyptian childhood as did her future husband. She was full of fun and adventure, and never lacked for a reply when she was caught and upbraided. She was much given to climbing over a public statue not far from their house, which depicted some member of the ruling house of Egypt. An

*Edith May Rowlatt, née Cornish, 1877 - 1965

Egyptian policeman caught her at this one day, and was taken aback when she explained to him in fluent Arabic that it was quite all right, he had nothing to worry about, for the Khedive Tewfik had himself given her personal permission to climb on the statue whenever she desired to do so. This bit of bluff wholly nonplussed the arm of the law.

On another occasion, she was brought forward at some reception, when still a small girl, and introduced to the Ruler of Egypt as her father's daughter. He asked her if she spoke Arabic, to which she replied "Oomaal"—an Egyptian dialect word meaning "of course" and rather implying "what do you take me for?" which much amused His Highness.

At one point in her early childhood this little girl and her brother both fell victims to a bad cholera epidemic in Alexandria and were desperately ill. The good old Scottish doctor sat up all night with them when the crisis came, and by sunrise was able to tell their parents that they would live. Their father, in his jubilation, insisted on the doctor, their mother, and himself opening a bottle of champagne and consuming it in the thin light of dawn.

Years afterwards, my mother was telling this tale in Cairo to some acquaintances. The story became garbled in the re-telling as is so often the case. Some time later, a lady came up to her and said, " Oh! Lady Rowlatt, do tell me: I have heard something so interesting. Were you really cured of cholera as a child by drinking champagne?"

The waterworks where these children lived had a large garden in which they played games such as any child delights in whose movement is not much restricted nor imagination over-curbed. One game involved tasting every green thing that grew in the garden. Nothing fatal occurred luckily. The worst was that a certain bush made their tongues burn and swell painfully but they were able to hold out till it subsided without the aid of authority, which perhaps was just as well as far as the future of the game was concerned. Outside the bounds of the garden lay a great attraction. There sat an old holy individual versed in the ways of spirits and of men. He held continual court in the open on the ground. Or rather, it was a mixture of court and consulting room. People came to be healed of ills of body and soul. They came for arbitration and advice; they brought their mules and donkeys, their babies and their grandmothers. All this could be seen and entered into by the children peering through the hedge.

A reverend air pervaded the scene, while the incantations and incense fascinated the English children who followed every move and debate with an awed wonder. My mother can still remember the wording of one of the doggerel verses often used by the old man in his ministrations. A rough translation of it is:

> "Sheikh Obeida, Sheikh Obeida
> Remove it from this
> And put it all in that."

The Sheikh involved was meant to take the pain from the sore spot by placing it all in some other object where it could do no harm. As the old man recited it his fingers moved lightly from the afflicted part to the object which was to act as the receiver, presumably of the evil spirit which was causing the pain.

Meanwhile the Rowlatt boys were finishing their education in England, with not a few scholarships and university awards to their name. The boys extracted much fun out of life in England—fishing, riding, boating or skating. There were great rejoicings when one of them rowed for Cambridge in the University Boat Race, though this event was saddened for them all by the sudden death, just before, of their much-loved father.

In a letter to one of his sons written about a fortnight before his death, he comments on some military campaigns of the nineteenth century which took place outside Alexandria: "I have lately been much interested in reading an account of the battle of Alexandria when Sir Ralph Abercromby was killed . . . after the British army landed at Aboukir in the teeth of a heavy fire from the French, they drove back the enemy as far as the present Mustapha Pasha Station—and then took up a position extending from Stanley Bay, straight across the plain on which our 'palezetto' stands, through Bulkeley Station and under Waterworks Hill to the Canal. The French occupied the old Caesar's Camp, and commenced the battle by trying to turn the right of the English army, which exactly occupied the site of our house . . . they failed in this attack as you know and ultimately retreated to what we now call the French lines. So our premises have twice been occupied by English troops—in 1801 and 1882."

Arthur Rowlatt's character was shown clearly by the many letters from England and Egypt on his death.

"His sons must recall with pride and honour his walk among men and his unsullied reputation. . . . Mr. Rowlatt's departure [from Egypt] was followed only by regrets and econiums of his excellence." "He gave me the impression of a mind thoroughly stayed on a Higher Power and so ready to meet life's changes calmly."

Two of Arthur's and Amelia's sons chose to return and work for Egypt which they had so loved from their infancy. Charles was eventually Director of Customs Administration, and Frederick, my father, became Governor of the National Bank of Egypt.

He started as a junior clerk in the London branch of the old Bank of Egypt. This was a weary time for him, sitting for hours on a high stool doing figures in a lugubrious city office; but he stuck it well, and by 1889 was promoted to Alexandria.

As soon as he arrived there, the old Egyptian-English link sprang to life once more. His mother wrote again asking for vegetable seeds, dried Egyptian food, and all manner of things. Old servants reappeared from nowhere to greet Fred with the warmth that only an old Egyptian friend can express.

Amelia sent them presents and tea and clothes from England, and followed once more their family ups and downs, sending them personal messages via her son. Her letters, too, became surprisingly peppered with Arabic words and exclamations. "Mashallah—the river is still frozen over."

Mary, Amelia's sister, writes to her nephew: "Your description of Aboukir Bay made me long to witness it all. I do yearn for Egypt, even the smell of bad seaweed. I am glad Mohamed goes on well. Salaams to him."

"Poor Mohamed. I am sorry his child is dead," writes Amelia. "Tell him I am very zaalan [upset] about it. I will get Sidney to go and choose a shawl for him at the Stores. . . . I am also sending a piece of two yards of blue spotted with white for Sidi Ahmed's waistcoat. . . . I promised Mohamed a railway rug, it shall come when I can get it." "I have written to the Stores to send you out . . . three pounds of tea in a canister to be labelled: 'For Sidi Ahmed,' which please place *yourself* in his hands. Also three pounds 'For Spiro's mother,' labelled so; it is not very far from the Bank. . . . Pa says 'Send us an *Egyptian Gazette* sometimes.' Pa has a corner in his heart for Egypt." This was shortly before his death. "We have Egyptian coffee every night. . . send us some bamia [a vegetable] in the spring, by someone. It is bought in the market dried and shredded, only during winter can it be bought. The first time Mohamed goes to town for anything he might buy us about four okes [an oke is two and three-quarter pounds] and keep it until someone is coming. The price is about fourteen piastres the oke, and the small kind is best." The bamia arrived in due course and was much appreciated.

Some of the younger brothers' letters now take on a pseudo-Byronic style, in mock operatic Turkish phraseology that defies description: "How is the world you live in treating you? That world of politics, sentiment and crime! You Oriental knave, your ugly face betrays your ugly mind. How now? I golfed at the Aldrich-Blakes this morning and beat them all. I only missed one drive in two hours, but then, unclean Giaour, wilt think I lie. Vile trespasser in the Land of Mohound, the Muezzin's cry stumbles in the miasma that rises from the frothy scum of infidels, thou usorious Frangi. We had champagne yesterday. How are all your comrades, itchy vultures replete of oats. We drove a patent rubber tee, nursling of Turks, and I lost a ball. But what care I. Oh wretched post-captain of a dahabiya. Nomad, I scorn thy beard. Thou slothful bat, me-seems thou art like the midday dog, gorged on the infinite offal of Zabalah—dull, somnolent, sublime."

Early in 1890, after her husband's death, Amelia Rowlatt decided to leave the house in England and join her son, Fred, living once more in the little Ramleh house. But just before she sailed, the news came of her son's promotion to be sub-manager of the Bank in Cairo. "I *must* congratulate you on your promotion," his mother writes. "Well done, it is most gratifying because it speaks so highly for you. . . . What comes from God (as this did) is best, and I must smother my feelings of disappointment about not being with you at Ramleh next winter.

"My boy, we must ask God's care of us and leave all in His hands. My sons have always been so very good and tender and loving with me . . . may God bless them and keep them upright and *staunch* in all things as they are now.

Fred Rowlatt as a young man, by his friend, L.M. Carver. Alexandria, 1889

"You can imagine how proud I am when I tell people that Fred is appointed sub-manager in Cairo—and they reply 'Already!'" He was aged twenty-five.

A letter of congratulation from one of his young brothers is written in a typically chaffing style, but contains one sentence unwittingly prophetic. "I am sure you will become a great boss. . . . When they start a Government Bank of Egypt as they possibly will do in the future, they will make you governor." The National Bank of Egypt was founded by Khedival decree in 1898, and in 1906, at the age of forty-one, Frederick Rowlatt was appointed Governor.

During the last years of the century, Amelia Rowlatt still enjoyed many things to the full, especially a gay evening. "Dined at the Savoy," she notes in her diary, "left early to go to dance at Continental, but alas, when we got there found it had been put off." And in the following year: "A lovely ball, enjoyed it much."

During 1901 her health deteriorated and she had considerable heart trouble, but her spirits were undiminished. "Very weak," she wrote on April 10. She shortly recovered, however, and "went calling, on a donkey." Later, she attended some party at Ramleh of which she recorded, "A stupid party—mostly old fogies."

On February 17, 1902—"Sixty-eight years today I have been on this globe." She continued her intimate touch with all the people of the country, especially the needy. "The poor Bedwin girl brought a leg of mutton as payment, so prettily, and refused to take it back. She sat with me here on the veranda, like a lady." And later on—"Take Mahboubah to hospital. . . . To hospital to see Mahboubah."

She frequently visited Fred in Cairo where he was now sub-governor of the National Bank of Egypt and she wrote in 1903 with evident satisfaction that she had travelled in a ladies' carriage, second class, for eight shillings and eight-pence—a journey of over one hundred miles.

On February 17, 1903: "Thank God that He has spared me sixty-nine years—so I've not died at sixty-eight as I expected." A few months after this, she became weaker and the doctor thought that treatment in England would be her only hope. She planned to leave with Fred and his newly-married wife. At the hotel in Port Said, waiting to embark, she died, in the land which she and her mother and grandmother before had so loved, where she had been married, and where all her children had been born. The *Egyptian Gazette*, writing at the time of her death, told how she had been esteemed by Egyptians, especially those who remembered her in her childhood and loved to claim her as a *"Bint al belad"*—a daughter of the country—one of themselves.

"Mrs. Rowlatt," this paper continues, "was one of the few remaining links which united us with the past of Egypt and was certainly the last Englishwoman who could remember the person, appearance and doings of the great Mohamed Ali himself. As a child at her nursery window, she could recall seeing the old Pasha driving up daily in summer from Ras el Tin to Kom el Dik in order to take the country air."

Hard Times, by Amelia C. Terry. "Dear Uncle Taylor in the Little Red House, Alexandria: 'Steamer in sight! Eh? Really one gets no peace in one's life in this country.'"

4

BIRDS, BEASTS AND BEETLES

I N the centre of the Nile, as it flows past Cairo, lies the island of Gezira. On that island was a wild, overgrown garden. And in that garden was a house. My sister and I were both born there and it became our much loved home for many years, till my father's death in 1950, when we returned it to the Egyptian Government, whose property it was. The family had lived there for forty-two years.

The Khedive Ismail had originally formed the Zohria Gardens, as they are called, to be an experimental ground for trees and shrubs which he ordered from India to see if they would nourish in Egypt. He succeeded well, and many of the present trees in the gardens and avenues of Cairo are the direct lineal descendants of the fine old giants who now, some eighty years later, reign supreme in the Zohria. One old banyan in particular has spread its tentacles downwards from its branches in all directions, and formed further trees around it in the true banyan fashion. It is a sobering thought that some of these large offshoot trees, whose trunks are now about two yards in circumference, used to serve as excellent giant strides when, as a small girl, I would grab their down-ward-growing rootlets which still hung several feet off the ground, like hanks of grey hair from some giant head. The banyan tree did not always seem a friendly giant to me, although I never hesitated to take such liberties with its hair. Sometimes, after swinging gaily round with heels in the air, I would pause and stare upwards into the world of dark foliage above, full of mystery and the unknown. Something would rustle overhead, probably a disturbed bat; a coldness would grip my heart and I would hurry away into the more sunlit parts of the garden.

When my parents first moved to this house, the Zohria was a wild dishevelled tangle of roses and undergrowth among the trees; but later the Horticultural Department of the Egyptian Ministry of Agriculture took it in hand, and made it into the beautiful and well-run experimental garden that it now is. Our own private garden too was a wilderness at first, worked at by one ancient son of Adam with no implements save his ten fingers. When my mother arrived and asked him where his tools were, he held up his hands, saying that God had given him none other than these. My mother set to work with a will and we eventually had beautiful lawns, a rose garden, herbaceous borders, a citrus grove, and great coloured splashes of creepers, bignonia, bougainvillea and clerodendrons, each name longer than the next, redolently Latin but with simple, beautiful flowers.

The bird life in this and the surrounding garden was a constant source of fascination, though the grounds are separated from the noise and dust of Cairo by little more than the Nile itself.   .

The garden has several big trees which add a great deal to the interest, for some of these trees are the citadels of the crows and some are castles of the kites—hereditary enemies. During the many years that I have watched birds in this garden, I have never known a crow and a kite truce; I see no reason to believe there has ever been one; the war of the Spanish Succession was the skirmish of a day compared with this ageless warfare. The battles sometimes take on enormous proportions; thirty or forty a side. I have rarely seen hand to hand, or should it be claw to claw, fighting. It is mostly strategical guerilla warfare. The kites, who never lose their dignity, are pestered and baited by the crows, who will come in a flight of three or four, squawk in a kite's face, then turn tail and fly off. After two or three sallies of this type, the kite loses patience, and with his shrill though beautiful cry, gives chase. Having achieved some reaction from the kite, the crows assume a justified indignation and return to the charge, six or seven strong. Soon there is a battle royal, everyone joins in, and the air is rent with caws and cries. As children we found these crow and kite fights absorbing and thrilling. Every crow flying away from the scene of action, was a messenger sent back at the risk of his life to get reinforcements, every kite flying forward ahead of his fellows, was their gallant captain, every huddle of crows cawing and nodding at each other on a neighbouring tree, was the general and his staff in consultation; and so on. Many is the time I have been dragged protesting from the window and made, quite rightly, to continue dressing or my lessons.

I know of no other bird who shows more palpably than the Egyptian crow what he would certainly be saying if he could speak. In the spring a whole family of crows, with much noise, will settle pointedly on a kite's tree near a nest. When the owner protests you can almost hear the crow saying in mock surprise: "Oh, dear me now, I quite thought it was my tree—fancy, children, this isn't our tree after all!" She will noisily gather her young together and fly off, but not before having wrecked the kite's afternoon peace. Besides being clowns they are really great villains, and in the spring, search every bush and hedge for small nestlings or eggs to devour. When I came into the garden and caught one at it, his every movement and expression seemed to say, "Now let me see, what was I doing on this hedge?—Oh, just walking along: extraordinarily nice thing, a hedge, to walk on in the spring, don't you think?" and he pretended to look innocently grieved when I chased him off. One year we put an old earthenware jar in a stand on the lawn, filled with water for the birds. The crows were terrified of it. They would come as near as they dared with their ridiculous sideways hop, then suddenly get in a panic and retreat hurriedly in disorder. Soon, however, they become only too familiar with it, and instead of clear, fresh water, it was always a soup of frogs' legs and bits of bread stolen from the gardener's meal.

The Cairo crow behaves, with any food he is unable to eat at the moment, in the same way as does a dog—he buries it. It would be interesting to know if this is a general habit of hooded crows or if the Cairo crows have invented it for themselves. I have often watched them carry off a piece of bread, dig it into the corner of a flower bed and camouflage the place by putting leaves and grass neatly over it with their beaks. They will also take a piece of bread which is too hard and dip it repeatedly in water by the garden tap until it is soft enough to please them. On some occasions a whole company of crows will take on a sort of mock solemnity and dignity. For no apparent reason, and usually at sunset, they will gather on the roof in rows and caw and caw together, then all will be silent for a moment or two before they start again, often led by a kind of choirmaster among them. "How the crows are praying tonight," our Italian maid would remark in awed tones.

As opposed to the crows, only once have I seen a kite lose his dignity. This one had become entangled in the long trails of bignonia venusta hanging from a tall tree and he was dangling head downwards, flapping feebly. We sent up a sporting garden boy to free him; it was a perilous climb, but he did it. The bird fell apparently senseless to the ground, breaking its fall on a rose bush. We laid its head in a saucer of water and left it. Five minutes later it drank some water, recovered and flew off. One thing the crows and kites had in common is that they both noticed instantly if we were having a meal in the garden. We could not leave the table for a minute without a crow flopping on to it and pecking at everything, or a kite with its beautiful swoop bearing down and neatly removing a titbit. A kite will remove food like this from a child's hand so quickly and dexterously that the child hardly has time to be frightened. In the same way, the kites carry off golf balls, as Gezira golfers know to their cost. If you happen to have a kite's tree in your garden you are, with luck, about all square at the end of the season, because after a few days when the kite finds the balls are not edible nor are likely to hatch into anything, it will turn them out of the nest, to be gleaned by the owner of the garden below. Once I was richer by a polo ball acquired in this way.

The two sorts of birds which get on best together are the bulbul and the sparrow. Both like to be near the house, both like the same type of small tree or large bush, and both go about in pairs or companies, fussy, cheerful and chatty. I have seen two sparrows and two bulbuls bathing simultaneously in a tiny puddle under the garden tap, while rows of friends and relations of each waited round for their turn. This alliance is of comparatively recent growth, because twenty-five years ago, the bulbul was almost a rare bird in this garden; they have increased enormously lately. The bulbul has some lovely liquid notes. One of his short snatches sounds just as if he is saying, "A *beau*tiful *cathe*dral." It was amusing to hear this being piped all over the garden in the spring of 1938, when Cairo's new Anglican cathedral was being consecrated by the late Archbishop of York.

About the strangest birds to be seen in the garden, though sometimes weeks go by and they do not appear, are three green parakeets. Ever since I can remember there have been three, a couple and a mad one, who dashes behind the others screaming across the sky. Many years ago, he inadvertently fell down our nursery chimney and was caught by the suffragi in the fireplace. The bird bit his finger badly with its curved beak, so he let it go, but ever after it has been mad—or is it for love? With only three of them . . . two's company even for parakeets. They used to come nearer to the house than they do now. I remember as a child being in my bedroom for three weeks with measles and feeling it was just bearable because, from my window, I could see these emerald birds eating the bohinia pods among the porcelain pink blossoms of that lovely tree. This species of parakeet was let out of the Giza Zoological Gardens many years ago to see if it would breed wild; there are several of them in the Zoo gardens living at liberty, and these few at Gezira; but I have seen them nowhere else.

Drama of another sort is provided by the little owls who live under the rafters of the house and there raise their families. Some of our guests, if not versed in the ways of Cairo baby owls, come down to breakfast looking white and worn, saying, "I'm afraid I hardly slept a wink all night—there seemed to be a man in my room; I heard him snoring most distinctly, just as if he had been under the bed or in a cupboard, but I could find no trace in the morning." To do them justice, the snoring noise of these young owls is almost identical with human snoring and does sound exactly as if it were in the room. One morning we found "the man" in the garden below, having fallen out of the rafters, a woolly white bundle with yellow eyes and a little yellow beak sticking out of the surrounding fluff.

For sheer decorative value, I think the prize goes to the buff-backed heron. He is common enough in the fields, but only occasionally honours us with his presence in the garden. Stalking elegantly across the green lawn, he looks like a fairy-tale prince transformed into a beautiful white bird. When he is in the act of catching frogs and beetles for his dinner, the illusion disappears; he fixes them with a hypnotic stare, stretches out his long neck parallel with the ground, waggles it from side to side in the most lunatic way, and then gives a sudden stab at his prey. Sometimes three or four of these herons will decorate the garden for a few days and then disappear again for months. A still less frequent visitor to the garden is the peewit. Occasionally on spring evenings, when the sun has just set, a flock of them wheel round showing the black and white of their rounded wings, and settle on the lawn searching for food. They are fascinating to watch, with their little runs of a yard or two and sudden halts, their heads on one side, listening, and their low cries one to another; but they are shy. These peewits roost on the lawn, but are off again in the early morning.

There are many other entertaining residents. The palm doves, for instance, whose chief characteristics are a fighting spirit (how they ever came to symbolise peace I cannot think) combined with marked idiocy which makes them attempt, day after day, to build on the shutters of the house. The shutters being closed every evening means the collapse of the twigs so laboriously collected. Then there are the beautiful families of hoopoes who carry on their heads the golden feather crowns, the gift of Solomon. When out walking one day, King Solomon found the sun too hot, so the Arab story goes. He asked if any animal or bird could help him. The hoopoes flew up and formed themselves into a close flock between Solomon and the sun. The king offered them anything they liked to ask for as a reward. They chose crowns of gold, though he warned them that it was a vain and unpractical thing for which they asked. Sure enough, a few days later the chief hoopoe came back and begged that the crowns should be removed: they were so heavy that all the hoopoes had stiff necks and could not fly in comfort. Solomon forgave them, and as they were truly penitent, provided them with beautiful light feather crowns instead.

The smallest and most endearing of the resident birds is the graceful warbler. It is about two inches long with another two inches of tail. Every year it builds a little domed nest in a lavendula bush near the house and lays five apricot-coloured eggs about the size of a fingernail. These little birds hop about eating insects off the bushes twelve inches from your nose, with no concern whatsoever.

Pride of place for colour and movement goes to the bee-eaters who are the dashing young men on the flying trapeze of the ornithological world. Chestnut brown, lemon yellow, and verdant green, they swerve and glide, float and dive through the air, searching for food in the very essence of self-confident abandon. In early summer in the fields they can be one moment high above your head, and the next moment so low and close that every feather is seen against the background of ripening corn.

Nearly every wild animal has, by now, disappeared from Gezira—except one large mongoose which can be seen from time to time in our garden.* I have not seen a fox for many years now. But it is encouraging to note that the ordinary garden birds, if anything, have increased. The Egyptians themselves take an interest in them. In the fine Agricultural Museum there is a beautiful collection of birds, one of the most artistically arranged that I know. An interest in, and protection of, birds has more than an intellectual or scientific value for Egypt, as her very life depends so much on the success of her crops and therefore to a great extent on that eternal battle between man and the insect pests, a battle in which many varieties of birds are man's staunch allies.

Reptile life was not missing either. There was one large bush past which, as children, we walked rather sideways with an occasional oblique glance, like a dog passing an enemy he does not feel capable of tackling that day, for a cobra was said to live there. Had not the gardener once found in it a nest of small, slithery, newly-hatched snakes? The darting little lizards were a very different proposition. These we loved. An old weeping willow was their especial habitation. It was gnarled and barren in the few winter months but, in early spring, about February, its hanging strands became supple with sap and the leafdrops of palest green broke out at the tips and soon covered the tree, falling to the lawn, a delicate cascade of pale spring green.

Under and around this tree darted the lizards. Sometimes you could hardly see them as they sped round on their highly important business. But sometimes they would stand so still that we children, on our knees in the dust, silently gazing,

* This last mongoose has now finally disappeared.

could see the beat of the lizard's heart against its shining skin. We never even tried to catch the lizards, they were too beautiful, but we hounded up hordes of black beetles, of the sort that inhabit open outhouses, scuttling under stones in the warm dust. We used to construct what we called black beetle farms, where we hoped they would breed; but they did not. Our biological knowledge was perhaps insufficient.

The more conventional of our hobbies was tending the patches designated as our own gardens. This pursuit, inevitable in the lives of so many children in so many generations, was much enlivened for us by the help of a Sudani chauffeur, Ahmed by name. Whenever we went on a desert picnic to a certain rocky terrain south west of the Pyramids we would gather white snail shells that abounded there and with these we decorated our gardens. Ahmed knelt in the dust in his smart blue suit and red tarboush earnestly designing patterns round the so-called flower beds of a few square feet. If a derelict nasturtium grew therein so much the better, but the snail shells were the thing. I still await a geologist who can tell me their origin and age. They look immensely old and are mostly uninhabited by snails but whether they have hung about that area for decades, centuries, or millennia, I know not. There is no such question however about the fossilised wood which can also be picked up in parts of the desert. It is not a product of yesterday. When energy and enthusiasm were sufficient, large hunks of this were also dragged home to embellish gardens, corners of balconies, and even schoolrooms, where their tenure was cut short by the cleaning zeal of servants. But in outside corners they stayed for ever till they became the fascinating haunts of spiders, earwigs, and nameless creatures with numberless legs.

Most of such insects we regarded as friends but the cockroach was an exception. In the old Ramleh house they came out in quantities during the evenings and from time to time we would organise a great round-up. We filled dried gourds with sand. The Egyptian gourd is a large affair with a much smaller top storey which can act as a handle. Grasping this firmly, we tore about the floor depositing the now heavy gourd fair and square upon any cockroach within reach. It entailed hopping with agility hither and thither to get the maximum bag before they all scuttled to shelter. Probably less effective than D.D.T. but how much more fun and surely a less ignoble end for the cockroaches themselves!

Only once in my memory has there been so bad a plague of locusts that they descended in swarms on the garden till it was impossible to walk in it without crushing them at every step. It was a calamitous year and all day long one heard the peasants in the neighbouring fields beating tin cans to scare the scourge away. Rather a vain hope. Driving to school in the old-fashioned Victoria we then had was quite an adventure, for the locusts would hit the coachman in the face if he did not continuously dodge them, and would bang around the fat pair of bays in a way they most disliked. The carriage wheels left behind them a slimy trail of mashed locust. School however was not called off.

Encounters with dangerous reptiles are but few and far between on the whole. My mother wandering about on the sandhills near Aboukir, in casual search for Graeco-Roman oddments, once saw what she thought was a small screw of old rope at her feet; on poking it with her sunshade however the rope became a horned viper, *cerastes cornutus*, a devilish little thing, doubtless the direct descendant of the one who, tradition says, so neatly dispatched Cleopatra in the same vicinity two thousand years before. We were sitting on the sand once, near the second Pyramid, when my mother noticed the servant who had come with us on a picnic that day, putting something carefully into his galabia pocket and pinning the flap down so that whatever was inside could not escape. On being asked what it was he produced a fully grown scorpion. "The baby was sitting on it," he said, indicating one of the children.

No reptile or insect has ever given me the shivers, I am glad to say, apart from poisonous ones. I remember once, on the return journey from a picnic, feeling an uncomfortable scratching up my spine. We had been sitting on the edge of crops by the desert. My mother commented on the fact that I was wriggling and restless even more than usual (I was about nine at the time). She looked inside the back of my cotton dress and let out a cry of horror. A vast mole cricket was prowling up and down my backbone. This creature was about four inches long, all legs and antennae. Removing it was quite a campaign which caused me much entertainment.

It is not so with birds, however. Much as I loved watching them, their close proximity made me feel quite pale. I am just as stupid about it still. Motoring in to Cairo along the Suez road, not so long ago, we gave a lift to a young Egyptian girl carrying an innocent-looking cotton bag. When we were tightly packed in the back of the car, I noticed that this bag, on the floor by our feet, was heaving around mysteriously. The next moment, out wriggled a half-fledged pigeon, followed by several brothers and sisters. I froze with fear, and in an artificially controlled voice, told the girl that I would deliver her safely in Cairo on one condition, that the pigeons were returned to the bag and the opening held tightly shut till we reached our destination, some eighty miles ahead.

The summers in which we did not travel to England were spent in the little Ramleh house outside Alexandria, so much loved by our grandmother. Here we played by the hour in the rock pools of the same bay where Amelia had caught her shrimps for tea, as we now did. And here we learnt to swim and dive, to know where the dangerous currents ran, which rocks cut our feet, and where stinging jellyfish lurked.

When still almost babies, we used to cling round our father's neck and he would dive with us on his back downwards through the blue sea, silver bubbles rising to the surface behind us. Our father was a great swimmer, well-trained in his childhood in the same bay where he now trained us. He kept an iron crowbar at the bottom of one clear pool. He would dive to this, and holding the bar to keep himself down, would walk about the bottom as if strolling in the garden. We would be left swimming above him, treading water in puppy-dog fashion and watching him below through the crystal water with infinite admiration.

In those days there were still many open spaces in Ramleh where wild flowers grew of the small tough sorts which alone thrive in these semi-desert wastes. One was a little echium which seemed to emerge blue, pink or mauve on the same plant, apparently just as the spirit moved it, and another a miniature red and green ice plant which flourished in the salty air. Here, and in the casuarina and gnarled pepper trees, we used to find occasional chameleons. It only required a little patience and stealth to capture one, but much more ingenuity was needed to tame it and keep it in good health. Some haughtily rejected the affection we showered upon them and refusing all flies proffered for their nourishment dead or alive, would contrive to escape in a few days' time. But with one we had a great success. Dear Kim, a saint among chameleons who thoroughly understood child psychology, gave just enough trouble to make us feel we were mastering him against all odds, yet obliged us with just enough intimacy to make us feel he loved us. We certainly loved him. He had about two yards of string, one end loosely tied round his waist and the other attached to a small mimosa tree over which he could clamber at will. But of course, every hour or so, the length of string was intricately entwined for its whole length round and about a complication of twigs and branches, the unravelling of which was a process.

At other times Kim would climb up one of our arms, round the back of the neck and down the other arm, a sort of Inner Circle. Or he would go up and down the lamp cord in our room accounting for every fly he met. Sometimes we felt he needed more exciting nourishment, something to test his hunting still higher. We would take him into the garden and place him under one of those large old-fashioned wire covers for protecting food and into this arena we would insert a grasshopper. The atmosphere of the bull ring prevailed. We watched every move with suppressed excitement. It was not very sporting I suppose, for Kim ran no risks while the grasshopper played his moves to avoid extinction. A chameleon shoots out four to five inches of tongue which lassoos its prey and springs back into its mouth with the burden, after the fashion of the paper tongues sometimes distributed at children's parties which extend on being blown and can roll up again instantly. So with adroitness and timing of his jumps the grasshopper could tire Kim's tongue muscles. The art being to wait still, long enough for the chameleon to have a stab, but then to move quickly enough for this to be abortive. Sometimes it went on sufficiently long for us, the umpires, to call the game off and free the grasshopper who jumped away covered with honours if rather shaken in nerve. But more often it ended in a catch and a crunch, with grass-hopper legs sticking out on both sides of the chameleon's mouth not unlike the handlebar moustache on a modern young man, before a second swallow finished off even these protuberances.

Other pets came and went with the usual regularity. One was a most spirited Egyptian donkey, white, large and powerful. I can quite imagine the Ancient Egyptians going forth to war on such beasts before the Hyksos invasion imported the horse. A battle charge would be just in their line. Ours pulled a little trap in which we all bundled. Off went the donkey at high speed but unfortunately our drive took a right-angle turn soon after leaving the front door. Whether the blood of his ancient race made him imagine that the dwellers in the Land of Kush or other foes lay straight ahead can never be told, but time and time again this donkey refused to slacken his speed or take the turn and we came to an ignomin-ious halt in a mutilated flower bed. Alas, he had to go.

Another character was a cat called Nora, of the stray poly-chrome kind. Nora could have had little education but she managed the art of life extremely well. Long after we had looked on her as our own special property, fed her and cared for her properly, a neighbour of ours was sitting on our balcony when Nora strolled across to pass the time of day and get a bite of tea. "Why, there's our cat!" (Maisie or Tibs, or whatever they called her), exclaimed the neighbour, "what is she doing over here?" Nora (or Maisie or Tibs) realised her tactical mistake and she disappeared for good; to try her luck at deception elsewhere I suppose. We missed her, though. A counterpart to Nora's dodge was once successfully brought off by an Egyptian cook engaged as culinary artist to some friends who took our Ramleh house one summer. It is quite usual in Egypt for the cook to live out and to come in every morning having marketed on his way. This enterprising man found two families who had meals at slightly different times and who both needed a cook. With the help of a co-operative kitchen boy in either house, he contrived to satisfy both families and draw wages from both, neither knowing for quite some time, that he was not giving them his undivided attention and skill.

We were months absent from the Ramleh house leaving it in charge of one Gooma, the grandson of Soubki who had been the Bedwin guardian when my grandfather first built this little house, and who then lived in a hair tent Bedwin-fashion pitched close by. Gooma had a prize fighter's figure and a resounding voice. Though they were now settled people and in our employ for more than a generation, there was nothing of the servitor about his ways. Far from it. Neither did he have the "oblige" mentality in any of its manifestations. Gooma and his family had a sense of democracy which verged on the autocratic. But this was not a pose or a reaction. It was natural to them.

He had a small brother with whom we used to play and from whom we learnt to blow on the thin curled tip of the reeds which grew wild, in such fashion to produce a little tune, low and vague like the buzzing of a bee. Good peashooters can be made from these reeds too. Our father taught us that. Gooma's brother was a markedly intelligent small boy, but in those days he ran around barefoot, with little or no schooling. Now, however, the change is complete. Gooma's son, a child unborn when we were small, today runs a housing agency in Ramleh, a well-managed and efficient business. His office is spotlessly clean with a bunch of fresh flowers on the desk. He wears well-cut European suits, and steps forward with a courteous welcome and the offer of coffee when any of us visit him there. Education, some culture, and some means have but polished the native self-respect of his like. Modernity has not here bred vulgarity.

During the long difficult years of my father's governorship of the National Bank, he always found time to spend Saturday afternoons with us children. However late he had to stay at the Bank on other nights and whatever pressure of work was upon him, Saturday afternoons were ours.

When we were in Cairo we would set off with both parents on tea picnics into the desert surrounding the Pyramids. The party usually hired camels at Mena, while the tea basket was loaded on to a donkey. Until we were about six or seven years old we too had donkeys, or we rode on our mother's camel, sharing the huge saddle with her. For many years in succession we had the same camels and the same man in charge of them, who came to look on these Saturday afternoons as their particular and rightful outings as much as we did. When we graduated to a camel of our own it was a great moment. First the forward lurch of the beast as he rises, which means a backward thrust for the rider if he wishes to remain on, and then just as suddenly the front legs are straightened and forward you throw yourself to counter the movement. When the camel finally stands up straight it seems verily like the top of the world to a seven-year-old. One of our first lessons in physical self-control took place on these camels. They were harmless old things really, but at the best of times a camel's falling lower lip and large yellow teeth are not prepossessing and they often gurgle and groan as they proceed. When a neighbouring camel's mouth bobbed up and down close to our pink legs hanging on either side of the saddle, the instinct to withdraw the leg slightly was very strong. Our mother encouraged us to relax and leave our legs in exactly the same position whether the camel's face was three inches away from us or not.

As our legs grew longer, we learnt to cross them in front of the saddle tree as the Bedwin do and communicate our wishes to the camel by drumming with our heels on its withers, or with the single rope attached to the halter round its nose. My camel was called Zarifa—the witty one. I loved her dearly, her dark brown eyes and long lashes, her ridiculous wisp of a tail, the blue beads threaded in her trappings to keep the evil eye off—everything about her I loved, even her camel smell which was not negligible.

We used to go along the edge of the desert where it verges on the crops, the Egyptian counterpart of Omar Khayam's "strip of herbage strown, That just divides the desert from the sown." Zarifa loved this. She would lower her four foot of neck and graze off little plants here and there in the sand, miniature wild mignonette, little scented stocks, or bunches of camel thorn, strange prickly fodder but succulent to her.

I thought this continual stopping for snacks was most infra dig and would pull on the rope and shout to her words solemn with warning of what I would do to her if she did not obey. But I am afraid, on viewing it in retrospect, that it was she who was in command of me and not vice versa, much as I thought so at the time.

Looking across the Nile Valley from the escarpment on which the Great Pyramid stands, one used to survey a lovely sight in some months of the year, which has now wholly gone.

As the Nile rose in summer it flooded its banks and spread its thick brown water over the fields for many square miles. The villages of mud houses rose above the waters, as islands in the waste. Here and there high dyke roads were above the flood and the palm trees had in proportion but their ankles under water. Not so the domestic animals returning to the villages from neighbouring dry land. They had nothing but their noses above water. The villagers went back and forth in narrow boats and in the evening the train of buffaloes would follow, their leader's nose roped to the end of the boat, and the small animals sharing the boat with their owners or held by their fore-paws just as depicted in the Ancient Egyptian tomb friezes.

We used to sail over these floods on moonlight nights, slowly and silently, save for the ripples from the prow. The smell of the mud where the waters had receded was acrid but not unpleasant, for the associations it evoked were of fertility to come. However, a smell it certainly was, not qualifying for the higher plane designated a scent.

In late autumn the floods subsided and the rich alluvial mud had yet again been deposited in age-old fashion on the Egyptian fields ready for sowing the crops once more. The sower would now stride over the mud as he scattered the seed, casting his bread upon the waters, knowing that it would return to him again after many days.

The Nile soil in this area is among the most fertile in the world. It is the colour of the richest plum pudding. The Ancient Egyptians called it Khemi, which also meant the Land of Egypt. This word has come into our language through Arabic, with the addition of *al*, the Arabic article, as alchemy. The idea of magic and mysticism inherent in Nature's annual refertilising of the soil has become woven into the very meaning of the word.

This old system of irrigation has here been replaced within the last twenty years or so by the more scientific form called perennial irrigation, a matter of canals and drains.

Sailing feluccas on the Nile itself during hot evenings under moon or stars continued after the irrigation sailing was no more. Here it was extremely easy to run aground on submerged islands of sand and silt. As the Nile fell in the autumn these emerged above the water, and the industrious peasant lost no time in ferrying over to sow his crops thereon and later to shield them from the sun and wind by rows and rows of reeds stuck in aslant for acre after acre.

On one Nile picnic the boat we were in stuck soundly. The rest of the party sailed ahead with the food and the drink and all contact was severed. A disaster. We were hours pushing, punting and drifting. Never have I developed such a thirst nor been so cut off from the source of its quenching. Eventually, hours later, again we ran ashore on a wharf used by that immemorial Nile craft, the ghiassa which plies up and down the river with merchandise from the agricultural lands of Upper Egypt. At that season and on that particular wharf the whole traffic was given over to onions. They lay in great heaps everywhere and covered ankle-deep the ground we had to tread. We waded in this yellow foam of onion skins through an atmosphere of onion as dense as a London fog with soot, until we found a café where the water supply was good. Quarts of it, with fresh orange juice, flooded down our desiccated throats.

Cairo – sketch by Amelia Terry

5

THE PEOPLE OF THE LAND

DURING all these years of childhood in Egypt, a great love of the country and people matured within me. The feeling was always unconsciously there, inherited from Sarah and Amelia and my parents' childhood, but it now slowly emerged consciously into the brain and heart.

This affection and understanding was nurtured by daily contact with the ordinary people of the country, especially the servants. We had an old bouab or doorkeeper; he was thin and long, with something of a Persian miniature figure about him, and his garments hung loosely in folds to his feet. Sitting on the bench by the door, he used to tell us long stories about the creation of the world, and about the doings of the great King Solomon, who was king of all the birds and beasts as well as of men, and who held rational conversation with them all. The old man, Radwan by name, was a frail looking creature, with a gentle, other-worldly voice, which invested his tales with mystery.

Bouabs are not all like Radwan. There are some town varieties who, owing to the geographical situation of the houses they are in charge of, have many neighbouring bouabs within close range. They gather at various points convenient to all, and there have chats about life in general for long stretches at a time. Worn out by the doings of the day, they retire to sleep the sleep of the just on their benches outside their own establishments. Thieves may come and thieves may go, but the guardians peacefully sleep.

When my father and his friends were young men and felt in jovial mood after a party, they would sometimes transport a sleeping bouab, bench and all, and deposit him outside some other house whose rightful doorkeeper would then be placed somewhere else, still quietly dreaming as the journey was made. What the doorkeepers thought on waking in the morning is not related.

Before Radwan's arrival, we had a very kind-hearted fat old party as bouab who, with his patience in sorrow and infinite faith in God, was a real saint. Once, when very young, I was climbing an orange tree. My foot became stuck between two branches and I could go neither up nor down. In slight pain and much fear, I yelled inarticulate screams. It was the old doorkeeper who came and rescued me, gently quieting my fears and taking my foot out of the wedged sandal. I was only about three years old at the time and felt quite sure that he had somehow saved my life. His gentleness and caring warmed my heart out of all proportion to the discomfort I had been in. We remained close friends until his death some eight years later, when he peacefully went to his Creator, dying suddenly one day at his post by the garden gate.

Our washerwoman was another favourite. She used to dance for our special delight, that curious Arab dance in which the muscles of the body are used more so than the limbs, especially the abdominal muscles. She was no sylph, in fact she was enormous, and the expressions she managed to get into her features had to be seen to be believed. We thought it the height of comedy and called for many a repeat performance.

Then there were the visits from old pensioned servants. These included Mohamed, a man of great age who had known the family generations back. He put on his best clothes to call, which consisted of a clean white turban and over his galabia a wonderful archaic ulster, which I presume had belonged to one of my forebears. It was made of thick tweed with a double cape and reached to the ground. His wrinkled old face, like a friendly monkey's, beamed between the turban and the ulster. Whatever the weather, I never remember Mohamed coming in any other attire.

At the further end of the scale was little Fatima, the coachman's only child. Her official visits were frequent, about once a month, I think. When left to play with us children for the morning, there was never any doubt who was the boss: it was Fatima. She was younger than we were but had as determined a character and as quick a mind as ever I have met. She chose the games, ordered us about and said who was to do what—a miniature general in an ankle-length, brilliant pink dress and tight blue jacket over it.

Poor Fatima. Up till we left the house in 1950 she still came once a month for a little financial help, some sugar, and some tea. Her husband, a feckless, intermittent seller of ice-cream, has abandoned her and she has lost a baby, but she has a young son about eight years old who shows all his mother's early characteristics. Perhaps he will be Egypt's first Labour Party Prime Minister.

Then there was the incomparable Hag Ahmed. He walked up the drive of our Cairo house once a fortnight when we were in residence, for a quarter of a century. His wise, kindly face was encircled above by a spotless white turban, and below by a short clipped beard which just followed the line of his jaw and chin. His white robe could well have been the prototype of Shakespeare's "driven snow", so white it was.

His clothes, the cut of his beard, and his deep, gentle eyes proclaimed him a holy man and a man who knew Islamic scripture and tradition. His title of Hag showed that he had made the pilgrimage to Mecca. But he was not a great preacher nor a professor. He did not visit us to propound religious truth, politics or philosophy. He walked up our drive with such dignity to come and iron our clothes. And this he did superbly well.

To Hag Ahmed, his Creator was ever present. The Kuranic saying, "God is closer to you than your jugular vein", was very real to him. His faith was his ideology in the sense that it affected the quality of his work, his character, his living, and the atmosphere he spread.

When, as a child, I would look into the window of his ironing room (an outbuilding near the main house), whatever worries or tragedies of childhood might be besetting me at the moment, they would dissolve as I stopped to pass the time of day with him and unconsciously imbibed his peaceful cheerfulness. Outside where I stood, the sun was hot on the back of my bare legs, but I stuck my head through the low window into the cool shade of Hag Ahmed's room. The thump of his old-fashioned iron and the smell of clean linen has remained with me for life, synonymous with peace of soul.

One day at the hour for Hag Ahmed's arrival, no white-robed figure came. But instead, to our surprise, a dapper young man walked up the drive in tarboush and suit of gent's dittos—Hag Ahmed's elder son. As he quietly set about his father's work he told us how the old man had been taken ill on a railway platform a few days previously. Some friends were with him, his son explained, and as they stood anxiously watching him where he lay on a bench, they saw his lips move. "Leave him," they whispered to each other, "he is talking to God." Old Ahmed just had the strength to lift his hand to his face and with his fingers he shut his own eyes and quietly died. And here was his son arriving, as a matter of course, to fill his place.

In viewing Hag Ahmed's life alone, one might be led to think that his qualities represented the "older generation, fast dying out," or some such saying, which might be true enough of some fine old men. But in his case there is, happily, more to it than that. Hag Ahmed's three grown-up children are wholly modern. They were educated at government schools. It is interesting to notice the different effect modern education can have on young people with the sure foundation of good family life, compared with those who have been taught no principles of faith. His sons wear striped lounge suits and like bright ties.

His daughter has high-heeled shoes and coloured jumpers. But the elder son has chosen, of his own will, to follow in his father's trade, and he brings to it all the aristocracy of service, learned from his father. The younger son has entered an Egyptian government university and hopes to be sent on an educational mission to complete his studies in England. The daughter is a fully fledged teacher in a government school. She has done a long spell at a school in a remote part of the country. As those acquainted with Egypt know, the difficulty has not always been to get the young men and women to qualify for their work, but to get them to give of their best, or even to go to the more distant parts of the country, away from cinemas, or fashionable restaurants. It is character that counts on these occasions, and Hag Ahmed has bequeathed character to his children.

They represent something of the quality of opportunity which is making itself felt in Egypt; but what is more significant, Hag Ahmed's children are modern shoots firmly grafted on to the old stock; the moral and spiritual qualities of Islam at its best. Not all the young people who are being introduced to the world of print have Hag Ahmeds for their fathers, nor the like of his daughter for their teachers.

A law to combat illiteracy has now made it compulsory for official employers to provide time and means, at their own expense, to teach any illiterate employees to read. When nearing the end of a morning's round of golf on the Gezira Sporting Club links, I have seen an anxious look creep into my caddy's face. "What is worrying you, Mohamed?" I would ask, and then remember that I should hasten on to the eighteenth, for now, at noon, the caddies all gather in the shade of the trees for their reading and writing lessons, where a teacher with a blackboard is provided by the Club authorities. "Would you rather miss school today?" I asked my sixteen-year-old caddy. "Oh no, ya sitt," he replied emphatically, with the light of enthusiasm in his eyes.

The four gardeners' numerous families were always turning

up in full force either to pass the time of day on some feast, or whenever they were in trouble. My mother was never too busy to see them, always giving of her best, whether it was a matter of bandaging a bad cut, advice about an unruly child, or mediating in some family quarrel. They usually left her comforted in body and soul.

The old idea of service, dying out in the world, was alive in those relationships. The interdependence of master and worker, and their equality in the eyes of God, was a very real thing. We knew that they could be relied on and that if we had special needs, they would drop their own plans, and help where help was needed. And they knew that their family troubles were our troubles, and they never hesitated to bring in the sick baby or the rheumatic grandmother, knowing that we, too, would stop what we were doing and give all the help in our power. It was quite usual for servants to stay until infirmity or death itself ended the partnership. Our head gardener had never worked for anyone else, coming to us as a lad under his father who was also our gardener. Over a stretch of some thirty-five years, we had but two cooks, Ali Badr of the flashing gold teeth, and old Mahmoud who used to give us picture postcards of shining, winged angels when we were small, because of our faith, I suppose, more than our characteristics.

The indoor servants who did the housework were Berberines, men from the borders of southern Egypt and the Sudan. Arabic was not their natural language but they learnt it as they grew up. In the evenings, sitting on a bench outside the back door, they used to talk their own tongue, a strange noise to our ears, of ejaculations and short truncated syllables. We once had a Berberine lad so unused to civilisation that he had never seen stairs before and went up them on all-fours. But they were mostly quick to learn, and when trained could be the best servants in the world.

When major hostilities broke out in the home among the staff, which can happen occasionally in every family, my mother would gather them all in. They would sit together round the kitchen table and a maglis or parliament would be held. My mother, as Speaker of the House, controlled affairs, giving all a chance to talk. This procedure went far towards settling the troubles.

There has always been a considerable amount of entertaining in Egypt, and it is inspiring to see how these men rise to the occasion with enthusiasm; nothing is too much trouble; they even welcome half-a-dozen unexpected guests for dinner at half-an-hour's notice. If a neighbour is giving a party and needs extra domestic help, it is usual to borrow servants for the function from friends, so you often find yourself in the strange situation of being waited upon in someone else's house by your own man.

From time to time the position for us was still further complicated. The house of the British General Officer in Command (when such a post existed) was just close to ours. The General was changed every few years, but his servants remained interminably, becoming as close friends of ours as were our own men. So, when first calling on the new General and his wife, perfect strangers, we would be shown into the room by the suffragi—an age-long friend. It was quite difficult not to have a chatty talk in Arabic with the servant—"How are you this year? How's the son? How's the old pain in the left leg?" and so on, before the eyes of a bewildered-looking lady, newly out from England, who would have been justified in thinking that we must have been lunatics.

One much-loved member of our household was the old Italian maid, Carolina, who added her bit to the mixture of languages by failing, after thirty years' residence, to pick up a single word of English or of Arabic, but instead, Anglicising or Arabicising her Italian according to the supposed need. Her original good Bolognese Italian would have served the purpose better in the end and, as we grew up, I am glad to say she resorted to it. Her lack of Arabic produced some strange effects in the household. The Egyptian washerwoman, for instance, always went by the name of Anna, a European name of which she and her parents were entirely ignorant. But the word ana in Arabic happens to mean "I." She had knocked on Carolina's door one day, and on being asked who was there, had replied "ana." This was quite enough to convince Carolina that the washerwoman's name was Anna—so Anna she remained.

One day, when aged about three, I scratched myself at play in the garden. I watched the thick vermilion liquid trickle slowly down my leg. The slight pain vanished as it dawned on me with the awe of discovery that it was this of which I was made. But it is not so easy with inanimate facts, to look backwards from mid-stream to the source and say, here and here I became aware of this and this. Yet I know with some certainty that very early on I realised that my lot had fallen among people with whom one could laugh.

As my sister and I moved from babyhood to childhood, we came in contact with the Egyptian populace beyond the confines of our immediate household. We were sometimes taken to visit a certain charitable institution in which my father took an active interest for many years. Part of it was a kitchen where the very poor could come at stated times for bread and soup. Whenever my father looked in to see them at a meal, they would all hail him as if he had been a fellow beggar, by saying: "You're late—we've finished it all—there's no food left for you!" This joke went on for years.

The ordinary people's sense of humour is indeed one of their most delightful traits. A joke, however feeble, is quite the best way out of any situation or awkwardness. Even with the old cab driver who takes you for a five piastre drive and frantically demands fifteen piastres. Instead of arguing with him, we learnt as we grew up to say some such stupidity as, "Are you *sure* you don't mean fifteen pounds?" and with a broad grin he would accept the legitimate fare.

As you walk about the small streets of Cairo you quite often see drastic-looking rows in progress. Fights to the death they seem to be, with the assailants holding each other by the throat and shouting at the tops of their voices, though their noses are only a few inches apart. Then perhaps a passer-by or a looker-on will make some joke, both fighters will relax their grip, shout with laughter, and the battle is over.

There is also the kind of traditional joke which goes on, repeated by word of mouth, for generations. Of such are the Tales of Goha. They consist of short incidents such as this: Goha had a donkey which he sometimes lent to his neighbours. A friend brought back the donkey one evening after having borrowed it, in a sad state, exhausted and beaten, so Goha thought he must put an end to his generosity. Next day when a neighbour came to ask for the loan of the donkey, Goha replied, "My donkey is dead." "But he can't be," said the man, "I saw him going to market yesterday." "I tell you my donkey is dead." Just then the animal in its neighbouring stall, lifted up its voice and brayed loudly. "There you are," said the man, "your donkey is alive and well." "What!" replied Goha, "you call yourself a friend of mine and you believe my donkey rather than me!"

And, in passing, one might allude to the type of unconscious humour found in such unpromising fields as the telephone directory. One that delights me is the names of small hotels and boarding houses which show a great range, often striking when seen in conjunction with each other—The Mabrouk ("Blessed," in Arabic), The Majestic, the Cromer, the Cosy. Or what about this valiant effort at internationalism? A flower shop called "The Flora Dora Omar Aly"?

It was on the back of the telephone directory that I saw the advertisement of a shop describing itself as "*le plus ancien magazin des nouveautés.*" What novel antiquities or antique novelties does that phrase conjure up?

Unconscious humour abounds in many walks of life and, for the observant, can be a constant source of pleasure. I think of the lady in royal blue velvet whom I watched visiting a Cairo exhibition one hot afternoon. Her high-heeled shoes, to which she was obviously unused, became more than she could bear. So, with no self-consciousness, they were removed and placed deftly on her head, peasant fashion, and there they balanced while she continued her tour in comfort. It is quite a common sight to see a country woman walking along with a basket on her head in which sits a huge gander en route for the market. And when, as can happen, she meets a friend also carrying a gander on her head, the effect is quaint. The women stand and chat animatedly while, on the top storey, the two birds' heads wave and nod at each other not a foot apart.

It is not only the women who have this amazing power of balance. I have seen a lad riding a bicycle in a crowded thoroughfare with both hands on the handlebars. He carried on his head a round tray a yard wide, on which were placed innumerable small bowls of yoghurt. He swayed left and right as he careered along in a maze of cars and trams, keeping his burden absolutely horizontal by adjusting his neck to the bends. No child needs to be taken to the circus in a country like this.

The smaller roads of Cairo and Alexandria can produce an entire army of characters, an array of colourful individuals conjured to mind by the words, street vendors. Gay or gloomy, humorous or intimidating, scallywags or stately, they people my memories of Egypt, in a grand parade.

The term, vendor, does not actually cover all this multitude, for some are buyers. Chief among these is the itinerant buyer of old clothes and empty bottles. He walks the roads of Ramleh and his cry is, oddly enough, an Italian one—"Roba Bechia; Bottillia"; no simple Egyptian can pronounce a "v" so vechia became bechia. One shameful day, we children copied his call as he passed, and into our courtyard he came, ready to negotiate with us for non-existent rags and bottles. Our confusion was complete as we anxiously watched him waver between anger and amusement.

I remember a saleswoman among this company. She sold eggs in a basket on her head, and at intervals uttered a call as eerie as a curlew's. It was a bald enough statement—the

Arabic for "Fresh Eggs ", but she managed to endow it with a ghostly something, fit to curdle any fresh egg. Her long robe touched the ground, hanging in straight lines from her shoulders, and her carriage was magnificent—a Grecian chorus woman stalking the Ramleh lanes in melancholy dignity.

Quite a different character was the old Syrian soap seller. He rode a grey donkey in whose saddle-bags were cakes of special soap made in Syria and exuding an excitingly aromatic oily scent. Our hair was washed with this. His legs dangled on either side, large yellow leather slippers hung loosely from the tips of his toes. Small differences of dress proclaimed him a Syrian, not an Egyptian. Recognising the various Near-Eastern races by such details is part of the knowledge acquired instinctively by anyone brought up in Egypt. Nobody ever said to us, "Look, his turban is higher on his head than is usual, and his blue galabia is shorter," but such distinctions are drunk in with no conscious effort.

There were one or two individuals to be met in the daily round who, for no good reason, filled me with terror. Most days, on the way to school, we passed a harmlessly mental Sudanese woman. She wandered quietly among the scrub on waste land by the Nile, scooping up bucketsful of dust and emptying them into the river, with what aim only her poor mind could tell. This humble figure focused for me three succeeding emotions, and my realisation of them. When I was aged about six or seven, it was unreasoned fear. At about eight years old, fear dimmed enough for me to know that if I could raise a laugh, even a forced one, the grip of fear would loosen further. So for the next year or so this poor woman became, to me, a figure of fun. Heartlessness had conquered fear and with it came the comforting feeling of victory. It was followed, however, when I was about ten or eleven, by an uncomfortable feeling, the birth of compassion edging its way into an immature heart, and throwing a new light on the laughter. And compassion, in its turn, won the day.

I am glad it did, for shortly after this, the old black woman disappeared, her task of filling up the Nile unaccomplished. I hope she found a peaceful grave. She probably did, for in Moslem countries, the mentally lacking are usually kindly treated. Ordinary folk consider that God has in safe keeping what is absent in the make-up of the feeble minded. It is borrowed, as it were, by their Creator and this gives them a special status.

The other figure whom I feared was a beggar who used to pass our house in Ramleh after dark when I was in bed. For years I never saw him, but his chant filled my heart with terror. He was heralded by neither shuffling feet nor tapping stick, so nothing but his voice could account for the fear he inspired. I could hear him approaching down the road, clearer and louder he came, till nothing existed for me but this unseen terror. Slowly the voice grew fainter as he passed, and my limbs less rigid. How curious is fear in childhood, and how wholly irrational! I looked with little more than casual curiosity at other beggars, and rarely shrank from the displayed stump of a limb or leprous-like skin; but there, in the voice of this invisible beggar, lay danger and evil. Who can tell, perhaps he was an evil man?

As my father lay in bed when a little boy in this same house, he would hear a noise some nights which did not frighten him, but filled him with the exhilaration of a sound symbolising important matters of the outer world. As he lay silently listening, he felt a party to mighty things afoot.

It was the sound of galloping hoofs across the waste land westward. He knew, for his father had told him, that this was old Admiral McKillop, of the Ports and Lights, in whom Ismail Pasha, then ruler of Egypt, had great confidence. The Pasha would send for him at any hour of the night for consultations; and the horse he rode could be heard thundering past our Ramleh house towards the Palace.

No such historic sound was heard at night by my generation, but several of the ordinary figures we knew as children are now no more.

One of them who, as far as I know, has disappeared from both highway and byway, was a peripatetic bard who recited his home-made ballads as he strolled along. The theme of his song was an invocation to the Almighty to bless the households within earshot. The master, the ladies, the children, the servants, were all specifically mentioned, ending up with "Maria, the Italian". This poet functioned in Alexandria which is largely cosmopolitan and it was a safe guess that some of the houses he passed contained an Italian maid, more than likely called Maria, and to be included thus by name, might well loosen the purse strings.

This departed poet filled a different role from the professional story-tellers who still exist, especially in the villages, and recite traditional stories of legendary heroes and of giants.

Just as some of these figures are typically Alexandrian, so others are more frequently seen in Cairo. The fact that the Cairo weather is somewhat warmer than in Alexandria, may account for the greater number of sweet-drink vendors to be seen there. Many of them wear the traditional skirt of a striped material predominantly red and yellow. One of the favourite drinks is a syrup made from locust beans, dark and of a Coca-Cola colour. Incidentally this latter liquid has seeped into Egyptian life most markedly; every last village in every last province has a Coca-Cola sign well to view. Football crowds are handed out paper caps and streamers which advertise it. This is a far cry in advertisement from the attractive clinking of two brass saucers used by the traditional sellers of syrup. Which will last longer, one wonders? It is interesting to muse on such matters.

Then there is the humblest and perhaps the oldest of the drink merchants—the goatskin water-carrier.

With back bent double under the weight, he moves through the small streets dispensing cool water to the thirsty young and old. Some of these old men (they always seem to be old) function under ancient endowments. Water, in a land like Egypt, means so much to people that, in times past, devout men have made provision in their wills for these Acquerii. Water is an honoured drink for most Egyptians. Their palates differentiate between various sources, and water from mid-stream of the Nile is specially sweet to them.

In our games as children, we enjoyed emulating the water-carrier. At least, I enjoyed it. My sister, being slightly younger, was naturally the goatskin. This inanimate role was dull per-haps, and certainly uncomfortable. She clung to my back, head downwards, I seized a leg and pulled it to the fore, and in our imaginations this five-year-old sandalled foot became the neck of the goatskin from which the seven-year-old water-carrier, staggering under the weight, dispensed drinks to the grateful world.

A man came to the house every now and then whose em-ployment would be hard to guess by anyone unfamiliar with Egypt. His tool of office looked something like a large one-stringed harp which he carried slung on his shoulder. He settled himself on a matting out-of-doors and forthwith various mattresses were brought from the house and placed before him. These he proceeded to unstitch. His job was to put new life into the cotton with which most mattresses in Egypt are filled. The pile of rather congealed and lumpy cotton was transformed, as he skilfully flicked at it with his strung bow, into a light and fluffy substance ready to re-stuff into the old mattress covers. It was fascinating for a child to watch, and had something in common with the miracle of egg-white being turned into meringue, added to which this whole process was accompanied by the gay twang of his bow.

Another visitor we loved to watch at work was the man who came to scour saucepans. The everyday cleaning, of course, took place in the kitchen, but this man was a specialist, hailed periodically for a total scouring. "I will whiten your pans," was his call, delivered with a beautifully modulated last syllable. He was accompanied by a little boy of seven or eight years old. This child was no mere adjunct or embellishment to the proceedings, he was the rotor arm of the engine, the hero of the piece. For he stood on his toes barefoot inside the pans and, by swivelling left and right, produced a fine finish to the metal with the ball of his feet in the centre and the tips of his toes in the angle. It was a dancing movement performed with his arms out, for balance, and every sign of enjoyment on his features.

Just as these and other daily met Egyptians became living, interesting people to us, so by degrees some of the story and personalities of Egypt's past came to life as we learnt more about it, often linking it with ordinary features in our own lives, immature though they still were.

One of a number of sketches of the Lebanon by Amelia Rowlatt:

Sittee Ammoon is a sister of one of the Emirs, or Magistrates, of the Lebanon and is one of the <u>few</u> Maronite ladies who continue to wear the Horn, the priests having waged a war against them. Sittee Ammoon's is of silver and nearly a yard long and much ornamented by precious stones and long silver chains hanging down from it and falling on each side of the face. The weight of this Horn is very great and so accustomed has this lady become to wear it day and night that she cannot walk or stand without it. It requires a great knack for a person to put on her own veil as the head must be bent so as to catch the veil on the point of the Horn as it is thrown.

6

BACKGROUND OF THE LAND

FOR some people, the history of Egypt is a gap hazily inhabited by Cleopatra, Saladin, and the Mamelukes, who waft in and out between two clearly recognisable points—the Pharaohs at one end and Farouk at the other. And yet it is one of the most colourful and dramatic histories that the world has ever produced. The history and art of Ancient Egypt makes absorbing study, but its immediate bearing on Egypt today is, to many people, remote. Therefore, it is interesting to remember that Lord Cromer thought otherwise. In a letter to Mr. Weigall he talks of "the value of archaeology which is really only another name for history, to the practical politician of the present day," and he adds, "incidents in ancient history frequently brought to my mind the facts with which I had to deal during my tenure of office in Egypt."* And Mr. Weigall, himself an Egyptologist, considered a first-hand knowledge of modern Egypt and Egyptians essential for the full understanding of Ancient Egypt. Be that as it may, to an ordinary individual like myself there seems no watertight compartments in Egyptian history, ancient, medieval, modern and contemporary.

A normal child brought up in Cairo can hardly fail to imbibe a sense of history, however fragmentary. Ours was a hotchpotch, but at least it was there, quite vividly encroaching on our daily lives. Most children have some object which can

* Arthur Weigall, *The Glory of the Pharaohs;* p. 83

be turned at will into a horse, elephant or aeroplane, and something against which they can measure the gradually increasing stretch of their arm. An old granite sphinx of doubtful dynasty served these purposes for us.

The sister of a well-known Egyptologist who had a little class of some nine or ten English children, was responsible for all the early years of our education. Once a year we were conducted round the Egyptian Museum and the objects explained so vividly that the great Pharaohs and nobles became to us lively men of flesh and blood and the outline of their way of living, so clearly depicted in the mural scenes and models, seemed as natural as the daily world around us. After each of these visits we had to write an essay on what we had seen. One year, I remember, the prize was a little earthenware offering dish such as is buried by the thousand in many Ancient Egyptian graves. To modern educationalist ears it might sound an odd prize for a nine-year old, but I treasured it dearly.

When much of your ordinary life happens to take place in Egypt over a long stretch of years, one of the fascinations of archaeology is the unfolding of the story from time to time almost literally under your nose. I remember a happy picnic we had as children at the foot of the Step Pyramid of Sakara, with the Egyptologist, Mr. Quibell. We sat on a mound of rubble and sand that had drifted up the side of the Pyramid which was then, as now, the oldest dressed stone monument known in the world. Little did we realise what lay beneath us.

Had we but had X-ray eyes, we would have seen below where we sat and strolled and chatted, wonderful fluted columns of delicate stonework, long ante-dating the Parthenon. As swimmers floating on the surface with a suitable gadget can see the glories of coral and rock below them, so we might have seen (had we possessed the requisite means) a great enclosing wall of fine white masonry and most skilful workmanship, unguessed at for that era.

A few years later, however, excavators were at work and there it was, revealed to normal view in all its beauty. It was the surrounding court, colonnade and temples of the tomb of King Zoser who built the Step Pyramid over his grave in the Third Dynasty, about a hundred to two hundred years before Cheops built the Great Pyramid. Zoser had a remarkable architect called Imhoteb who must have been a man of great genius, as heretofore only mud brick or wood construction are known, and dwellings made of reed or papyrus bound in bundles. A most interesting architectural connection can be traced between those earlier materials and this sudden fine flowering in stone.

During the digging and studying of this area we would sometimes stay with the excavator, Mr. Firth, and his family in a house on the edge of the desert looking due east over the Nile valley below, to the desert hills beyond. In the face of these cliffs east of the river are great black holes like eye sockets in a skull. They are ancient quarries from which the Egyptians cut limestone for the Pyramids, floating it across the valley in the flooded season, then dragging it up to the western desert on sledges or rollers.

There were moments of deep peace and happiness in that house at Sakara. The simplicity of life on the edge of the desert (anyhow for a guest) was like balm after the complications of Cairo—emotionally and practically. Mr. Firth took us down a great tomb shaft he was working on once, many metres deep. The air was stifling and it was impossible to stand upright, but it was most exciting. And there, at the bottom, literally in the bowels of the earth, was a wall covered with blue-green glazed tiles, a beautiful phenomenon of those early days which is thought to be derived from the reed matting of pre-history.

Evidence of all eras is scattered together over the Sakara area and some grave material lies on the surface. The winter evenings were cold and we used to gather ancient bits of wood to warm ourselves with, but we always had to bring it for expert inspection first, to make sure it had no inscription or

CABINET · PORTRAIT
ALEX. XUEREFF   RAMLEH

Sidney Terry, from a portrait by F. Green.
Malta, 1841

Peter Taylor, 1870

Mercy Friend Taylor, "Aunt Mo"

Arthur Henry Rowlatt

Amelia Caroline Rowlatt

Josiah E Cornish,
my mother's father

The Waterworks House, Alexandria

The Cornish Family in the garden of the Alexandria Waterworks, about 1887.
The girl in the sailor suit is my mother.

The Bank of Egypt, Alexandria, after the British bombardment of 1882

Tents of the British army at Ramleh, 1882.
The area is now called Mustapha Pasha and Rushdy

The staff of the Bank of Egypt, about 1896. Fred Rowlatt is standing, fifth from right, behind Mr. Colbeck, the manager

The National Bank of Egypt, Cairo, soon after its foundation in 1898

The Rowlatt Family: Aunt Pollie (Mary Terry), Arthur and Amelia.
Back row: Fred, Sidney, Jack, Juliet and Charles.
Wyelands, Ross-on-Wye, about 1885

Fred Rowlatt with his mother, Amelia,
and her sister, Mary Terry,
at the Ramleh house, 1901

My parents, about 1907

Miss Ellen Chennells

Henriette Devonshire,
noted Orientalist

Mr. Harris and Miss Selina Harris

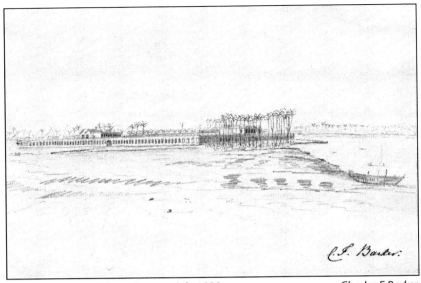

A view of the barracks at Rosetta, July 1830.   *Charles F Barker*

INTERIOR OF THE NEW OKELLA AT ALEXANDRIA.

Interior of the new OKELLA at Alexandria.   *Charles F Barker*

Sketches from the Commonplace Book of Mercy Friend, 1830.
Charles Fiott Barker was the son of Sir John Barker, British Consul at Aleppo
and later Consul-General in Egypt, 1829-1833.

painting on it worth preserving. Ptolemaic or Roman stuff made lovely fires. During one visit I had a birthday. Near my plate at breakfast was a small pottery jug of the Saitic Age. I noticed it, but with the idiocy of youth I dared say nothing. "Perhaps it's not for me," I reasoned. "Being Egyptologists, they probably use that sort of thing for salt and pepper—it's an extra cruet, I expect." So I decided to make no comment. At the end of the meal my attention had to be forcibly drawn to it. I have always been afraid that they may have thought I did not want it, which was far from the case. Both Mr. and Mrs. Firth died in the following years. I hope they know that from then till now the little jug always stands on a table in whatever room happens to be mine.

The Reisner's home in Giza, under the shadow of the second Pyramid, was another favourite place. Dr. Reisner was then leading the joint expedition of Harvard University and the Boston Museum of Fine Arts. It was he who found, in a shaft over one hundred feet deep, the alabaster sarcophagus and funerary furniture of Queen Hetep-Heres, mother of King Cheops, the great Pyramid builder. The reconstruction of this queen's carrying chair must be one of the most striking examples of skill, scholarship, and patience in the whole annals of archaeology. The wood had quite decayed, but every bit of detailed inlay and decoration has been pieced together in its original order, and put on a new frame.

The Reisners were so hospitable and kind. Their mud brick house had more comfort and charm than many a Cairo villa.

An outing we often enjoyed as children took us to the great temple immediately below the second Pyramid. This was built about five thousand years ago by the Pharaoh Chephren as a solemn place of worship, facing due east so that the first rays of the rising sun could penetrate the holy place. We called it our "playground" and leapt about the fallen granite and limestone blocks, joking and laughing, in high spirits. I suppose the Pharaoh and his priest took it in good part, for they never haunted us nor sent a granite rock toppling off the Pyramid to crush us as we jumped about irreligiously and noisily in the sunlight, which they could well have done with all the alchemy of Ancient Egypt at their disposal.

Travellers through the ages have written such fascinating accounts of their first impressions on seeing the Pyramids that I often wish I could remember the first time that I saw them. I sometimes go back hopefully into my memory, thinking that the mechanism of the mind might reveal it to me. But it has proved a vain search, not surprisingly perhaps, for I must have been only a few months old.

The Pyramids are creatures of more moods than a film star. In the early light of morning they are a delicate shell pink rising through a chiffon mist. They have a dream-like quality as if the first puff of dawn wind would blow them away. But at midday, there they still are, tawny brown, yellow, deep cream, or golden—all friendly colours against the delphinium blue sky. In the high summer they and the sky behind them can be colourless with heat; and in the winter a wind can howl round their ice-grey stones to penetrate the bone. On a moonless night the Great Pyramid is hardly discernible save where it blocks out the stars. But a midget human, passing below it, feels, rather than sees, the immense form hovering there like a giant in a fairy tale nightmare, waiting in the darkness ready to pounce. I am happy to record, however, that in the last five thousand years or so the Great Pyramid has not been known to pounce, nor is it likely to do so in the next five thousand. It did not even rebel when I piously chipped off a small corner of one of the mammoth blocks as a tangible bit of Egypt to take to boarding school in England. I planned to take a bottle of Nile water, too. This project was nipped in the bud by unreasonable adults. They amply made up for it though, by posting me lengths of sugar cane from time to time, and a wonderful sweet, halawa simsimia, made from honey and sesame oil. The school took this in its stride, showing greater width of vision than did Miss Farenden's establishment over Amelia's edible odds and ends from Egypt. But it must have been trying for the school authorities to find chewed sugar cane behind the passage radiators, instead of just the usual apple cores.

A favourite spot of ours lay south of the Sphinx towards Sakara. It had been a Ptolemaic burial ground and it was quite easy to find fascinating relics here. Blue mummy beads were the chief treasures but broken ushabtis were also prized especially if the remnant of the statuette showed a foot or a bit of the head with its ceremonial beard. Occasionally a sacred eye of Horus winked at us out of the sand and was borne off in triumph to be the find of the season and *pièce de résistance* for whatever drawer or cigarette box constituted the museum of the moment. My finger tips still respond, in imagination, to the search in the depths of a pocket among sand and fluff for a lost treasure which had to be found before being sent to bed if the Egyptological world was not to suffer loss.

The less fascinating relics lying about this Ptolemaic cemetery were, of course, human bones. But these were so whitened with age and so much part of the landscape that on the whole they lacked personality, and we would brush aside a rib or two, and even a bit of jaw with teeth still in it, quite unperturbed, as we settled down to our afternoon cup of milk in the business-like way that children do, or munched our bread and jam with its coating of Ptolemaic dust on which we were so often nourished. I remember though, from time to time, picking up some bit of clean white bone which took my fancy. It was a piece of skull once, I recollect, with the join across the bone so delicately fretted and interlocked, so beautifully worked. And as I gazed at it I became aware in a new way that this had been part of warm flesh and blood, that a personality had been clothed by it who had known tears and joy, love and sorrow, and the pulsing movement of life as I knew them. I was deeply awed but not afraid. Perhaps I shall meet the owner of that skull one day and we can compare notes together in the familiarity of the hereafter.

Some years, when older, I used to visit a little house at

Abydos, on the edge of the desert. Here I stayed with those who were then at work copying frescoes of the great temple of Seti and his son Ramses II. In addition to the pleasure of my hostess' company, this little mud brick bungalow was always full of charm. The mode of living here was almost as simple for us as it was for the Egyptian peasants in the neighbourhood. A fellaha made the bread, our food came from the village, our milk from the village buffalo, and we washed in a flat, yard-wide tin called a tisht, in true Egyptian fashion.

A red hollyhock had grown up outside the veranda window and, sitting there in the evening, one could see through its leaves and flowers to the pale desert beyond—a possibly unique view. I spent many hours climbing over the fine nineteenth dynasty temple close at hand, or just sitting on high, in an angle of the mammoth stones, alternately reading and watching the birds.

Some of the birds, such as hoopoes and wagtails, would run about the honey-coloured temple, while others like kestrels and an occasional harrier would be circling solemnly, high in the blue above. The very dullest-witted could not but muse on this ancient land from such a vantage point. On the temple walls, Ancient Egypt is depicted in the detail of its agricultural life, its natural history, its trade, and recreations. Below, between the village and the fields, backwards and forwards, passes Egypt's peasantry of today, and not a break in this life has there been for five thousand years and more. The place where the sculptor's knife cut the stone all those eras ago looks like the incision of yesterday. Yet it was work done to honour a king dead over a thousand years before Rome conquered Britain.

It was mostly through friendship with archaeologists that the history of Ancient Egypt became to me a vivid background to life in modern Egypt, though, in a sense, familiarity with it began much earlier, when we ran up and down the Sphinx's back, after the manner of chicks on a hen, or played hide and seek with the children of the French Director of Antiquities in the Museum garden that was then full of dispossessed Pharaohs and redundant gods. Crates of Museum paraphernalia, statues and portions of statues, made an excellent setting for our games of chase, and a grove of ficus trees provided shade in which to rest when weary from jumping back and forth over half a Horus. But sometimes a melancholy mood would overcome us as we played there. Influenced no doubt by the Ancient Egyptian atmosphere, the Cult of the Dead would enthral us. Once, I remember, it was the obsequies of a dead sparrow upon which all was centred. The French archaeologist's child had a true Egypto-Gallic sense of mourning. A cardboard box made a passable sarcophagus, some of the smaller children were detailed as professional weeping women and the whole affair went with a swing.

I have not penetrated this region for what seems like dynasties but is, I presume, only decades. Near this spot there is now an imaginative garden. A pond with reeds and Nile water-lilies puts one in mind of papyrus and lotus. Clipped marjoram borders entwine in Pharaonic patterns. Whenever I visit the Museum nowadays I say to myself: "This time I will not stop to inspect the little garden. The wind is cold—or the sun is hot—or I am late." But I always do stop and it always gives me pleasure; it may be for its own sake or is it possibly for the sake of that dusty patch whose successor it is, where children laughed and leapt over the Pharaohs and over the flowers? "My name is Ozymandias, King of Kings, look on my works ye mighty and despair." Not having been mighty we had been in no way intimidated by such ideas—nor by the thought, for that matter, of Champollion's or Mariette's ghostly disapproval.

On other occasions I would perhaps be lying on a bank of yellow sand in the sun watching a large square-faced beetle pushing a ball of dung laboriously up a slope backwards with its hind legs, when my father would explain how this was the same type of scarab beetle that the Ancient Egyptians so often watched perform this feat, and how they chose it for one of their symbols of the sun-god, thinking perhaps that in that round ball were the scarab's eggs which would hatch by germination from the sun's heat.

Or down by the sea at Ramleh we would bring him beautiful mauve shells to admire, and would be told that this was the very sort of shell, the murex, from which the Tyrean dye was extracted of old, that coloured the imperial purple robes of emperors.

And so, one way and another, without much mental effort, the outlines of the great story fell into place.

Menes the first unifier of Upper and Lower Egypt was eventually followed by the Pyramid builders of the Third and Fourth Dynasty with their capital at Memphis south of Giza. These were the giants of the Old Empire. The tale of unity and strength, division and decay, is the theme throughout. The Old Empire dissolved in anarchy, but not for long. The Twelfth Dynasty ushered in a fine new epoch, the Middle Empire, in which art and commerce were revived. The Hyksos Kings, foreign rulers of Semitic origin, held sway for some of this time, till a strong Egyptian King of the Seventeenth Dynasty arose and expelled them. Some experts have thought that Joseph lived and that the Exodus took place during the Hyksos regime, but this is only a guess. The New Empire, initiated in about 1550 B.C., chose Thebes as its capital, where modern Luxor now stands, in Upper Egypt.

Such great names as Queen Hatchepsut, and Tothmes, the conqueror, dated from this time, when the Egyptian Empire stretched south to the Sudan and east and north through Palestine and Syria up towards the mountains of Asia Minor. About the middle of the fourteenth century B.C. came the strange experiment of King Akhnaten who, abandoning Thebes, built his capital at Tel al Amarna and developed a monotheistic religion, the worship of the disc of the sun. It lasted but his lifetime. The old priesthood prevailed and the next Pharaoh returned to the ways of his fathers. The great

Ramses II was soon to reign and under him Egypt again reached the heights of power from which she had tottered while the philosopher king had shut himself up at Tel al Amarna. But it was not long before signs of decadence were once more apparent. Assyria and Babylon were menacing powers. Esarhadon and Nebuchadnezzar both penetrated Egypt, and finally Cambyses of Persia dominated the whole scene. Egypt fought bitterly to regain her independence but to no avail. When Alexander of Macedon appeared on the horizon nearly two centuries later he was hailed as a deliverer. It is striking how Alexander lingers in the memory of the present Egyptian peasants. Perhaps this has something to do with the fact that he took pains to identify himself with the old deities of Egypt as the Pharaohs had done before him. He went out to the Temple of Ammon at Siwa, in the western desert, and spent some time alone in its columned courts.

Whether he followed this line as a policy or a faith, it is hard to say, but he has certainly left a mark on the common people of Egypt today. The Egyptian peasant knows Alexander by the name of Abu Qurnein, the Father of the Two Horns, from the headdress in which he was depicted on some temple walls, consisting of two cows' horns, a symbol of one of the Ancient Egyptian gods. When a certain workman on a dig hurt his leg badly with a falling beam, a few years ago, he did not call on his Creator nor on any Moslem or Christian saint to aid him, but he called on Abu Qurnein, the young conqueror of two thousand years ago.

As is well known, Alexander left no living heir, and his prodigious empire was divided between his generals. Egypt fell to Ptolemy, and he and his warring descendants ruled her for some three hundred years. Cleopatra, the last Ptolemy, let Egypt drop from her beautiful hands and Rome caught it. Cleopatra died, and Augustus inherited.

Egypt was famous as the granary of the Roman Empire, and coins bearing the stern profiles of Rome's emperors can still be found in the desert sands and crumbled dust round old towns—Diocletian's great hooked nose and Hadrian's less austere features.

In a remote part of Coptic old Cairo, there stands a Roman bastioned gateway. It rises among small dwelling houses and Coptic churches, and is deeply impressive. It has now been cleared of rubbish, and the immediate surroundings much improved, by the endeavours of a well-known Coptic family. But when we visited it in my early years, the first thing one was aware of was the squeaking of myriad bats, followed soon and overwhelmingly by a bat smell of great power.

I did not mind the bats, in fact they added considerably to the pleasurable awe of the place; but they have so entered into my constitution that neither improved conditions nor the mere passage of years have ever been able to disassociate for me bats from Roman bastions.

This Coptic quarter of Cairo is most interesting. The word, Copt, is derived from the Greek, Aigyptioi—Egyptian. It now signifies the old race of Christian Egyptians. They are lineal descendants of the Ancient Egyptian race, and their Coptic language, now used only in ecclesiastical ritual, is derived from the Pharaonic tongue. They were among the very first converts to Christianity outside the immediate area where Jesus worked. Some of them claim that St. Mark himself evangelised them. Therefore, the churches gathered in this quarter are of great antiquity; all are interesting, some are beautiful. The exteriors show almost no sign of what they are within. The plain walls are, for the most part, built in with small, inconspicuous houses, down narrow lanes. This camouflaging of religious buildings was natural in past eras for any community with a minority religion. The relation between Christian and Moslem is an important factor in Egypt's internal situation.

The eye of imagination goes back some seven hundred and fifty years and sees a humble figure dressed in brown robe and cord belt walking doggedly along the streets of Cairo through bastion and gateway, past sentry and guard, up steps, down passages until he finally reaches the great Ayubite Sultan of the day.

Tradition has it that St. Francis was kindly received. ". . . the Soldan began to feel great devotion towards him, as much for the constancy of his faith as for his contempt of the world (for albeit he was very poor, he would accept no gift) and also for the fervour of martyrdom he beheld in him. From that time forth the Soldan heard him gladly, and entreated him many times to come back, granting to him and to his companions freedom to preach wheresoever it might please him; and he gave them also a token, so that no man should do them harm."*

An old Coptic gentleman stood on his balcony a few years back; in the silence of the evening he was talking to himself, rather than to me. He looked across the Nile, which shone a silver-green in the dusk, to the Valley of the Kings beyond, indescribably beautiful and still. He nodded towards the tombs of his ancestors, the Pharaohs, and murmured, "They were the fire. We are the ashes." This may have mirrored the mood of a sad old man near the end of his life, but it is far from the truth. The Coptic community could have a vital contribution to make to a new Egypt.

A Coptic service in one of these churches can be a refreshing mixture of ceremony and of family life. Incense abounds, canticles are chanted in the Coptic tongue, and the priest is treated with great deference. At the same time, whole families down to the very newest arrivals, attend the church. Some Coptic babies are christened when very tiny and confirmed immediately afterwards, with the result that congregations at Communion Services are liable to include Communicants of a few weeks old. The deacons who assist at some services can be quite little boys, who entertain themselves by hopping about in play when not actually needed at the altar. Another link with pre-Arab Egypt is the popularity among modern Copts of the old names. I have shared a taxi

* The Little Flowers of St. Francis. Chapter 24.

with Isis, heard Ramses upbraided by his mother for eating too many sweets, and once danced a waltz with Sesostris.

Egyptian history of the next nine hundred years was the period which came to life for me most vividly as I grew to know and to love the scene in which it was set. Behind the open streets and neon lights of modern Cairo lies a wonderful world. This is the city of the Arab rulers of old.

The first Moslem invader arrived in the year A.D. 641, and battered on the gates of the Roman bastions. His name was Amr ibn Aas, one of the leaders of the newly risen Arab army which was flooding north, east, and west from the desert lands of Mecca and Medina. The peoples were strengthened and united by the faith of Mohamed, their prophet.

It is always striking to see the ordinary Egyptian man quite simply saying his prayers wherever he happens to be at the appointed hour, the cook in the kitchen, the chauffeur by the garage, the peasant in the fields. The women mostly pray in their homes, or in certain mosques specially favoured by women, often built round the tomb of some saintly woman. All this I saw around me. But what were the foundations of their faith? I gradually began to learn something about it.

The rules for washing head, hands, and feet before prayers were strictly carried out under the stable tap by our outdoor servants, and I had, of course, watched it from childhood. On Fridays, the Moslem Sabbath, the mosques are crowded to overflowing, the call to prayer and the sermon are sometimes cast by microphone hundreds of yards around. But far the most magic of muezzins in my memory, chanted from his minaret unaided by device. His call to prayer floated through the clear air of Helwan. We had been sent to this healthy but unromantic place to recover from measles. There certainly exist people who have found an enchantment in Helwan (apart from some engrossing neolithic remains in the neighbourhood) but the place is not redolent with charm. This beautiful voice, however, calling men to remember their Creator and be thankful, fell on at least one pair of ten-year-old Christian ears and Helwan is remembered with gratitude. It was not quite so purely elevating as perhaps it sounds. For it was linked in my mind at the time with a new delicious form of biscuit which we munched in quantities during this stay. I remember standing on the balcony eating one with conscious relish while my mind and heart were just as consciously open to the quality of the muezzin's voice and the content of his words. "H'm," I noted to myself, "there seem to be two very different forms of satisfaction in this world, nor do they have to cancel each other out." But I digress.

About ninety-two per cent of Egyptians are Moslems. The prophet Mohamed, the founder of their religion, was born in Mecca towards the end of the sixth century A.D. He was, we are told, born after the death of his father and he lost his mother when only a few years old, so was brought up by relatives. He belonged to an important Meccan family, but was one of the "poor relations." History is not very clear about details of his early life, but it is supposed that he was sent out for a time to learn the language and ways of the desert Bedwin. He certainly travelled with camel caravans which traded with other communities and possibly other lands. He may even have been as far as Egypt.

We next hear of him as the conductor of caravans and the husband of a widow of means, called Khadija, fifteen years older than himself.

In those days, Arabian tribes all had their own deities whom they worshipped in the form of stones, sticks and other idols. A certain large black stone in Mecca was supposed to represent the particular deity of that part. Mohamed and Khadija worshipped this. It is certain that Mohamed had dealings with Jews and Christians as he travelled round and from them must have acquired much. After deep thought he turned against pagan worship and formulated in his own mind a faith based on the essential unity of God who created the world and man. He felt himself called to a divine mission by God to end paganism and spread the worship of the one God.

At this time he started receiving what he believed to be divine inspiration, sometimes directly from God, and sometimes, so it seemed to him, through the Archangel Gabriel. He used to have times of retirement and contemplation in which to receive guidance. These messages, written down and collected together, form the Kuran. Though Mohamed believed himself to be the mouthpiece of God, he was diffident about calling himself so, and at first only spoke of it to his immediate relatives and friends. His wife, Khadija, was one of the early converts.

As time passed, he and his small band of followers preached more openly and appeared to plan, with care, round the people whom they wished to change, some of whom were people of influence. It was not long, however, before a quite formidable opposition arose and at one time it became so bad that Mohamed and his friends were barricaded into the quarter of the town where they lived.

When they were eventually let out, Mohamed worked mostly on the outskirts of Mecca among strangers coming in and out of the town to trade. Many of them listened keenly to his message and he had several invitations to go and work in their own towns. But he did not feel it right to accept at first.

Some of his staunchest new converts came from a town to the north of Mecca, now called Medina, and there he sent one of his close friends to encourage them in this new way of living. A moral code was forming among these pioneers in which such things as adultery, theft, and lying were forbidden.

The opposition in Mecca, far from abating, had heightened to the point at which its leaders decided to do away with Mohamed. They arrived secretly at the place where he was thought to be, but they were too late—he had fled. He had chosen Medina as his refuge. The journey had apparently been carefully planned with camels, guides, and necessities provided. The party had spent the first night in a cave in the opposite direction from Medina so as to confuse any enemies who might follow them.

From this time onwards, Mohamed's mission went ahead. He incorporated much from Jewish and Christian sources into his religion; the faith of Abraham was a great inspiration to him. The chief prophets of the Old Testament are spoken of in the Kuran and Jesus is given a place of honour and reverence. Some of the great truths of His life, such as the Virgin Birth, are wholly accepted by Moslems. To his followers, Mohamed is the latest prophet sent by God, therefore has the fullest revelation, but they are forbidden to speak of him as being better than Jesus, Moses or Abraham, who are to them all divine messengers of God. Moslems talk of Christians and Jews as People of the Book (the Bible and Talmud) and they feel a great theological affinity between the three great faiths.

The word Islam, which was the name given by Mohamed to his faith, means "submission"—total submission to the will of God. This is evident in the ordinary Arabic conversation of every type of person however modern they may be. Such a saying as *In sha' allah* (if God wills), is the phrase used when speaking of something you would wish to happen, or *Al hands lilah* (praise be to God), is the correct answer when someone asks you if you are well and the answer is in the affirmative.

The injunctions left by Mohamed in the Kuran cover the whole of ordinary life and are often based on common sense hygienic principles such as abstaining from pork, a dangerous meat in a hot country before the day of refrigerators. The whole Islamic religious and civil law is based on the sayings and revelations of the Prophet. It would be more accurate to say that the one code is at the same time religious and civil, for no difference is made in Islamic law. Nor is there an order of priesthood as such. A sheikh who leads the prayers in a mosque is a man learned in the Kuran and tenets of the faith, who has studied them long and acquired a theological reputation, but there is no initiation ceremony for him to perform or clerical body to join.

The five minimum requirements of a Moslem are the recital

of the Creed—"There is no god but God and Mohamed is his Prophet"; the recital of prayers at set times during the day; fasting during the month of Ramadan; the giving of alms; and the pilgrimage to Mecca, the latter to be done if and when possible. It would be wrong, for instance, to go off leaving behind you an uncared-for family. The successor to the ancient black stone is still in Mecca. After Mohamed had won all the Meccans to belief in the one God he did not destroy the old stone but kept it as a sort of geographical rallying point for the new faith, devoid of any worshipful quality in itself. As the present-day pilgrim reaches Mecca he has to stop several miles out and, be he a millionaire or a beggar, he is then clothed in two cotton garments only. Bareheaded and barefooted he makes his way to the central mosque surrounding the stone.

The following verses of the Kuran give some idea of its nature: "Put not God with other gods or thou wilt sit despised and forsaken. Thy Lord had decreed that thou shalt not serve other than him; and kindness to one's parents whether one or both of them reach old age with thee. Say not to them 'Fie,' and do not grumble at them, but speak to them a generous speech. And lower to them the wing of humility out of compassion, and say 'O Lord have compassion on them as they brought me up when I was little.'

"Your Lord knows best what is in your souls, if ye be righteous, and verily He is forgiving unto those who come back penitent. And give thy kinsman his due, and the poor, and the son of the road; and waste not wastefully, for the wasteful were ever the devil's brothers, and the devil is ever ungrateful to his Lord.

"But if thou dost turn away from them to seek after mercy from thy Lord, which thou hopest for, then speak to them an easy speech . . . .

"And draw not near to fornication; verily it is ever an abomination, and evil is the way thereof.

"And slay not the soul, that God has forbidden you, except

for just cause; for he who is slain unjustly, we have given his next of kin authority; yet let him not exceed in slaying. Verily he is ever helped.

"And draw not near to the wealth of the orphan, save to improve it, until he reaches the age of puberty, and fulfil your compacts, verily, a compact is ever enquired of.

"And give full measure when you measure out, and weigh with a right balance; that is better, and a fairer determination.

"And do not pursue that of which thou hast no knowledge; verily, the hearing, the sight and the heart, all of these shall be enquired of.

"And walk not on the earth proudly; verily thou canst not cleave the earth and thou shalt not reach the mountains in height.

"All this is ever in the sight of your Lord and abhorred."

(E. H. Palmer's translation. Chapter 18, verses 23-40. *Sacred Books of the East* Series.)

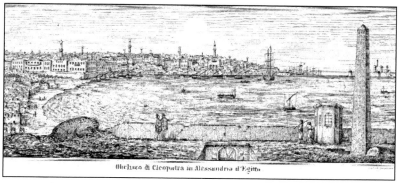

Alexandria's eastern harbour, mid nineteenth century, showing "Cleopatra's Needle" before it was removed to the Embankment, London

7

THE TALE OF THE LAND

As I grew up I began to be seriously interested in the art and history of pre-Ottoman Islamic Egypt. The well-known Orientalist, Mrs. Devonshire, a French lady of charm and scholarship, took parties to visit the Islamic monuments of Cairo.

Mrs. Devonshire's help and encouragement to me was a privilege and I accompanied her regularly on these tours. I could be of a little use, too, in such things as taking energetic members of the party up minarets and so on, for Mrs. Devonshire was quite an old lady. Very occasionally, if she was unwell, I would conduct the party. After my initial nervousness I enjoyed it. On one occasion I fairly breezed through the afternoon, letting myself go on all manner of historic detail. Only after the return did I realise that one of the members of the party was a most eminent Orientalist who probably had known all I was holding forth about, before I had been born.

The expeditions I most enjoyed were when two or three keen Orientalists, including perhaps some visiting professor from Europe or England, would set out to see a special monument, little known and further afield—and I was invited to go with them. The conversation was, at times, above my head but I drank in what I could, and had the run of Mrs. Devonshire's library for further investigation. I look back gratefully to those experiences and all they opened for me.

Some of the mosques we visited, in the ordinary parties,

were also off the beaten track for tourists. Gems of the eleventh to fifteenth centuries were deep in the old city of Cairo, down little lanes so narrow that our horse-drawn carriage could not always get round the corners in one turn. One such favourite of mine is the mosque of Aslam al Bahay, hidden away under an arch among the labyrinth of medieval Cairo. Aslam had been a slave to the Sultan of his day, but was given his freedom and rose to the rank of sword-bearer. But as was the case with so many of these men, he fell into disgrace, spent some years in prison and forfeited his possessions. Though the curve of fortune ran often suddenly downwards, yet, as long as the victim was still breathing, there was always hope for the reverse action. And in Aslam's case it happened. From his liberation until his death in 1346 he lived in freedom, surrounded once more by wealth and respect, having built this beautiful mosque.

The design is of two large bays and two triple arched divisions surrounding a central court. Above the prayer niche, showing the direction of Mecca, is a fine bit of plasterwork which is unusually decorated with green and brown faience. Another comparatively rare feature is a broad band of faience round the drum of the dome on the outside. It is in the form of an Arabic inscription done with large letters in dark brown decorated with delicate green and blue arabesques with designs in between, on a white background. The interior of the mosque has some coloured marble decorations, and in the funerary chamber the carved wooden tomb is original fourteenth century work, as is part of the glass in the window.

Some of the inhabitants of these remoter parts did not often penetrate into modern Cairo; a group of Europeans was quite a sight for them. Crowds of children used to collect and follow us round, sometimes shouting "Nasrani"— (Nazarenes, i.e. Christians)—or just staring, their eyes popping out of their heads with curiosity. Occasionally they had to be kept at bay by a special policeman who accompanied Mrs. Devonshire on the trips. The adult population of

these parts behaved well, though consumed with curiosity
themselves. I heard one mother telling her child to leave us in
peace, "for after all," she said, "are they not sons of Adam
like ourselves?"

Many of the doorkeepers of the mosques and their children
became great friends of ours. However dirty the little street
outside, every mosque in use was kept clean inside. Men and
boys would often be at their devotions as we entered and
would continue quite unselfconsciously in our presence.

The keen pleasure of finding, sometimes quite suddenly,
that one has begun to master a branch of study, broke in on
me during these trips. Much of Islamic architecture in Cairo
can be dated by the form of lettering used in inscriptions, the
type of decorating and the ground plan itself, and, in some
cases, by the amount which the roadway has risen above the
level of the floor. Learning to recognise these signs and
deducing facts therefrom was a new and exciting experience,
on the wings of which I learnt with relish the history of those
times.

Egypt was at first administered by governors appointed by
the Caliphs from Damascus, and then from Baghdad, successive capitals of the great new Arab empire. But it was not long
before the governor developed into a more or less independent
ruler. The well-known Ibn Tulun was one of these. By the end
of the tenth century, Egypt was ruled by another dynasty of
Arab rulers, the Fatimites, called after Fatima, the Prophet
Mohamed's daughter. It was they who founded the city we
now call Cairo, which finally succeeded to the past towns that
had been built near by.

Astrological omens carried great weight in those days.
Mars, known to the Arabs as the Conqueror of the Heavens,
was in the ascendant, so the new city was named The
Conqueror, al Kahira, which is easily traceable in our word,
Cairo. This Fatimite era was one of lavish living and of
immense wealth and power, which subsided from time to time
with shattering rapidity into periods of poverty and starvation.

Nasir-i-Khusrau, a famous Persian traveller of the eleventh century, has given us a first-hand description of Fatimite Cairo. The riches were stupendous. Many thousands of people lived in the royal palace, and the number of palace servants ran into five figures. He saw great galleys on the Nile. The streets were fine and well illuminated at night. He describes the young ruler of the time as being simply dressed and clean-shaven. Nasir-i-Khusrau saw him riding on a mule to some festival, but the ceremonial umbrella carried over his head was encrusted with jewels.

It is interesting to note, in the trends of this past history, how the people's morale and character seemed to stand firm through the first stages of wealth. Goods were sold at fixed prices, and any shopkeeper discovered cheating was taken round the streets on a camel, ringing a bell and declaring to all passers-by in what manner he had been dishonest. Somewhat later, the great riches appear to have eaten into the soul of the place. We get descriptions of drinking bouts with amber cups, of immense banquets off gold plate, of fabulous jewelled clothing, of chess played with gold and silver pawns, and a ruler out of touch with his people, idling in his palace and scoffing at the faith of his fathers. After this, with deadly speed came the crash. The ruler's own family had to move to Baghdad to escape starvation.

One of the earliest Fatimite sultans, al Hakim by name, was a madman. From the top of the great gateway of Bab al Nasr you can look down today into the ruins of his spacious mosque. He came to the throne of Egypt in A.D. 996 at the age of eleven. A year later he was responsible for his first political murder—the first of many. His actions and the laws he issued were weird, cruel and illogical, showing as time went on that they undoubtedly came from a distorted mind. He was given to wandering round these very Cairo streets at night, to the terror of his subjects. Many are the stories told of his cruelty and of his dealings in black magic. One of his generals, returning from a successful campaign, arrived unannounced into the ruler's presence to tell him the good news. It was an ill chosen moment, however, for he disturbed al Hakim at one of the grimmer perpetrations of his disordered mind. He knew his master well enough to realise that the best course was to go home and put his affairs in order. His apprehension was fully justified, for within a few hours his head was off. Al Hakim had a strange, perhaps hypnotic, influence over people. In his later years he claimed divinity and many believed him. In course of time came the inevitable revulsion against him, and nearly all his intimate friends were murdered. One, however, Darazi, escaped to Syria and founded there the remarkable sect of Druses, mysterious to this day. Al Hakim himself eventually disappeared when wandering alone on the Mokatam heights above Cairo. His clothes and his dead donkey were the only traces of him found.

Not all these Arab rulers behaved thus. One of them was a quiet, pious man who would sometimes sit at the corner of the street dressed like the poorest of his subjects. He would weave baskets as he sat there, and talk to the passers-by about the necessity of a spiritual life and devotion to the Almighty.

The Fatimites built a fine fortified wall round Cairo, portions of which stand today, with three magnificent gateways. They were built in 1087, just twenty-one years after William the Conqueror invaded England.

These gates lie deeply in the old town. An antique guardian used to keep the key to the wicket gate leading into the wall by the Bab al Nasr. He carried a candle and beckoned you silently on, into the dark, musty and dusty passage within the wall. Arrow slits threw some intermittent light as one proceeded, and there were small guard houses built out at intervals. The old guardian had a fine sense of the dramatic. He would point to a damp patch on the wall as you passed, and murmur the one word, "blood", which he firmly believed it to be.

Before the days of artillery, these walls were indeed impregnable. They were built by people with a thorough knowledge of military architecture, ahead of anything known at the time. Some of the same devices are seen on crusader castles in Syria and castles of that era in France. But they were all just later in date, and may well have been copied from this Cairo master-piece.

The old man led you on until the top of the wall was reached by a fine circular stairway. When Napoleon took Cairo, he manned these walls. They are castellated outwards, but he added a defence on the inside, too, for fear of a rising within the town. He inscribed the names of some of his French commanders on the towers along the wall. It is curious to see them still—"Tour Corbin", "Tour Milhaud"—as a reminder of his brief authority here. The wall crosses the top of two great entrance gateways. You can look down through the holes for boiling oil and other missiles, on to the street below, crowded with inhabitants going about their daily business.

In spite of the melodramatic tenor in much of medieval Egyptian history, I have rarely heard of a ghost story. But there is an old twelfth century corner of Cairo where, if a psychic visitor of today became aware of the past, he might hear a ghost saying in Anglo-Saxon tones, "'Ere, Bert, pass the next perishin' stone, will yer?" For here is a small portion still standing of the fortifications built by order of Saladin, in the construction of which he was said to have used prisoners from the Crusader armies. This spot, in the Citadel of Cairo, loomed large to me as a child, because here the English history, learned as an ordinary lesson from my governess, and the Egyptian history slowly coming to life all round me, met at a tangible place.

Within the Citadel walls there exists a deep well. Its diam-eter is large enough to allow of a sloping spiral path which descends from the top, high above the level of Cairo proper and the Nile, until it reaches water level far below. Down there in the old days an animal turned a water wheel. The buffalo, or whatever it had been, was brought down when young and never taken up again, so we were told. Donkeys then carried the water in skins up the spiral ramp, turn after turn, to ground level far above. In common parlance it is called Bir Yusef—Joseph's Well. Needless to say it had nothing to do with the patriarch of old, though the ordinary Cairene of these parts believes it to be the well in which Joseph was thrown. But it was almost certainly built, or cleared, by Saladin whose first name was Yusef—a sufficient fact to account for the confusion. As children, we would sometimes be taken right down to the water level of this pit. Pad, pad, down and round, round and down the ramp we would go, getting more silent and more awed at every step, till at the bottom we would gaze at the broken relic of the water wheel, our minds a confusion of pictures in which Saladin, and the party of Ishmaelites, interwove with the certain sensation that Australia could be but a few feet below where we stood.

Saladin, who was of Kurdish origin, wrested Egypt from the decadent Fatimites. His dynasty was short-lived and was succeeded by the rule of the Mamelukes who reigned from 1250 to 1517, during which time Egypt was the head of a large empire stretching through Palestine and Syria to the river Euphrates. The Mamelukes originated as the Sultan's personal bodyguard, a *corps d'élite* of picked Turkoman and Circassian slaves. They were given the best military education of the day and were treated with respect.

The circumstances in which they seized power were singular and intimately connected with a remarkable woman called Shagret al Dur, meaning, in Arabic, Tree of Pearls. She was originally a slave of Turkoman origin, belonging to the Caliph of Baghdad, but was later sold to the Egyptian Sultan Saleh, a great nephew of Saladin's and last of his dynasty. She was a favourite of his and he married her. In November, 1249, this Sultan was away in Damascus fighting, when the news reached him that the French, under King Louis IX, had launched another Crusade and had actually landed in Egypt, which meant that the Sultan had to hurry back and face this greater danger.

It so happened that Sultan Saleh was ill at the time, but he was a courageous man and immediately set forth on the tedious journey south and west across the desert of Sinai, though he had to be carried in a litter for most of the way. On arrival, he endeavoured to organise his army and camped near the town of Mansura some ninety miles from Cairo, with the idea of stemming there the oncoming Crusade. Probably owing to his illness, Shagret al Dur accompanied her husband on his new campaign.

Had the French forces known it, they could have pushed on from the coast and smashed the Egyptian army, for Saleh's illness had increased—he was, in fact, on his death bed. But the Crusaders dallied on their way. This delay made history for it launched the melodramatic career of Shagret al Dur.

When the Sultan died, she it was who took control of the situation, civil and military. Firstly, she had his body embalmed and sent to Cairo secretly. Then she announced that he was still ill in his tent and unable to see people though he would be better in a few days' time. A doctor, a eunuch, and a faithful slave shared her secret, the doctor visiting the royal tent daily to give semblance of truth to the story, and the slave forging his late master's signature to orders of the day, which were actually commands framed by Shagret al Dur herself. As a finishing touch, food was daily prepared and taken to the royal "patient's" tent.

It was not long before this amazing woman had her military forces in disciplined array. She had seen to it that reinforcements and part of the river fleet from Cairo came to their aid. Eventually the French Crusaders arrived on the scene and faced the Egyptians across a canal which, with the town of Mansura, exists today. The battle started leisurely with nothing but skirmishes and the mutual capture of a few prisoners. But February 9, 1249, dawned a fateful day.

A Bedwin traitor showed the Crusaders a ford across the

canal and over they came, taking Shagret al Dur's troops by surprise in their tents. The General who had been acting immediately under the Queen's orders, was killed as he hastily mounted his horse to fight. It boded ill for the Egyptians but, again, lack of strategy on the part of their opponents gave them a second chance.

King Louis's younger brother, Count Robert d'Artois, in command of the second column, dashed ahead of the main party in his enthusiasm, which meant a straggling attack, instead of a united one. The late Sultan's Mamelukes rallied and led a furious counter charge. The battle raged all day. When night finally fell, fifteen hundred Crusaders had been killed and King Louis was a prisoner of Shagret al Dur's. One of the fallen is commemorated in Salisbury Cathedral where his mourning family placed a fine recumbent statue of him, telling how he gave his life at Mansura in 1250. The plight of the Crusaders was indeed sad, for an epidemic broke out among the remainder. One of their number, the historian Joinville, describes how being ill, he asked a priest to say a special Mass by his bedside. Half-way through, the priest himself fell a victim of the illness. Joinville rose from his bed to help the fainting man who was just able to finish the Mass. "But," commented Joinville, "he never chanted again, for he died."

In the meantime, Sultan Saleh's son arrived from abroad where the news of his father's illness had reached him. Shagret al Dur now announced the Sultan's death and handed over the reins of government to this young man, her stepson, Turan Shah. His rule was not a success. He was efficient but cruel, and the Mamelukes came to the conclusion that they would rather have Shagret al Dur as a ruler, who was efficient and just in her dealings with them. Turan Shah was soon murdered by them, with the connivance of his stepmother who once more became the acknowledged sovereign.

Coins were struck in Shagret al Dur's name and she was mentioned in the weekly prayers in the mosques, as had been the custom with preceding Sultans. By all accounts she was a judicious and wise administrator. One of the first things she did was to make peace with her erstwhile enemies of the eighth Crusade. King Louis was freed for a ransom, and his troops evacuated the coastal towns which they had still held.

The Mamelukes, who had virtually placed Shagret al Dur on the throne, now wrote to the Caliph of Baghdad who was still titular head of Islam and supposed to give or to retain his blessing from such appointments. A reply came back leaving no doubt as to the Caliph's views on such an unorthodox idea as a Moslem woman ruler—"Since no *man* among you is worthy of being Sultan, I will come in person and bring you one." Shagret al Dur seems to have had no personal ambition for the career of ruler, well though she filled the role, for on receipt of this message, she graciously retired. The Mamelukes appointed in her place one of their number to be King. But they did not plan to give up their popular Queen as easily as that. The new King was immediately made to marry her, and, probably by prior arrangement, he left most of the administration and decisions in her capable hands.

It was not long after this that Shagret al Dur's life turned from triumph to melodramatic tragedy. The cause of it was her fierce jealousy as a wife. She must indeed have been a fiery and interesting character. Regal power she was able and ready to lay down but when rumours reached her that her husband was contemplating marriage with a Princess of Mosul, nothing filled her days and nights but thoughts of revenge.

A famous Syrian historian of the fourteenth century has left us a detailed account of how the Queen's suspicions were confirmed. A group of her husband's personal prisoners were passing under a balcony of the Citadel Castle one day on their way to a dungeon. They guessed that Shagret al Dur might be within earshot. One of them raised his voice and speaking in her native Turkish tongue, said: "By Allah, Princess, we are quite ignorant of the cause of our arrest but when al Moezz [her husband] went to ask the hand of the Princess of Mosul, we expressed our disapproval on your account. For we owe everything to your kindness and that of your late husband. Al Moezz, vexed with our reproaches, had conceived a hatred against us and treated us as you perceive." Shagret al Dur apparently signed to them with her handkerchief that she had heard and understood.

She soon picked a violent quarrel with her husband, after which he left the Citadel for a favourite summer house of his, near the polo ground. A few days later, Shagret al Dur despatched a message to him telling of her affection and submission.

After a game of polo he returned, unsuspecting, to the Citadel, when he went straight to have a bath and change after his game. Events now happened rapidly. Five assassins attacked him in the bath hall. Hearing his cries for help, it is reported that Shagret al Dur relented and, rushing in, told the assassins to stop their work; but they shouted back the answer: "If we spare him now he will spare neither us nor you."

Shagret al Dur seems to have done all she could to hide the crime, announcing that the Sultan had died suddenly and even introducing professional weeping women into the castle. But it would have taken more than that to avert her fate, and well she must have known it, for al Moezz had adherents.

As soon as the truth was out, she lost no time in collecting many of her jewels which she proceeded to pound in a mortar to prevent them adorning any other woman. Imprisonment followed soon and her own assassination was not long deferred, by the order of a former wife of al Moezz whom she had forced him to divorce.

Her body was thrown on to the rubbish heap outside the Citadel walls, where some of her faithful followers collected it and gave it burial in the beautiful mausoleum she had built against her death.

There it stands today—so little known. A charming mosaic is still visible in the prayer niche, representing a Tree of Pearls against a golden background. The quietness all around seems a curious memorial to this turbulent woman who was able to rule all except her own human passions.

On the way to the house where we had lessons every morning with other English children, we would pass by a road called Sharia Shagret al Dur. It was a peaceful little road with quiet residential houses and gardens on either side and was beautifully lined with blue jacaranda trees. The first burst of blue in the spring coloured the scene above our heads, and later, as the flowers dropped, the colour spread in a thick carpet at our feet. This, too, seemed a strange memorial to one whose life had been neither peaceful nor quiet.

Cairo during these eras, from the tenth to the sixteenth centuries, was a strange mixture of barbarism and culture, of savagery and civilisation. A standard was set in design and workmanship which has probably never been surpassed anywhere since. The joy of beautiful things beautifully done speaks clearly, from the wealth of objects left for us to enjoy today.

In the world of letters and science, these centuries produced men whose names are still known the world round—philosophers, historians, astronomers, and mathematicians. The study and practice of medicine was amazingly advanced. Sultan Qalaun, a Mameluke Sultan who ruled during the thirteenth century, founded a hospital in Cairo which had separate wards for different diseases, a section for women patients and a section for men. It had baths, kitchens, and a dispensary. It also possessed a lecture room where the leading doctors on the staff instructed students. One hears of a surgeon who did not hesitate to perform a cataract operation on a patient who was blind in the other eye, so sure was he of succeeding. So perhaps it is not surprising that Egypt can still produce some of the world's leading doctors and surgeons.

Qalaun also built himself a beautiful mausoleum, and a mosque which is used today for services and prayers. When it was new, however, the holy men of the time refused to pray in it for three reasons. Firstly, they said that the Sultan had stolen columns from other buildings for the construction. Secondly, they declared that the money with which to build the mosque had been taken unjustly by force. To this the Sultan replied that when he was out riding in the desert one day, his horse had kicked up something with its hoof, and he had found it to be a casket of treasure which he had used for these works; but in this he was not believed. The third reason was that a noble lady with a great many slave girls had been peremptorily turned out of her house, which happened to occupy the site desired by the Sultan for his mosque. But it must be said in Qalaun's favour that he had good points, and he relieved the people of several unfair taxes.

In his time, Cairo was the chief town in a state of the first importance. Deputations and ambassadors arrived at the Ruler's court to negotiate treaties with him, from such people as the Kings of France and Sicily, from the Tartars, and even from as distant a place as Ceylon.

The great Arab historian of the fifteenth century, al Maqrizi, describes the return of Sultan Qalaun from a victory over Mangour-Timour, the son of Houlagou the Mongol, in the year 1281. "The Emir Sherif al Din Jaki," he says, "went from the Sultan's tent to prepare the ambassadors who were in Cairo and to lead them out to meet the Prince. Their reception was on Saturday the twenty-second day of the month. The Sultan was under his flag, having in front of him the Tartar prisoners some of whom carried broken standards. These captives, as well as the drums of the Tartars and baggage of Mangour-Timour, were led towards the Bab al Nasr, they crossed Cairo to the Bab al Zuweila and from there they went to the Citadel."

Sultan succeeded Sultan in meteoric succession. Most of them fought their way to the top over the corpses of their adversaries, and consequently few rulers died in their beds. Cairo and Damascus were both capitals. These cities were linked by an efficient pigeon post service, which took letters from one town to the other in a few days. One of the well-known Mameluke rulers was the Sultan Baibars, whose tales of prowess are still related by professional story tellers in the smaller Egyptian coffee houses. One of Baibars' boasts was that he could play polo in Cairo and Damascus in the same week, covering the distance of some four hundred miles by means of a chain of fresh horses posted across the Sinai peninsula, through Palestine and into Syria. It was a remarkable feat. He is also credited with having swum the Nile in full armour.

The Sultans administered their large empire, sometimes with rough justice and foresight, always with vigour. At the same time, they led their armies in major campaigns against the Crusaders and Tartars. The old Arab chroniclers give us graphic descriptions of this warfare, and they show how the common people of Cairo followed the fortunes of war with enthusiasm. They were kept well posted with news. One of these historians describes the scene in Cairo at a moment when the news seemed bad, though victory was gained in the end. "The people put extreme zeal into their prayers," he says, "and all applied themselves to reciting the Kuran. Gathered together in the mosques they cried aloud and gave themselves up to fervent prayer. That same day, pigeons arrived with perfumed wings, bearing letters also perfumed, announcing the great news of the Tartar defeat. Postal runners arrived as well with despatches confirming the news. Loud music was heard: Cairo and the Fort of the Mountain [the present Citadel] were imposingly decorated and an order transmitted to the different provinces prescribed the same signs of rejoicing."

This amazing succession of Mameluke Sultans lasted till 1517 when, after some valiant fighting, they fell before the all-powerful Turkish army of Selim I. The Turks fought with powder, artillery and muskets, weapons the Mamelukes had not mastered, partly through disdain of anything more than personal courage and physical strength in battles.

At the last moment, they hired a few cannon from the Republic of Venice at vast expense, but they had no time to be trained in their use. So the last ruling Mameluke was hanged by the Turks over the Gate of Zuweila.

For the next three hundred years, Egypt lay half dead as a province of the Turkish Empire, ruled by governors from Constantinople. The vigour of her previous life died down to mere embers. A few good Turkish-style mosques were built with slender minarets like sharpened pencils, and some charming examples of what is called sebil kutab were constructed and endowed. These consisted of a room for free schooling, built above an enclosed fountain where the poor could get drinks of water. But works of art comparable to those of Fatimite and Mameluke times ceased to exist.

There are a few specimens of domestic architecture left to us today, dating from the times of the Turkish domination. These are of interest, for practically nothing in the nature of private buildings has survived from earlier days. The last one to be lived in privately by an Egyptian family is the eighteenth century house of Sheikh Sehemy. I never visited it while the family were still in residence, but used to go there frequently in latter days.

Standing in its shady garden, or wandering from room to room in the house, it needs no effort of the imagination to see the life which went on here—the merchants passing in and out, as they pass in and out of the pages of the Arabian Nights. The inhabitants of this old house must often have heard bands of Mamelukes riding through the narrow lanes of Cairo, with clang of weapons as they went. For although the Mamelukes as sovereign rulers fell for ever beneath the Turkish cannon in 1517, their descendants roamed the country for centuries after. They were little more than brigand bands, but sometimes assumed real power, acting as local dictators. And as ever they remained fighters. It was their army that met Napoleon's forces at the Battle of the Pyramids, to resist, but in vain, the great Frenchman's entry into Egypt.

It is at this point in history, 1798, that the Sultan of Turkey sent an official force to Egypt, with the object of helping his allies, the English, oust the French from Egyptian territory. Turkey could not possibly have foreseen that in doing this she sowed the seed which was to produce so great an internal change in Egypt. One of the subordinate officers of the Turkish force was a certain Mohamed Ali.

The history of the early nineteenth century in Egypt is the history of Mohamed Ali. He was born in 1769 in Kavala, on the borders of Thrace and Macedonia. His parents, of Albanian yeoman stock, had lost several children at an early age, and tended to over-protect their much-loved son. This solicitude worried Mohamed Ali, who set about counteracting it by a self-imposed discipline. Years later, when speaking to Prince Puckler Muskau, he described it thus : "At the age of fifteen I resolved to vanquish myself. I often fasted for days together, or compelled myself to refrain from sleep for a similar period, and never rested till I had outstripped all my companions in bodily exercises. I well recollect our laying a wager one very stormy day, to row over to a small island, which still remains in my possession. I was the only one who reached it, but although the skin came off my hands, I would not suffer the most intense pain to divert me from my purpose. In this manner I continued to invigorate both mind and body."*

Mohamed Ali was a very young man when he was sent to Egypt to fight the French. A certain bold cavalry charge won him renown. This was the same man who, in his old age, was frequently seen by my grandmother, Amelia Terry, when, as a little girl living in Alexandria, she looked out of her nursery window.

Mohamed Ali decided to stay on in this country. His personality soon made itself felt. During the next few years following the Battle of the Pyramids, Egypt was in a chaotic condition, with the Sublime Porte wielding authority on the

*Puckler Muskau, *Egypt under Mehemet Ali*. London, 1845; Vol.1, p. 318

one hand, and the Mameluke chieftains on the other hand, in continual strife, both among themselves and with their Turkish overlords. By 1805 the sheikhs of Cairo elected this young Turkish officer as Pasha, and he was later confirmed in this position by the Sultan of Turkey.

By any standard Mohamed Ali was a remarkable man. His enemies and his friends alike admit it. Although Egypt was technically part of the Turkish Empire and paid annual tribute to Constantinople, yet to all intents and purposes Mohamed Ali became an independent ruler, even to the point of securing the Sultan's consent to his position becoming hereditary. He was the great-great-grandfather of ex-King Farouk.

Though some of Mohamed Ali's methods were crude, to put it mildly, such as his well known murder of the remnant of the Mamelukes, yet he expressed a love of Egypt and a sense of mission to her people. "It is true, I have to overcome many a severe struggle," he said, "and perhaps for this very reason I have become more closely and ardently devoted to my adopted land. I had neither rest nor peace; Egypt appeared to me like a poor naked helpless child which, for centuries, had been stupefied with sleep, to whom I was now to be everything—its father and mother, its master and servant, its teacher and judge; and often when lying sleepless on my couch, have I said within myself: can a single Mohamed Ali be sufficient to rear, to clothe, to instruct, and to train this child? Even now I feel dubious of success; yet, perhaps in spite of every obstacle, it may be accorded to me by God, to whom I owe so much, and to whom I have always applied for direction."*

As early as 1815 he uttered a strange and partly prophetic statement. He said in conversation with the great traveller, Burckhardt, that "England must some day take Egypt as her share of the spoil of the Turkish Empire, for the big fish swallow the small."** From the first Mohamed Ali looked

* Puckler Muskau, *Egypt under Mehemet Ali*, p. 276-7
**Valentine Chirol, *The Egyptian Problem*, p. 42.

westward for inspiration and help in his project, primarily to France, but also to Italy, Austria and England.

Though from a military standpoint he originally met the French as an enemy, yet he was deeply impressed by the thoroughness and vision of Napoleon's group of savants, who did such fine historical and scientific work during their brief sojourn in Egypt. It was Mohamed Ali, for instance, who saw the great possibilities in cultivating a new form of cotton plant proposed by the Frenchman Jumel, thus laying the foundations for most of Egypt's economy. He made a great bid for an educational system in Egypt. In 1822 he set up the first printing press, having seven years previously sent a lad of sixteen to Milan to learn the whole mechanism and art of printing. He simultaneously trained a group from the University of al Azhar to become the first compositors.

Through the lead of Mohamed Ali, Egypt was at this time wide open to European thought, culture and experience; even the political philosopher Bentham wrote the Pasha pages and pages of advice. Some of those who came to help were undoubtedly sincere, and loyally served Egypt; but there were others, rascals and adventurers, who seized every opportunity of feathering their own nests, and took personal advantage of Mohamed Ali's enthusiasm for reform. In this respect Europe has had something to answer for in Egypt.

With almost no prepared material, he created an army and he built a fleet. His army captured the Sudan, and wrested (though temporarily) Syria, Crete, and parts of Arabia from Turkish dominion. He rebuilt some of Cairo, and made the present Sharia Mohamed Ali, copied from the Rue de Rivoli in Paris. This road leads up to the Citadel crowned by the famous mosque, which was founded by him and in which he was buried at his death in 1849.

A son, and then grandson, succeeded Mohamed Ali for brief reigns.

Egypt's next ruler was Said Pasha, another son of Mohamed Ali. He had some good ideas, but lacked the strength of character to carry them out. It was Said Pasha who granted England a concession in 1854, for the founding of the Bank of Egypt, which establishment my grandfather, Arthur Rowlatt, joined in the following year. For England already had certain financial interests in Egypt, and was anxious to keep a control of them, even indirectly. The number of Englishmen employed in the Bank was negligible, nor was English the language used for transactions. It was, strangely enough, Italian. A relic of this is found in the Alexandria Bourse to this day, where a wonderful mixture of official phrases can be heard. "*Stabene*" shows agreement, quite logically. But the negative of it is "*mastabenish*"—the prefix and suffix being the negative form in colloquial Arabic, added to the Italian phrase.

By far the most historic concession granted by Said Pasha to Europeans was that of 1856 to the Frenchman Ferdinand de Lesseps, for the construction of the Suez Canal. Although he never lived to see its opening, Said Pasha's name was honoured by the naming of the new town Port Said, which grew up around the entrance to the Canal.

In view of the Anglo-Egyptian agreement on the Canal Zone signed in 1954, it might be of interest to survey the varying western views about the Canal in the early days of the project.

On November 17, 1869, some six thousand visitors gathered in Port Said to attend the opening ceremony of the Suez Canal. Among them was a little English boy of four years old, complete in breeches gathered below the knee and Victorian jacket. He was my father, Frederick Rowlatt, who accompanied his father as a guest of the Khedive Ismail, Said's successor. The ceremonial opening of the Canal was a brilliant sight, which this small boy never forgot.

The Empress Eugénie of France, aboard the Imperial yacht *Aigle*, led the stately procession of sixty-seven vessels, southwards. Northwards from Suez came a flotilla of Egyptian warships, until the two columns met halfway amid general rejoicing and triumph. The Crown Prince of Russia, the Emperor of Austria, Prince William of Hesse, and the Crown Prince of the Netherlands were among the Royal guests; but English names of like calibre were absent.

What was England's early attitude to de Lesseps, that visionary Frenchman, as his enterprise moved from project to accomplishment? It was curiously obstructive.

For England, the Canal project crystallised all the age-old mistrust of France. Herein lay a threat to her lucrative trade round the Cape of Good Hope. There must be no canal. Had Napoleon's Egyptian adventure succeeded, he and his band of scientists would surely have dug the canal of which he had dreamed, in spite of the false theory of those times that the waters of the Red Sea were thirty feet higher than the level of the Mediterranean. England however had then faced a Napoleon with a Nelson and the scheme sank for the time being as surely as the French battleships sank in the Bay of Aboukir. That had been an incident which England could understand and oppose in her own way. But here was a French idealist who with immeasurable patience, perseverance and will-power was pursuing his ideal peacefully to its logical conclusion.

It was a new situation in a new dimension, but England still evaluated it in outmoded Napoleonic terms. The thing must not take place. Direct enemy action was out of the question, for England and France were fighting side by side in the Crimea for much of the time. But other ways were employed. The British Consul General in Egypt was instructed to persuade the Ruler of Egypt by any means in his power that the scheme was nonsensical.

In Constantinople, Queen Victoria's ambassador, the redoubtable Lord Stratford de Redcliffe, who wielded great influence with the Sultan, managed most effectively to hinder the essential ratification of the concession. Even after Great Britain had eventually given an undertaking to be neutral, means were found for obstructing de Lesseps. Lord

Palmerston continued to hold forth in Parliament thus: "It is an undertaking which, I believe, as regards the commercial character, may be deemed to rank among the bubble schemes which from time to time have been palmed off upon gullible capitalists." Even *The Times*, it is regrettable to note, dwelt long on the hazards of nature such as tempest and sand which, from the haven of Printing House Square, appeared unsurmountable obstacles to the success of the scheme, though de Lesseps, working on the desert spot, assured the world to the contrary.

Was it any wonder that the usually patient de Lesseps wrote to Richard Cobden, "How can it be imagined that people on the Continent will believe in the sincerity of England, in her great zeal for universal progress, civilisation and public wealth if it sees that England, where public opinion reigns supreme, allows her Government to continue its incredible opposition to the Suez Canal, a private enterprise, in the origin, constitution and object of which there is nothing to awaken any suspicion of political rivalry?"

From the start de Lesseps envisaged the Suez Canal Company as having international backing. Accordingly shares were reserved for various leading countries. There is a certain poignancy in reading these statistics today. One column shows the amount of shares reserved per country and the next column is headed, "shares applied for and allotted." All countries save two accepted at least part of the amount offered, and some required extra shares. Great Britain was offered 80,000 and the U.S.A. 20,000. These were the only two countries against whose names the word "Nil" appeared in the second column. Alluding to this, de Lesseps wrote to a colleague, "All their efforts [the British] are now directed to deterring their compatriots from subscribing to it, because in their innate pride and insular arrogance, they believe that their example will prevent other nations from investing money in it. We are now in the course of destroying their last illusions."

This was in 1858. Disraeli's spectacular purchase of the Khedive's Canal shares is too well known to need recapitulation: * it took place sixteen years later, in 1874, by which time England had awakened to the importance of the situation. It is only fair to emphasise that in spite of her confessed self-interest in the matter, when England did change by realising that her line of obstruction was a mistaken one, she took steps to admit it and to make certain amends in her own particular style. Lord Derby speaking in Edinburgh said, "We have the greatest consideration for M. de Lesseps. We acknowledge that instead of opposing him in his great work, we should have done better to have associated ourselves with him." Queen Victoria invested de Lesseps with the Grand Cross of the Star of India, a generously worded message of congratulations on the opening ceremony was sent to him from Her Majesty's Government, and finally, he was made a Freeman of the City of London. It is to be hoped that the Frenchman recognised in this act the restitution it was undoubtedly meant to convey, and ignored the slight touch of irony in the situation.

Where, it can justifiably be observed, did Egypt herself feature in all this? The question could be partially answered by remembering that up to 1914 Egypt was still, in the last analysis, part of the Ottoman Empire—that sick and dying man. (This domination had lasted since 1517.) In ink and paper terms this was true; but in flesh and blood terms, the thousands of men who laboured with soil and sand to make the canal a reality, were Egypt herself—Egypt's own flesh and blood. Thousands, perhaps millions, of their descendants form part of the rank and file of independent Egypt today. For them it was but natural that the Canal Question symbolised bitter feelings, a conscious bitterness towards England's later policy mistakenly or not, and an unconscious backwash of bitterness against the Great Powers of the early days, including Turkey herself. It is not surprising that their desire

* 176,602 shares for which he was paid £3,976,582.

at last to be masters of the situation should go deep.

In many aspects Egypt now stands on the threshold of a new era, and her relationship with England is one of the most important of these aspects. For Egypt, the differences in this new era are apparent. Yet it is an equally new era into which England is stepping. May it be that we too realise its significance? Already the comparatively small national squabbles that raged round the Suez Canal in the early years have a Ruritanian ring to them, and the vast national quarrels of the first and second World Wars in which the Canal was a vortex, are surely outmoded. The ideology of Moscow owing allegiance only to itself, and to which any loyalty of country or race is wholly subordinate, is now the actuating element. The understanding of this ideology and the framing of an inspired alternative to it is the one pertinent setting today for any treaty between free nations. It is a change in essentials, and calls for a change in national character to match the hour.

When de Lesseps was made a member of the Académie Française, a fellow academician used this sentence in his speech of welcome: "You possess in the highest degree the secret of greatness, the art of making yourself beloved." Is this not an art which, if in humility acquired, would fit the free powers of today for new leadership?

"Our tents at Ramleh, August 1860."   Amelia C. Rowlatt

8

THE TALE CONTINUED

FROM 1863 to 1879 Egypt was governed by the Khedive Ismail. He made some attempts at much needed reform for his country, and did achieve a certain amount; but unfortunately he had little financial acumen, nor was he well advised. Ismail spent exorbitant sums of money on building palatial residences for himself; a relic of one of his summer palaces stands today desolate among green clover fields, just outside Cairo. One hot summer evening I wandered over it with one or two friends. The sunshine fell through dusty windows on to the strange ornamental lake in the courtyard, where the green water lay heavily. The only living creatures we disturbed were stone curlews, whose cry echoed eerily, and a few descendants of former black slaves, who greeted us quietly with the natural good manners of their kind. The weird atmosphere of Turkish palace life a hundred years ago hung in the air. The ghosts gently receded ahead of us, as we went from room to room in silence.*

The building of so much which was to crumble so soon was not wholly Ismail's fault, for there were only too many self-seeking Europeans around of dubious character, with plausible advice on what to do with money. The financiers of Europe fed him with capital in an irresponsible way and then clamoured for their governments to take action when the interest payments were not forthcoming.

---

* This palace and garden has since been renovated by ex-King Farouk and is now a public park.

From fear of bankruptcy, Ismail sold his Suez Canal shares to the British Government, which gave Britain greatly increased financial interests in Egypt. It was felt in Europe that the bondholders, both French and English, must be protected.

The outcome of several missions of inquiry into Egypt's finances resulted in the setting up of what was called the Dual Control. An English official superintended the revenue and a Frenchman the expenditure. The state of affairs began to improve as far as finance was concerned, but co-operation on this basis did not appeal to Ismail. It seemed hopeless to these officials to try and proceed, with the Khedive so often opposed to their efforts; so in 1879, at the suggestion of England and France, the Sultan of Turkey deposed the Khedive and appointed the latter's son Tewfik in his place.

Two years after this the first rumblings of a revolt became apparent. It was led by an Egyptian army officer called Arabi. Lord Cromer, in one of his reports on Egypt,* says that it was more of a rebellion against Turkish mismanagement in Egypt than primarily anti-European. Yet the unpopularity of the Dual Control had much to do in forming it. Neither the Sultan himself, nor the Khedive and his Egyptian government, stood up to this revolt, which by the early summer of 1882 took on a serious aspect. Europeans were threatened, as indeed were Christian Egyptians too. Mob violence seemed imminent.

Women and children were hastily evacuated; but my maternal grandfather, at that time director of the Alexandria Water Company, naturally refused to leave, as he was responsible for the water supply, a vital necessity which it was his business to keep available so long as Alexandria was in any way inhabited by the living. A most adventurous time awaited him. Many of his staff and workers fled, so he had to do a great deal of the actual work of the installations himself, by night and day. He never went unarmed, even when snatching a hurried meal. Sometimes the captain of one of the British

* No. 1; p.2. 1905

men-of-war would send a boat for him, and a request that he should come and confer with them on board ship; and sometimes he had to visit the Egyptians, for part of the essential waterworks lay in the territory occupied by Arabi Pasha. This had to be inspected regularly. It was naturally to the advantage of the rebels to have a water supply working, so they used to meet my grandfather on the border of their territory, and provide him with a guard of their men while he was at work.

One day Arabi sent a message to say that he himself wished to see over the waterworks. My grandfather had no idea if this was to be a more or less friendly inspection, or if the Egyptian leader planned some attack. It would have been unpolitic to have met him with a display of arms, so my grandfather, being an engineer and most resourceful, thought of another device.

He constructed a system of steam jets at regular intervals throughout the premises. These were controlled by frequent inconspicuous means. Had Arabi or his men shown any sign of hostility during their conducted tour, steam jets could have been loosed instantly on the whole party and created utter confusion. It was a bold scheme, for my grandfather would have suffered severe burns with the rest. But, mercifully, the visit went off without incident. My poor grandmother, as a refugee in Beirut, had no idea for weeks whether her husband was alive or dead.

The Rowlatts were by then in England, but an old friend, Mr. Calvert, Acting Consul in Alexandria, wrote to Mrs. Rowlatt on June 6, 1882: "The street and especially the square, were filled with people, full of apprehension. Few went to bed that night [May 27], or those who did had not much sleep. . . . I only slept at daybreak. All night long, I heard carriages passing to and fro between Ras el Tin and Rosetta Gate, full of Egyptian officers. . . . All financial Israel has left, taking their money with them. . . . The natives are beginning to feel the effect of the crisis. Many are taken away from their fields, where their presence is much required, and cultivators cannot obtain advance on crops. Shopkeepers have desired their agents in Europe to keep goods. In a word, if this crisis lasts, great misery will be the result. . . .

"I do not think there will be any danger run by the European population. If there were, surely Italian, Austrian, Russian and other vessels of war would come here to protect their subjects; but none have come."

The British, French and Greek fleets had come, however, and were waiting outside Alexandria.

The next letter Mrs. Rowlatt received was from a humble employee of the Egyptian Telegraph Company. It was dated June 23, 1882, and said: "Dear Madam, me, my mother and sister send our best respects to Mr. and Mrs. Rowlatt and family. We suppose that Mr. Rowlatt and all the family know that a revolution took place on the 11th last which gave much trouble to the people in the country. . . . The staff of the Telegraph have asked for a safe place to work, the reply was that if anything wrong should happen we must get into bottles [!] and hide ourselves in them or go and hide ourselves in the charcoal. A great number of shops are smashed to pieces, many of the shops are closed; also from three to four hundred persons killed and wounded on the same day of the revolution. . . ."

After this outburst, the British men-of-war bombarded the forts where Arabi's revolution was centred. Arabi, a fine man in his way, retreated to Tel al Kebir and prepared to resist. The British again invited the Sultan to step in and quell the revolution, which was after all in his own territory, but he was loath to do so. The French and the Italians were asked to co-operate but refused. So British troops were landed and finally suppressed Arabi's army at Tel al Kebir in September 1882.

Thus ended the first organised round of the nineteenth century in which the native Egyptian sought to free himself from foreign domination. This rising had focused the genuine hopes of a few idealists, notably Sheikh Abdou, that it might prove to be the starting point of a truly popular and national movement.

In view of later events in Egypt it is interesting to remember Sir Valentine Chirol's report on visiting Arabi during the latter's exile in Ceylon: "He told me frankly that though he had mistrusted us intensely in those troublous times all he heard from Egypt since the British Occupation had satisfied him that we were doing great things for the fellaheen to whom he himself belonged and he could not but be grateful to us for having befriended them. But, he added, in almost the same words which an Egyptian statesman used to me, who was for many years one of Lord Cromer's most loyal coadjutors, 'there will be no assurance of peace in Egypt so long as the Turkish house of Mohamed Ali has not been turned out of the country.'"*

So there the English were, for good or for ill, right in the middle of Egypt and thoroughly involved in her affairs. Lord Dufferin, then British Ambassador in Constantinople, was sent to Egypt to advise on this curious situation. He laid down a scheme whereby the country could be administered efficiently, order restored, and a degree of prosperity reached. The man to whom this task was entrusted was Sir Evelyn Baring, afterwards Lord Cromer. He came from India with the reputation of being rather autocratic in his ways, and some wit circulated the following verse about him:

"The virtue of patience is known,
  But the frailty of humans is such,
  That in Egypt we'll say with a groan,
  There's an 'evil in bearing' too much."

But from his arrival in 1884 till his retirement in 1907, he shouldered his laborious task with courage and absolute integrity. He lived frugally and simply, sparing himself no effort to fulfil what he felt to be right.

At the outset of Lord Cromer's régime in Egypt, the policy of Mr. Gladstone's government appeared to be that the British

* Valentine Chirol, *The Egyptian Problem*.

authorities should aid Egypt to restore peace and order, should guide the Khedive in doing so, and after a reasonable stretch of time, that they should retire from the scene. No major reforms were first envisaged. But the policy from Westminster vacillated back and forth, this way and that, till it was not easy for "the man on the spot" in Egypt to follow any clearly laid down plan from London. So naturally circumstances began primarily to dictate action.

It soon became apparent that, at least on the face of it, many far-reaching reforms would bring an easing of the burden of life to millions of Egyptians suffering hardship and wrongs. The starting of one reform led to another and another. Key posts were taken over by Englishmen to assure the smooth running of these reforms. Administrative influence was removed at many points from Egyptian hands and transferred to British.

As sure as the wake follows a ship, unpopularity followed these well-meant efforts. There was the opposition of the good men who, in some cases, suffered with the guilty a blow to their pride, and there was the opposition of the guilty who found themselves no longer able to live off the poor by devious means, such as diverting the precious irrigation water on to their own lands *ad lib.*

The Englishmen in those early days of the Occupation had chosen a hard furrow to plough, but for better or worse they manfully rolled up their sleeves and ploughed it. There were still grave financial difficulties which had to be gradually overcome. The nucleus of a modern Egyptian army was formed, and the best irrigation experts set about vast schemes to control the waters of the Nile, which to Egypt is her literal life blood. Few could deny that these efforts laid the foundations of modern Egyptian prosperity.

Yet, human nature being what it is, Egyptian feelings here and there were hurt, resistance here and there crystallised, and on both sides many minds remained open, but many hearts were closed. Lord Granville felt compelled to write to Lord

Cromer (Sir Evelyn Baring as he then was) in these terms: "It should be made clear to the Egyptian Ministers and Governors of Provinces that the responsibility which for the first time rests on England, obliges H.M. Government to insist on the adoption of the policy which they recommend and that it will be necessary that those Ministers and Governors who do not follow this course should cease to hold their offices."

So the machinery of administration went forward with many excellent material results throughout the country. The ancient system of corvée (forced unpaid labour) was finally abolished, except when public danger from high Nile floods made it necessary to call men out as an emergency.

Early in 1892 the Khedive Tewfik died suddenly. He had always been a friend of Lord Cromer's. His son Abbas Hilmi succeeded him. It was not an easy position for a young man to find himself in and he started by making his own opinions felt, as many a young man in his situation would have done, whatever his nationality.

Abbas Hilmi deposed his Prime Minister whom the British trusted, and put in his place one whom they did not. The young Khedive was made to understand the error of his ways. It would be idle to say that there was not friction in some quarters after this incident. But it must also be said that many real personal English-Egyptian friendships were founded during these years, both among the British officials and the educated Egyptians, as well as between the British and the fellaheen.

Lord Cromer ever had in mind the moral advancement and character building of the modern Egypt he felt himself called on to help create; but there is an almost wistful note about it in some of his reports. "As regards moral progress all that can be said is that it must necessarily be slower than advance in a material direction. I hope and believe however that some progress is being made. In any case the machinery which will admit of progress has been created. . . ."*

* From Lord Cromer's annual report to the British Government, 1903.

He was also most particular about the conduct of the British community under his paternal charge. If any young man got into trouble, Lord Cromer would know of it. A reprimand would be forthcoming, or if he thought really seriously of the incident, the young man would get a notice to say that the next boat home to England sailed at such and such a date, and would he please be on it. When in 1906, my father, Frederick Rowlatt, was proposed as Governor of the National Bank, Lord Cromer at first opposed the appointment, on the grounds that Rowlatt was too young. But when, in spite of this, his appointment was confirmed, Lord Cromer sent for him and told him frankly how he had been against it, but now that he actually was Governor he [Rowlatt] could count on Lord Cromer's full backing. He gave my father one piece of advice: "When in doubt, do nothing." "No, sir," the young Governor replied, "when in doubt I shall come to you." And through the next year, which was Lord Cromer's last in office, they worked in close collaboration.

In the early years of this century there were definite stirrings of a nationalist movement. Under the leadership of Mustapha Kemal many Egyptians began to voice their opinion that now was the time for self-government in Egypt and that it could best be achieved by themselves, for themselves, and in their own way.

In June, 1905, a most unfortunate incident occurred which created misunderstanding on both sides for years to come. Some British soldiers were marching from Cairo to Alexandria, and *en route* five officers went to the village of Denshawai to shoot pigeons. Round every Egyptian village are flocks of semi-wild pigeons kept for food and for manure. No one is allowed to shoot them without permission from the head man of the village. These officers misunderstood a guide who was with them and, thinking that they were at liberty to shoot, did so. The villagers were of course deeply angered. They planned and carried out a revenge in which they attacked the officers; two were wounded and one died, of sunstroke it is thought, as he lay on the ground in hiding from the Egyptians. Drastic action was taken against the peasants by a court including English and Egyptian judges. Four were sentenced to death, others had various prison sentences and seven received fifty lashes.

On the anniversary of the Khedive's accession, January 8, 1908, the Denshawai prisoners were pardoned and released. And in the following month Mustapha Kemal died. But seeds of a national spirit had been sown, and much trouble and heart searchings for both English and Egyptians lay ahead.

Many people would agree that the British have had certain powers of creating order and stability in other lands than their own, of setting up communications, producing good water supplies, founding administrative machinery that actually works, and holding up a standard of justice and integrity. In Arab countries the expression *Kalam Engliz* (the word of an Englishman) was sometimes said at the end of a long collo-quial argument by one of the parties. And the meaning of those two words was "I have told you once, I am not saying it again. I mean what I say and I am holding to it."

In many an Eastern country where the British have taken over, budgets have balanced, trains arrived at stations when due, and judgments have been given in favour of the poor man with-out a bribe, for the first time. Where and how is it that we fail?

Is it that in seeing good material fruits of our labour to hand, an unconscious but none the less real superiority has set in? And in an atmosphere tainted with this, human relation-ships freeze and wither.

The art of winning people's hearts can only be accom-plished by freely giving of the heart in the first place. The very good itself in our achievements may have blinded us to this fact, and so we proceed for years on end doing the right thing in the wrong way until sooner or later the peoples on whom the benefits are conferred feel like saying (and do say) "Go—take your irrigation and roads and schools and sanitation—but go—for heaven's sake—go!" Then we find this attitude difficult to understand and stick in our toes.

During the first world war some Turkish prisoners lived in huts near our house in Egypt. These men were set to cultivate land close by, and among other things they raised a fine crop of onions. One morning every onion plant was found wilting. A bevy of agricultural specialists arrived, fearing some new plant epidemic. They gazed at the crop and questioningly scratched their heads, for they saw no sign of blight or disease. Suddenly one expert thought to pull up a plant and found that there was no onion and no root, but just a bunch of leaves stuck in the ground. Plant after plant was pulled up and the same discovery made—nothing but leaves.

The Turkish prisoners had thought one evening how nice an onion or two would be with their supper. Under cover of darkness they had consumed every one and had carefully replanted the leaves.

The Agricultural experts had at first sought here and there in their expert brains for the reason of this ailing crop, only to find a simple but fundamental reason. Its foundations were lacking.

A broadminded and highly educated Burmese lady once said of the British, "You have given us material improvements of every sort, you have given us freely of the fruits of your head and your hands—but you have not given us your hearts so it is almost impossible for us to love you." Who can hear such a statement without thinking of what St. Paul said nineteen hundred years ago—". . . it profiteth me nothing".

It is so easy for us to listen only to the old peasant who straightens himself up at the name of some past Englishman—Cromer, or Kitchener—and says to you with obvious sincerity "Those were good days"; as they have often said to me. It is right and just that the old peasant should remember those days happily and with pride, but he may not be the pointer by which to set our compass.

Whether we like it or not it is the young men in the European suits who stream out of the universities every evening on their way home and hang on to the back of the trams three deep, laughing and joking: they are the pointers. What is going on in their hearts should make us think. And the young women too. Their opinions may not be so complimentary, but behind the bluff, the immaturity, and the exaggeration, it is good to try and understand some of the insecurity, hurt self-respect, frustration, and bitterness they have inherited.

It is a solemn thought that millions of past and present pin-prick injuries to the spirit and souls of men and women are the things which eventually bear the harvest and which become translated into terms of oil, military zones, pacts, or whatever it may be, without at their source having been that at all.

At the outbreak of the second Sikh war, John and Henry Lawrence, the well-known administrators, took two differing views of their situation. John was outraged at the treachery of the Sikhs and horrified with them for breaking their word. But Henry followed the line of thought that possibly, just possibly, there had been something wrong in the English which had been the original cause of the Sikhs having acted as they had done. In family life enlightened people are quick enough to see this principle. The father, who when he heard his small son swearing, went straight off and beat his elder son, was acting on it.

The diplomacy of the open heart and of humility may be simple but it is not easy to pursue. Nor is this surprising for it is a new dimension of thinking, a stretching of the minds and souls of men. And who will have the moral courage to begin with a simple apology?

After the entry of Turkey into the first World War, Great Britain's position in Egypt became strangely anomalous. Egypt was still, on paper at least, a part of the Turkish Empire; and here was England, at war with Turkey, yet administering part of her territory. So on December 18, 1914, H.M. Government declared Egypt to be a British Protectorate, and Prince Hussein Kamel was nominated Sultan of Egypt. The old Khedivate existed no longer.

Sultan Hussein succeeded his nephew Abbas Hilmi whom the British Government had finally asked to abdicate chiefly owing to his pro-German sympathies. The new Sultan was a quiet, dignified and gentlemanly man. Soon after his succession to the throne, those who followed Egyptian politics became increasingly aware of the name of a certain Saad Zaghloul.

When Lord Cromer had spoken at a great gathering in the Cairo Opera House on the occasion of his retirement in 1907, Saad Zaghloul was sitting near to him on the platform, and he was the only man in Egyptian politics of the day whom Lord Cromer mentioned by name. He had joined the Nationalist Party in the early days of Mustapha Kamel and was later to become the great champion of the Nationalist cause.

Zaghloul was of peasant stock. He had a good brain and a large heart. This, and his fine command of oratory, gave him great influence over the masses whom he could sway at will. He had some of the attributes of greatness. The party he formed was the well-known Wafd, which stood for total independence for Egypt. The timing and the manner of bringing this about, as upheld by Zaghloul, did not satisfy the British Government, and years of bitter clash resulted, with Zaghloul both in and out of the Premiership and in and out of exile.

It might not be out of place to quote here from one better fitted than I am to survey some of the factors which led up to the temper of the time. "During the years preceding the outbreak of the war, Great Britain had made little attempt in Egypt to redeem the pledge she had published to the world. She had neither admitted Egyptians to a responsible share of the government of their own country, nor had trained them to take the place later of Englishmen who were controlling the administration. The tendency had been in the contrary direction. With the exception of a few individuals intended for a scholastic career, no educational mission had been sent to Europe. Young Egypt, desirous of entering the civil professions, had had to accept training from Englishmen who lectured in English, and possessed but little practical experience of the subjects which they professed to teach. It is not perhaps surprising in these conditions if Egypt regarded the state of affairs as unsatisfactory, or if that dissatisfaction slowly developed into a sentiment more pronounced, and more bitter. If some of the causes of the changed attitude of the people towards the Occupation sprang from the praiseworthy ambition upon the part of Englishmen to heap prosperity upon the country, it is hard to deny that Great Britain took little or no pains to study the psychological side of the situation. Great as were the material benefits which she had conferred upon the inhabitants of the Valley of the Nile, they were obscured by her obstinate reluctance to cede to the government any share of the authority. Egypt, oppressed and tax ridden had accepted uncomplainingly a foreign occupation. Freed now from her former miseries, she wanted political freedom; and, by the irony of fate, the chains of subjection were pulled the tauter." *

I once watched two children at play together. They thought out a fine game, involving make-believe horses, carriage, ladies, gentlemen and coachmen. The dominant child organised it among several children with care. "You be the lady. You are the horses. You be the coachman, and here is the carriage."

The other child who had shared in the original idea said, rather tentatively, "What am I to be?"

The answer came back: "Oh, you'll be the little dog that runs behind."

The game went splendidly, but I noticed the expression of "the little dog" as it ran behind, and it boded no good.

During the 1914-1918 war, an Egyptian Labour Corps and a Transport Corps gave invaluable service to the Allied cause by their work both in Egypt itself and in some cases as far away as France. But the formation of these corps was at great

* Lt.-Col. P. G. Elgood, C.M.G., *Egypt and the Army.* Oxford University Press, 1924.

and sad expense. The British Army desperately needed extra labour, but the Egyptian peasant resisted all persuasion to leave his fields and volunteer. Added to his natural disinclination for service of this sort, he had been told at the beginning of the war that nothing would be required of him except his neutrality. But the needs of the British Army became such that desperate measures were resorted to. The Egyptian local government was appealed to in the provinces, and it was made clear that if the requisite number of recruits was not forthcoming, it would be they, the officials, who would suffer.

This immediately led to tyranny of the worst sort. Pressgang methods were resorted to and personal scores settled by marching off unwilling peasants to the nearest labour depot, with no warning and by force. I well remember passing a small crowd of country people at this time. The men had been rounded up for service in the Labour Corps, and the women were wailing behind them with that peculiarly grief-stricken mourning of their kind. Being a small child, I had little idea what it was all about; but the picture remains with me so vividly across the years that I still cannot pass the spot where I saw them without the scene and the lamentation clearly before me.

A great bitterness grew in the hearts of the fellaheen against the British as a result, and when it came to requisitioning their precious animals, even the she-camels, their confidence in British justice was at a low ebb. They could hardly be expected to understand the desperate military need of the time. That such a situation should ever have arisen is a tragedy. But the last straw was to come, and in this it is difficult to see a thread of justification. A great campaign was initiated at Headquarters for contributions to be made to the work of the Red Cross. That Sultan Hussein and the wealthy Pashas of the towns should contribute is one thing—they did so generously; but quite another thing was to whip up demand in the countryside, where the nature of the campaign was utterly misunderstood. Again the unscrupulous small official came into his own, with the idea that a large subscription list from his area would open the gate for his own personal advancement, in some unspecified way. Money was extracted from wretched men and women who could certainly not afford it, and who were left with but one idea, that the British Army had ordered this to happen. Some bewildered old people even got it into their heads that, if they did not pay, a red cross was to be branded on their arms—they, devout followers of Islam. It takes more than a generation for such mistakes to die down. Feeling ran high, and blood ran too. Englishmen were murdered, some shot at in broad daylight in main thoroughfares, others killed secretly and brutally. From 1914 to 1922 Egypt was under martial law. This terminated in 1922 when a big step forward was taken in Anglo-Egyptian affairs.

The British High Commissioner communicated to Sultan Fouad (who had succeeded his brother Sultan Hussein) that the British Government intended to recommend to Parliament a Declaration to Egypt which read thus:–

"Whereas the relations between His Majesty's Government and Egypt are of vital interest to the British Empire; the following principles are hereby declared:—

1. The British Protectorate over Egypt is terminated and Egypt is declared to be an independent sovereign state.

2. So soon as the Government of His Highness shall pass an act of indemnity with application to all inhabitants of Egypt, martial law, as proclaimed on November 2, 1914, shall be withdrawn.

3. The following matters are absolutely reserved to the discretion of His Majesty's Government until such time as it may be possible by free discussion and friendly accommodation on both sides to conclude agreements in regard thereto between His Majesty's Government and the Government of Egypt:

(a) The security of the communications of the
    British Empire in Egypt;
(b) The defence of Egypt against all foreign aggres-
    sion or interference, direct or indirect;
(c) The protection of foreign interests in Egypt
    and the protection of minorities;
(d) The Sudan.

Pending the conclusion of such agreements the *status quo* in
all these matters shall remain intact."

The British Parliament sanctioned the Declaration on
March 15, 1922, and the Sultan immediately addressed a
royal rescript to the Egyptian people, in which he proclaimed
Egypt to be an independent Sovereign State, and assumed the
title of His Majesty, King of Egypt.

There was not much public enthusiasm over this, but two
years later to the day Egypt's first Parliament assembled, consisting of a Chamber of Deputies and a Senate, with Zaghloul
Pasha as Prime Minister. It was not long, however, before the
reserved points in the above Declaration became great stum-
bling blocks in the pathway of Anglo-Egyptian affairs, which
was marked by tragic outbursts of violence, and mistakes on
both sides. One of the worst of these was the senseless murder,
in 1924, of Sir Lee Stack, Governor-General of the Sudan and
Sirdar of the Egyptian Army. The punitive measures taken on
account of this murder were severe, and covered a wide range.

Lord Allenby, the High Commissioner who drew up the
demands, had been under great strain during these difficult
years. He had earlier been sympathetic with the Egyptian view
and had struggled for the abolition of the hated Protectorate.
There is no doubt that he was now convinced of the justice of
his ultimatum and the need for severity. But it is reasonable to
suggest that part of the wording might have been differently
expressed. The communication sent to the Egyptian Prime
Minister contained the sentence, "His Majesty's Government
consider that this murder, which holds up Egypt as at present

governed to the contempt of civilised peoples, is the natural outcome of a campaign of hostility to British rights and British subjects in Egypt and the Sudan founded upon heedless ingratitude for benefits conferred by Great Britain." Such a phrase as "the contempt of civilised peoples," lives in the heart of a nation long after it has forgotten that it had to pay a fine of half a million pounds.

So, one way or another, it is not surprising that the "free discussion and friendly accommodation" mentioned in the Declaration of 1922 were sought after by both parties as successfully as the chasing of a will o' the wisp might be. Abortive negotiations followed each other with monotonous regularity. Sometimes the Egyptian delegation would visit the British Government in London, sometimes British spokesmen would hopefully come to Cairo for talks; but the results were much the same, till finally in the summer of 1936 agreement was reached—mostly owing to fear of Mussolini's intentions in North Africa. By this Treaty the British troops were to evacuate to the Suez Canal Zone, and Great Britain was to be represented by an Ambassador instead of a High Commissioner, Egypt also sending an Ambassador to London. The *status quo* in the Sudan was to be maintained, and Egypt herself would be responsible for the safety of minorities. The repudiation of this treaty in October, 1951, and subsequent events, are present-day history known to everyone who reads the papers.

In 1936 negotiations on the Egyptian side were conducted by Mustapha Nahas. He was born in 1881, a year before the bombardment of Alexandria, in a small town to the north of Cairo. His family were in fairly humble circumstances, but he showed marked ability at school, and in due course took up a legal career at which he did well.

When a young man, in the early years of this century, he joined the original Nationalist Party under its leader Mustapha Kamel. For the next few years politics claimed his attention. The fortunes of his country were deep in his heart and active in his mind; but he kept at his profession. In 1918 when Saad Zaghloul was forming the Wafd, his attention was drawn to Nahas. He approached him with an offer to join the Wafd and embark on the stormy sea of politics.

Nahas, who was by now an able judge, felt a strong desire to throw in his lot with Zaghloul, whom he greatly admired, but there were difficulties in the way. The Nahas family, of peasant stock, were not wealthy, and at this time the future Prime Minister was keeping not only his immediate family but also providing for numerous relatives who could not be wage-earners. He felt unable to leave his work and accept Zaghloul's proposition. But Zaghloul was determined that a way could be found round this dilemma. He had prophesied to himself a powerful political career for Nahas, and if family finances stood in the way he himself would provide what was necessary to remove that obstacle. So all was fixed, and Mustapha Nahas threw himself into the volcanic politics of the time.

When Zaghloul died in 1927, a national and much mourned hero, it was Nahas who succeeded him as President of the Wafd. Leaving on one side the rights and wrongs of his nationalist policy, all would agree that it was a difficult position to fill.

Nahas Pasha became Prime Minister in 1928, and had a short and stormy passage with Lord Lloyd over an Assemblies Bill which the High Commissioner thought extremely ill-advised, but to which Nahas stuck with prodigious determination. This ended in his dismissal from office, but brief though this premiership had been, it showed that he was both powerful and popular.

From now he was ever near the forefront of the fray, and often collided head on with the High Commissioner and the British Government. He gave trouble and received it.

During the last World War, Egypt held to her agreements with Great Britain, both in the letter of the law and in the spirit. Egyptians manned many important points in lines of communications such as the railway westward toward Alamein, and men gave their lives in so doing. Nahas Pasha chose a moment during the war when things looked about as difficult for the Allies as they well could be, to make his most determined and public declaration to stand by Great Britain and her cause.

On one of the Moslem feasts of Bairam that fell during the war, Nahas Pasha saw that every wounded British soldier in Egypt received a small personal present from him, and many are the British convalescent officers and men who have enjoyed trips on the Nile as Nahas Pasha's guests at his expense.

He had at first a simple touch with high and low and a natural love of human nature. One of his childhood friends, less gifted than was the young Nahas, started earning his living as a gardener, and remained a gardener. When the Prime Minister visited the town where he worked, the gardener used to come and see him or he would visit the gardener. It was just a meeting between two old friends.

All this makes it doubly sad to see how power, wealth, and the wrong company eventually corrupted his character, first neutralising his good qualities to impotence, and then proceeding to build up elements of actual wrong, till his country which once loved him had little alternative but to turn wholly against him.

Throughout much of Nahas' political career he had an enemy with whom the crossing of swords was but thinly veiled, a man forty years his junior, with whom he rarely agreed, but one whose star has now set for fundamentally the same reasons—the love of power, wealth, and bad company.

Farouk was born on February 11, 1920. The day is clear in my memory, for a favourite guinea pig, the plaything of some of us children in Cairo, produced a baby guinea pig on that same day, which much-loved animal we respectfully called Farouk after the baby Prince. Farouk was indeed loved and welcomed, and became a thoughtful, well-mannered boy. As a small child he was fairly strictly brought up. One of the Queen's ladies told my mother at the time how, when about three years old, Farouk ran round to everyone he could find in the Palace one day, saying, "Do you know, I'm a fine fellow; I'm a Prince, I'm a very important person." This news he had just discovered from some servant. He ended by running into his father's study with the same tale. King Fouad dealt with him peremptorily. "You are not an important Prince," he said, "you are only a silly little boy." Farouk, much cowed, went round to everyone he had spoken to before, and told them he had made a mistake, and that he was only a silly little boy after all.

At the age of sixteen he inherited his kingdom, to all appearances a young man really wanting to know his people and do his best for them. What went wrong, why, and when, may be discovered by some future psychologically-minded historian.

I first saw Queen Farida, his first wife, when she opened a Horticultural Exhibition. It was before the public were admitted and we were only a small party to receive her. She was newly married, very young and with great charm, she looked thoroughly at ease, chatting in French, English or Arabic as she went. When amused she would laugh lightly and freely like a child. She was but seventeen years old. The next time I saw her was at a formal presentation of foreign ladies to the new Queen at Abdin Palace. Again I noted her charm and gift of putting people at their ease. One elderly lady was walking backwards after her presentation to the Queen, as was the custom, before regaining her seat some ten yards away. She looked perilously near running aground on a tiger skin or a lamp, which would certainly have foundered her. The other ladies sitting round were too nervous to say anything, but young Queen Farida saw the danger, and called out in her natural way, "*Eh—attention, Madame, prenez garde!*"

Now the Egyptian court is no more, the last vestige has gone from the world of the old Turkish Imperial etiquette. It lingered on at Cairo in various ways; one was the form of curtsy used by ladies before the Queen. It was elegant when properly done. As you bent downwards, your right arm made a sweeping gesture towards the ground, and then up over your head. This represented the ancient Oriental idea of putting ashes on the head as a sign of humility.

It was old Turkish custom that prevented other members of the Royal Family taking Farouk to task in any way whatever, now that he was King. A senior and respected member of the family told my parents one day how distressed he was about the first signs of Farouk's bad conduct. "Even I," he said, "can say nothing to him."

In those early days he and his Queen were in love. When the late Archbishop of York visited Cairo at about this time, he was received by the young Farouk who sat the Archbishop next to him at dinner. "I am a lucky man," said the King to the Archbishop, "I have married the woman I love." It was shortly after this that Farouk asked if he could see over the new Anglican Cathedral in Cairo (the land on which it was built was sold to the British Community for this purpose by the Egyptian Government, at a purely nominal fee). At one place the King suggested that a bronze railing would be better than the wooden one that was there. He had this bronze rail constructed and presented it to the Cathedral, where it still is, engraved as the gift of King Farouk.

How idle it is to say that human nature cannot change, either for good or for bad! Poor Egypt, her need was not for a mixture of Sultan Abdel Hamid and Henry VIII. Early in 1948 was the first time that I, personally, heard displeasure expressed at the way King Farouk was living, though it had been well-known everywhere long since. Many must have had serious forebodings; but his picture still hung in office, home and shop, and most speeches worthy of the name contained fulsome tributes to him. The type of people whom I heard speak their mind in private were the steady, good-living type of worker, butchers, cooks, gardeners.

Yet Farouk was no fool. Did he foresee his fall? He is said to have given out one day that in five years' time there would be but five kings left in the world.

"And who will they be, Sir?" asked his hearer.

"The Kings of Hearts, Clubs, Diamonds and Spades," replied His Majesty, "and the King of England."

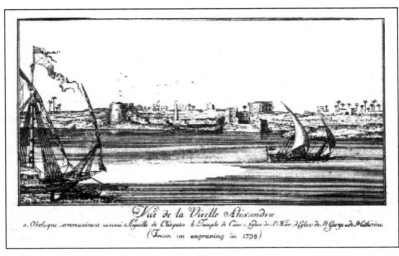

Vue de la Vieille Alexandrie

9

NEW IMPRESSIONS

WHEN I left boarding school in England in 1926 and returned to Egypt a young woman of eighteen as opposed to a child, there were of course new aspects of Egypt to experience. In those early days, few Egyptian ladies accompanied their husbands to formal functions and dinner parties. Therefore girls such as my sister and I, straight from school, helped to form the female element at royal or government banquets.

This brought us in passing touch with Egyptian leaders of all sorts to whom we chatted away with what seems, in retrospect, extreme *naïveté*. I remember sitting at dinner next to a Minister of Waqf (a cabinet post concerned with religious foundations); he was a cultured gentleman of the old school, in turban and robes, added to which he was a profound classical Arabic scholar. I discovered in the course of conversation, that he did not know the Arabic word for cape gooseberry, which fruit we were then eating. At least he did not know the vernacular term which I had learnt as a child from our gardener who always called it, "the lady in the mosquito net," alluding to the casing which covers the fruit proper. This knowledge I imparted to the elderly scholar with great satisfaction on my part, not realising that it was tantamount to informing a university professor of literature about a term used by an unlettered peasant for an obscure fruit, and imagining that by so doing, I was adding considerably to his necessary sum of knowledge. To think of it only, makes me now embarrassed. These ministers and government officials treated our immature efforts at conversation with invariable patience and courtesy.

The King's receptions at Abdin Palace were formidable affairs. The buffets would have groaned had that ridiculous expression ever been applicable to a laden table. They were stacked with such things as ox heads made of *foie gras* from which real ox tongue protruded, ships in full sail made of cake and the rigging of spun sugar; cooked pheasants with all the main feathers replaced so that the birds looked as if they had just alighted in an autumn stubble field. They did not remain that way for long, though. The guests made short work of most things. Some would line up in phalanx close to the table and stay there till all was consumed. I became quite clever at piercing the throng round the buffet and laying hands on a roll of bread and anything plain which I would there and then make into a sandwich and squeeze my way back with it for my father. He could only eat simple food and as he grew older the physical exertions needed to procure it on these occasions were rather more than he could manage.

These receptions were magnificent in their own way. Fine men of the Egyptian royal guard lined the main staircase in full dress, carrying their lances. The waiters in scarlet and gold dispensed the food from golden plates. But even in those days it was an anachronism which, not being voluntarily tempered to the times, had later to be swept away by compulsion.

Occasionally my father would be summoned to the Palace to see King Fouad privately, and they would have a quiet meal together in a simple setting. It was once enlivened by a hard piece of fried toast which, when my father cut it, sprang across the table and hit the monarch in the face—at least so my father related.

Palace banquets featured in our lives long before we were old enough to attend them, for our father would sometimes bring us back a handful of sweets from these functions. He would come into our bedroom when he returned, uninhibited by qualms of conscience about waking us up in the middle of the night. He would push his top hat under the mosquito net and in it we found the sweets. His decorations glistened in the half light from the open door, his shirt front shone and we were much impressed.

Some of the official government receptions for visiting royalty or notables were enlivened by entertainments. Dazzling ladies of ample proportions pirouetted about alternately with startling acrobatic turns. I remember one such evening when it was an entertainment in itself to watch the reactions of a rather prim middle-aged lady, the widow of an English statesman, who, visiting Egypt, had been included among the guests. She was unstrung to begin with by a fiery turn wherein a girl was swung round by her feet at top speed and a man jumped lightly over her head each time she came round.

Then, to prepare for the next dancing number, the drugget had to be removed from the floor. Our chairs were on the edge of this drugget, so in rushed a wild-looking individual with waving hair, waving galabia, and with his mouth full of protruding nails. He proceeded to turn the grandees off their chairs with an imperious wave of the arm and to haul up the drugget from beneath their embarrassed feet.

Such incidents are taken without comment in Egypt, where in curious ways, and at surprising times, democracy is carried to its logical conclusion. But to the visiting English lady, the onrush of this apparent madman, brandishing a hammer and ordering her off her chair, was indeed a shock.

At an evening reception of this sort, I remember slipping away for a moment to talk to one of the performers who had just accomplished her turn. Her name was Fatima, she was aged ten, and with her elder brother to help, had done the most amazing acrobatics. I found her peering through the ornamental palms at the other numbers, having changed into her "off duty" attire, a maroon satin dress cut on the cross to just below the knees and little white socks. Her family were paid £10 an evening, she told me, and had two or three engagements a month. I thought it more amusing to peer through the palms too, and chat to Fatima, than to sit on my gilded chair in front.

How many parties are remembered for the keen incidental pleasure of doing what the party did not exist for you to do! My partner and I slipped out from a formal Residency dance one evening and spent half an hour trying to mesmerise a tame marabout stork in the garden. It was an ancient bird that had seen more than one High Commissioner come and go. It did not respond to our efforts, but we did enjoy ourselves. And once, at Shepheard's Hotel, we found a devious means of climbing on to the glass roof of the dance hall and watching the strangely foreshortened figures below, looking so idiotic in their solemnity, so we considered. But we extracted the savour of danger from the nights when the English General in Command gave receptions in his illuminated garden, and we were not among the guests. We would then creep up to the garden hedge, close to our own garden, and lie in the ditch at its base watching the grandees strolling up and down a few feet from us, as they made polite conversation, oblivious of our presence. Every now and then a sentry with fixed bayonet would stump past us on his side of the hedge, and that was the moment not to cough or giggle—hardly to breathe.

It was also a joy to return to the doings of the Egyptian Horticultural Society. This is an institution which holds first-class shows on a big scale three times a year. The display and quality of flowers and fruit, amateur and professional, was often most impressive. But, as in all flower shows worthy of the name, it was much enlivened by the human element. The final minutes before the competitors had to leave and the judges to enter, were crammed with incident. The secretary and his supporters would herd people to the door, or attempt to, rather like a sheep dog for once bettered by his sheep. Within five yards of the exit someone, whose exhibit was at the far end of the huge hall, would think of an improvement

"Our little house at Ramleh"   Amelia C. Rowlatt, 1868

Our Cairo home for forty-two years

Radwan, our doorman at the Zohria

Looking towards the willow tree where
the lizards lived

Entertaining Australian troops at the Zohria, 1914-18

Rowlatt and Barker cousins
near Mena House, about 1920

The author aged about ten

Soubki, the Bedwin head of the family
which for three generations guarded
our Ramleh house

The Mokatam Mountains – Cairo and the Citadel in the distance.
The artist, H. Calvert, was an old friend of Arthur and Amelia Rowlatt.

Two men, one on a donkey, head towards their village at dusk.   From an old family album, artist unknown.

Cairo Brownies about 1920, the author standing third from left

At Mena Swimming Bath with my sister, Pamela, 1931

Fred and May Rowlatt at the Zohria

My parents picnicking at Sakara on top of Zoser's temple

Ismail Mohamed, Abdelmohsen and
gardeners at the Zohria. Ismail afterwards became
head gardener to President
Gamal Abdel Nasser.

Mohammed Dahab, head
suffragi at the Zohria

Ali Dahab, suffragi at the Zohria & front row centre, in his Nubian home

"View on the Nile near Abd-el-Mandour"   Amelia C. Terry, 1850's

in his display and dodge back among the crowd of pursuers with the turns and twists of a rugger match.

The actual gardeners as opposed to the owners had their particular system of finally freshening up the flowers so carefully and lovingly arranged. They filled their mouths with water and sprayed the whole exhibit through the sole agency of the mouth—a most skilful performance which never ceased to fascinate me. Sometimes it fell to my lot to judge the class of gardeners' bouquets. It is interesting to look back over the years and note the change in style produced by these simple people. In the early days of the show, their efforts were often crude in colour and form, but have improved out of all recognition, till in latter times they made bouquets which would grace any West End florist's window.

Judging these arrangements was quite a difficulty, as each gardener developed his own style (admittedly sometimes a reflection of his employer's wife's style), and one came to recognise the hand at work on what was supposed to be an anonymous bouquet. There was one very solemn old gardener who invariably wore a calf-length blue galabia with a hem-line high in front and low behind, and a felt hood, as distinct from a hat, also up in front and down behind, the effect of which, combined with a magnificent handle-bar moustache, was outstanding to say the least. Unfortunately his style of flower arrangement was equally outstanding, and I had to put his personality, which was endearing, firmly out of my mind when judging this class.

The Horticultural Department showed skill and imagination in their spacious exhibits. One year a wonderful lawn effect appeared made of seed germinated on wet sacking, therefore transferable at will. The mind behind this idea told us that he had once gone to a fancy dress ball in a suit of mustard and cress grown in like fashion. He admitted to having procured the first prize, and bronchitis.

There are fine gardens of great botanical interest in Egypt today where anyone keen on horticulture will get a warm welcome and can find an equally keen Egyptian ready to discuss the latest ways of propagating this or of pruning that.

But there are other strange little gardens which gave me pleasure of another sort, seeing them again after the years in England. Wherever a peasant guardian of some Ancient Egyptian site has his small hut overlooking the tombs or temple in his charge, here he attempts to raise a few square feet of garden. The very nature of his preserve is sand and stone and he is usually far from a water supply with no means of importing soil. Yet it is amazing what he can achieve. A castor oil bush may flourish in one corner with its decorative leaves and reddish spiky fruit. Maize, pale green and slender, can send up tall stems. The Egyptian radish called figl grows in rows, nourished by drips from the porous water jar which stands in a corner by the hut to catch the breeze and cool the drink.

The tin which serves as mug and watering-can rests on the wooden lid of the jar and is used to dispense to the vegetation what water the guardian feels he can spare. White stones, pebbles or whatever geology affords him from the neighbouring land, often mark out the beds in these tiny patches. As the sun sets in the Sahara behind, the owner of such a garden can be seen sending his sundown prayers over the other Egyptian desert, eastwards to Mecca. He is often a Saidi from Upper Egypt and wears a black robe and white turban. He is a dignified figure as he bends and rises with hands held palms up to heaven, praying between his patch of living green and his dusty acres of the dead.

It was during these first winters in Egypt after boarding school years, that I became aware what divergence of views and what misunderstanding could flare up between some of my English friends and the people of the land in which they found themselves. My new companions were usually the young officers and married couples of the regiments stationed in Egypt. They spoke little or no Arabic, and often misunderstood the man-in-the-street. The Egyptian, on his side, would sometimes do things which happen to madden an Englishman, things often harmless enough but occasionally harmful, such as beating his beast of burden.

When this happened, the passing young Englishman would leap out of his car and start beating the Egyptian, leaving me breathless and miserable, on the fringe of the scene. What was needed was a quiet and rational conversation, pointing out the advantages of helping your horse instead of beating it. I have seen such a conversation in which the co-operation of the driver was immediately gained; but without knowing the country or the language, it was difficult for the Englishman to get started. If an animal is found in bad condition, there are now two wonderful hospitals for animals run by joint Egyptian and English effort, the People's Dispensary for Sick Animals, and the Brooks Hospital. In many cases an introduction to either of these places is the answer to such situations.

On one occasion, several of us settled down to a picnic on an apparently vacant bit of sandy waste near the desert edge. An Egyptian peasant shortly arrived in a tearing rage. One of the men of our party stood up to him and the situation looked menacing. My requests, to let me at least find out what had upset him, were granted. It took some moments to make myself heard, during which time I waited nervously under the shower of curses and the brandishing of a mattock. When this subsided, it appeared that we had been sitting on a seed bed. Never have I seen a seed bed look more like waste ground, but none the less it made the owner's wrath understandable. It was obviously the occasion for an honest apology and a small sum to compensate. The old man slowly cooled off, and I thought we had only just made good. But we had not gone a few yards when he caught us up, this time with an apology himself and several cucumbers as a peace offering.

This ended happily; but there were other times when it did not. Incidents, often trifling in themselves, would leave hurt feelings on one side and plain rage on the other—sometimes an English fault, sometimes an Egyptian. But whichever way it was, it always left me sad and anxious, feeling equally loyal to both parties.

It is only fair to say that there was always a number of men and women from the English regiments stationed in Egypt who took a most understanding interest in the people among whom their lot had temporarily fallen. They availed themselves of all opportunities to learn more about the country and the people. It took considerable strength of character and enterprise on their part to break away from the rut limited by bridge, cocktail parties and polo, but those who did were repaid. Any genuine friendly touch was certainly appreciated.

In those years the ordinary man was thinking about and experiencing new things. His attitude to medicine and doctors for instance was undergoing a change. He was more willing to go to hospital than he used to be, though he still kept some quite decided ideas about his treatment. He had less faith in a medicine which tasted pleasant than in one which tasted nasty. I knew of one hospital which, when dealing with simple people, put an artificially disagreeable taste in the medicine if it did not naturally exist, for the doctors said that it really did make a psychological difference to the patient's recovery. The sick man often chose a local anaesthetic rather than a general one, for he was happier if he was able to follow more or less what was happening. Consequently local anaesthetics were given even for an abdominal operation, and the patient's nervous system was so good that he stood it successfully.

There was one hospital with such a good name that devious means were sometimes resorted to for gaining admission. This was the anti-rabic hospital where the patients underwent several weeks' treatment consisting mostly of injections. They naturally did no work, were given regular meals and had what, in their eyes, was a fine holiday at government expense, provided they came for treatment before it was too late to avoid the terrible tragedy of hydrophobia. So one way and another the glowing accounts of life in this place given by returning patients were too much for some of their hearers in a distant village. One of them fixed a donkey's jaw—the jaw bone of an ass in fact—on to a kind of tongs. A forceful jab at a man's leg with this device, for a small fee of course, could produce such a bite, that with the aid of a few circumstantial details in the telling of the tale it would get the patient safely into this haven of rest in Cairo. Some time elapsed before the plan was uncovered.

However, there is really a considerable advance in grasping the meaning of modern medicine, especially among the types of persons such as gardeners, small shopkeepers and so on. The chauffeur of a friend of ours gave his master a concise and understanding description of a blood transfusion one of his relatives had undergone. That sort of man a few years back would not have been able to do this at all. And yet, at the same time, you have the old type of treatment by holy men, and charms and ancient remedies going strongly still, right in the middle of the biggest cities and often with amazing success. A garden boy of ours suffered for some time with strange backaches. We sent him to hospital where they took trouble in trying to cure him but could not discover how the pain originated. After a short relief the pain returned. Eventually he asked for several days' leave to visit a holy man whom he knew. He came back saying he was cured, and has since had no recurrence of the trouble. He told us with pride, and apparent pleasure, how he had been held down by three men while a hole was burnt in his back and a pea inserted which had to be kept in the wound to prevent it from closing. Kuranic recitations and prayers accompanied this performance. A kitchen boy of ours was also cured of bad neuralgic headaches by a saintly individual who pricked his temple hard with a lot of pins stuck into a handle, and an oily mixture of some sort was applied. We had done our best with aspirin, doctors and all we could, to no avail.

There is a great deal of real simple faith among these people of Egypt. Naturally much of it has some superstition attached. If you stand near the Bab al Zuweila, one of the eleventh century gates in Cairo, many of the women who go through it about their everyday affairs will brush their hands over the old door in passing and then rub them on their faces or the faces of the children accompanying them. The spirit of a holy man is said to inhabit the door which is stuck over with little votive offerings of hair or rags put there either in thanksgiving or to acquire virtue. Then there is the tomb of a sheikh among palm trees outside Cairo where friends of ours had land. If the owner made some such suggestion to his headman, as: "I think we will grow mangoes here," he got a reply like this: "Yes, certainly, that would please the sheikh." Or when he said, "What about cutting down that old tree?" and the answer was, "Well, I'm not sure that the sheikh would approve of that."

You also hear stories such as this, which was told me by an acquaintance who firmly believes that the blight of cotton-leaf worm, some years ago, attacked the fields of the bad and irreligious man and left the crops of the good and pious. He, himself, he affirms, was staying with a good man, whose fields seemed free of the worm though his neighbour's were badly affected, for he never gave a tenth of his crops to the poor, which is the Islamic rule. But to their dismay, on closer examination, they found some of the cotton worm beginning to come over the boundary on to the good man's land. They watched horrified, and the owner began to search his conscience to see where he had sinned. "But," said my friend, "as we stood there watching the field, down came a great flight of crows, settled on the ground and started to eat every caterpillar that had strayed off the bad man's land on to the good man's land."

The intermixture of superstition among the uneducated part of the population, takes an inclusive rather than an exclusive form. A Moslem Egyptian peasant woman, for instance, is quite likely to pray for the recovery of her child at the tomb of a Christian saint after having thoroughly invoked Islamic aid. She follows the principle of leaving no stone unturned.

There is a huge and ancient sycamore tree at Mataria near Cairo, under which, tradition states, the Virgin rested with Jesus on their flight into Egypt. (It is the same one from which my grandmother, Amelia, took a twig to send to her family in Kent, as a memento of Egypt, in 1852.) This tree is covered with small votive offerings. Most of them, but by no means all, are from Christians.

The outer realms of modern medicine can also be happily merged with superstition, in the minds of some simple folk. A French lady, much loved and revered by many poor people of Cairo, was asked by one of them for a note of introduction to a hospital so that the sufferer would get good attention in the crowded out-patient department. Meeting one of the family later, she asked how the patient was. "Oh, he is much better," was the reply. "We couldn't get him to hospital, but we soaked your letter in water [to make a charm of it] and then he drank the water into which the ink had melted—and it helped a lot."

Admittedly, this took place a good many years ago. It would be rare to find a case quite like that nowadays.

Even if the simple people are apt to hold on to some primitive ideas, it does not mean that they are not able or willing to take in new ones, as the following experience shows.

Just before the outbreak of war in 1939 Egyptian women flocked to A.R.P. and First-Aid classes. This catered for the more educated among the townswomen. It was suggested to me by a public-spirited lady who lived some five miles out of Cairo that I might try to bring some elementary first-aid information to the poorer type of Egyptian women in a neighbouring village. With the help of a friend, I attempted the task.

Preliminary negotiations were made through the village sheikh who co-operated fully. The schoolhouse was lent to us after school hours and even the old doorkeeper dressed in a discarded British Army jacket of venerable age, offered us his one-eyed service to keep off small boys and other idle individuals who might find their way into the building out of sheer curiosity and disturb us. This he did regularly throughout the course, bringing with him a great whip, a suitable symbol of authority he thought, but which was for show more than for use. He always gave our room a special clean before our arrival, and at the end considered himself amply rewarded by the smallest tip and a little bag of sweets for his children.

The lantern by the light of which we worked during the last half of each lesson was a favour lent free of charge by the owner of the little village shop.

Quite a concourse arrived the first day aged between fourteen and forty, and considering that many were illiterate, they were most quick and practical in picking up the points. We concentrated our instruction on the hygiene and minor home accidents side of first-aid, thinking it unnecessary at that point to link it in their minds with the possibility of actual warfare. But we had not reckoned with the impact of world events. War and rumours of war were naturally rife in the papers and on the wireless, and our ladies shortly jumped to the conclusion that if they came too regularly and were too proficient they might be whisked off to some far-flung battlefield, to minister there. Not realising any of this, we were sadly disappointed to find an almost empty schoolroom awaiting us one day.

All came to light, however, after consultation with the sheikh, and we were able to explain that what they were learning was to help them in their homes in any circumstances, and that if war came to their doorsteps suddenly out of the skies, it would be of special value. They all trooped back in good spirits and we continued. At first there was not much discipline, and punctuality was a virtue unknown, but as we proceeded both these qualifications improved; the one by stern disapproval and marked attention to those waiting quietly for their turn, the other by a much appreciated system of reward. Those who attended all the lessons and arrived on time were promised small prizes.

One of the joys in teaching Egyptian women of this type is their strong sense of humour, to which one can unfailingly appeal in cases of discontent, grumbling or jealousy. We also found it an effectual weapon in the actual tuition, for they would always laugh heartily at a demonstration of the wrong way of doing things, especially if accompanied by a little dramatic action. I am afraid at times our Arabic gave them something well worth a laugh. We discovered on the first day that we did not know the word for a vein; after several abortive attempts to describe what we meant, we succeeded by calling it a "hose pipe for the blood." Our pupils gave full and natural outlet to their own histrionic instincts. If one of them was putting splints on a companion's supposedly broken radius, for instance, "the patient" would groan and moan and look most realistically in pain.

After six lessons we held a short oral and practical examination. The results were quite creditable. It was a very informal examination with the questions slightly modified to suit each pupil's capabilities. The younger, who could read and write, had more complicated questions about the circulatory system and so on, while the more elderly who had had no sort of teaching or education of any kind before, were given simpler questions of hygiene and bandaging. Then if we knew, for instance, that Fatima or Karima had had to attend an aunt's funeral the day we had done artificial respiration, we took that into account too.

This little course had nothing official about it whatsoever, but we felt that it would be encouraging for the women to be given, at the end, just something in writing to keep. The local man of letters offered to write out, in the beautiful Arab script, a simple certificate to say that So-and-So had attended so many talks on First-Aid in such-and-such a year and had taken a test. This, we felt was sufficiently non-committal. So imagine our consternation on first seeing these certificates shortly before presenting them, to discover that the enthusiastic sheikh had added to each the words, "and she has passed the examination brilliantly." It was too late to alter anything for the less brilliant members—but perhaps it was a fault in the right direction. After all, Ancient Egyptian priests frequently wrote out certificates for the dead to use as *laissez-passer* through hell, stating the bearer's total innocence; a blank space was left for the name, and they were handed to all comers. Anyhow, we had a triumphant passing-out ceremony in the presence of local notables. The students were very much dressed in their best, all demonstrated something they had learnt and received their certificates. They cheered us, we cheered them, and together we cheered the notables.

Before and after this small effort, there have of course been many large ventures undertaken by Egyptians to teach the poorer people health and hygiene. Private enterprises, Government schemes and Point Four projects are among the largest in the Middle East. Some of the educated Egyptian women did fine work to combat the terrible malaria scourge of 1944 and the relapsing fever of 1946.

On these occasions well-to-do Egyptian ladies went most courageously into the homes of the very poorest where thousands were dying or starving for, in some cases, no one in the immediate neighbourhood was left with sufficient strength to work. These ladies, for the most part, had never before been in contact with conditions approximating to this. But they rolled up their sleeves and went into the thick of it. Nor was it on their doorstep; many took a twelve hour train journey to reach the bad spots.

An isolated cholera outbreak created another emergency. The Government dealt drastically and, in the end, successfully with this. Among other measures they scattered disinfectant powder from low-flying aeroplanes over vast areas of town and field. The whole population of the large towns was inoculated against the disease. This entailed much hard work on the part of professional and voluntary medical units, and included a good deal of persuasion and quieting of fears, as thousands of the population had never had an inoculation in their lives.

There was, at times, much howling and screaming among the infant citizens, who feared they knew not what. As often as not, the injection was finished before they realised it had begun, and tears gave way to smiles of relief when they were told it was all over. Many, however, came most willingly. In one instance, a doctor was surprised to see a toothless old woman waiting again in the queue, whom he recognised as having had her full dose the day before. "Ah," she said when questioned, "this is just what I need. I have not been well for a long time. But I feel so much better since you gave me the 'needle' yesterday. Just once more, please, and I will be quite cured."

A characteristic of the everyday Egyptian which seemed to me to develop further in these years was his sense of decoration. As is well-known, the decorative work of the Ancient Egyptians was remarkable and so was the work during the Islamic ages, down to the early sixteenth century. That much of this latter was done by ordinary workmen is shown by the type of article decorated, for instance, the earthenware water jugs such as are in use today. At the base of the neck is a little filter of perforated earthenware which could so easily have been some holes to act as a sieve, but these medieval workmen often made the most delicate patterns out of this filter. One, in the Museum of Islamic Arts in Cairo, is a peacock in lace-like perforations. There is another instance of these old Egyptian workmen's love of design for its own sake. It is a small metal object also in this museum, inlaid with copper and silver. One of the narrow bands of inlay has come out and there, in the socket, is a tiny pattern, done just for the joy of doing it, as the inlay had been hammered down on top of it immediately, and it had remained hidden for hundreds of years.

There is much of this feeling in the workman of today. He still makes beautiful *mushrabia* (wooden trellis) work with almost no pattern to guide him and even the brasswork in the bazaars, done sometimes by quite small boys, shows a fine sense of pattern and skill; the same can be said of the traditional coloured tent work. The authorities of the Islamic Museum once had a fragment of beautifully carved, most intricate plaster work needing restoration. A quite uneducated worker in plaster took one look at it and sketched out the remainder of the pattern without a moment's hesitation.

The above instances show the sense of decoration among people whose craft calls for it. But there is another sort of decorative sense which is apparent in everyday trades, such as the butcher, surprisingly enough, who, on high days and holidays, sticks a trail of purple bougainvillea into the scrawny half of a sheep, a rather doubtful embellishment. And the vendors of vegetables and fruit who arrange their shops or stalls with infinite care so that the colours and forms of their wares make a lovely sight. The wayside booths of earthenware goods are beautifully arranged too, not highly coloured like the fruit, but with all the natural browns and beiges blending one into another.

Sometimes real imagination is shown. I once watched a grand parade in a country town on the occasion of a feast day. The various trades of the place had decorated lorries or carts in appropriate style. The Nile fishermen held their nets aloft as though they had been triumphant banners from the wars. The tailors had attached coloured galabias, some only half finished, to their old lorry and these fluttered in the wind most merrily. The butchers had two red hunks of unspecified meat fixed as ornaments on either side of the driver. The rest of the car was mercifully draped in greenery instead. Workers from the government irrigation department had somehow rigged up a pump from which gushed cochineal coloured water. A sweating individual in another corner of the lorry worked a hand pump as hard as he could, which in some miraculous way drew the water round again ready to pour forth afresh as the lorry proceeded. Thus they paraded with music and applause through lines of cheering inhabitants, their hearts swelling with local pride.

Then there are other spontaneous and surprising ideas, not always successful but most expressive. On feast days the bicycles hired out by the hour for small boys to career round on, have coloured paper threaded through the spokes of their wheels and, as they dash along at high speed, the effect is quite startling. Sometimes domestic servants get ideas of decoration in their work. The cook of a friend of ours was told, before a party, to make the dish of fish look as elegant as he could. The hostess was rather taken aback when the dish was served with the backbone of the fish stuck straight up in it, like the mast of a ship, with small carrots and turnips stuck alternately on the bones all the way up it on either side. Another friend asked her servant to buy, during her absence, a screen to hang in the doorway to keep the flies out. You can get them made of bits of bamboo and beads in simple patterns. The servant chose what he thought was a lovely pattern right across it; but alas his mistress was not pleased, for the pattern was in writing and it read, "coiffeur".

When it comes to clothes and fashions, the ordinary Egyptians of the town let their decorative sense rather run away with them, especially in children's clothes. I remember seeing a small girl of about five dressed in a flannelette dress, the pattern on it being bathing belles, each beauty in her bathing dress covered about a foot of material, so that only three or four of them were on the dress at all.

Nor are such fanciful patterns a new phenomenon, for Miss Amelia Edwards in her book, *A Thousand Miles up the Nile*, published in 1873, writes: "Among certain fabrics manufactured in England expressly for the eastern market, we observed a most hideous printed muslin representing small black devils capering over a yellow ground, and we learned that it was much in favour for children's dresses." Among these horrors it is still a joy to see all the peasant children and some of the town children dressed in their own traditional clothes, which combine gaiety and dignity so perfectly.

That latent artistic talent lies in many an ordinary Egyptian is shown by an interesting experiment at the Higher Institute of Education in Alexandria under the Art Director. Three wholly different types of Egyptians were given a chance to express themselves through the medium of painting. The first consisted of students from the modern Egyptian universities, the second, theological students from the ancient Islamic University of al Azhar, and the third group was formed from members of the Institute's own servant staff.

This last group were incorporated with the experiment solely on account of the great interest they took in the other students' work while they tidied the drawings away and cleared the rooms. The director would find these servants, mop in hand, poring over the work of the students and holding animated discussions among themselves about the merits or otherwise of the designs before them. They even started surreptitiously removing some specimens which they took home and tried their hand at copying. Nor did they merely copy them, but started adding original details of their own. The Director felt that at this point something definite must be done. Being a broad-minded man with his heart wholly in his work, he did not discharge the servants for over-stepping their cleaning duties, but gave them his official and organised backing.

In his own words, "I gave one of them a new paint-box, paper and pencils, and told him to go and look at the actual subject instead of a picture of it. The next day, I saw him working on a bunch of flowers which he had picked from the garden. The result was surprisingly good and his fellows came and asked if they might have the same materials and see what they could do. They showed remarkable independence of choice and treatment of subject in the colours they used.

"Feeling that they should be encouraged, I projected some of their work on to a screen. They were very excited and asked to see more, so I showed them some of the best work of Group B as well as some of the best work of Islamic painting and pottery. . . . Next they began to go with the students on visits to art exhibitions and museums. All this stimulated them to further effort and they worked with great energy.

"In imitation perhaps of Group B [the theological students]

they often wrote verses about their own works or even explanatory notices. One of them put, as a title for his painting, 'The Duck Princess'. It shows a duck swimming down a river next to a sailing boat. In the foreground is part of the river bank with trees and flowers and some peasant women filling their pitchers at the water's edge. The duck itself is very big and is placed right in the centre of the picture, so that it dominates the whole scene and makes everything else look disproportionately small. 'Why did you paint the duck so big and the other things so small, when it isn't really like that in nature?' asked one of his fellow servants. 'I wanted to show that the duck is a princess, independent and heedless of the boat or the noise of the women or the wind in the trees. She is bigger than them all,' was the reply. . . . In Ancient Egyptian art this device of enlarging size to symbolise importance was often used."

The students in the other two groups are mostly training to be teachers. Their art studies are in the nature of a hobby, an additional creative enriching to life, but many of the results are most promising. The Director plans to keep in touch with all three groups during their careers by holding exhibitions, publishing their works in magazines, and writing notices of them.

The students of the modern universities are, in a way, the least interesting as artists, lacking the spontaneity and freedom of the other two groups. One of the theological students tells how a new world opened for him when, at the age of twenty-eight, he found himself attending the art lessons at the Institute. As a small boy he had keenly modelled horses and camels of Nile mud, but his father had disapproved of such mudlarking, especially as it included making models three foot high, and planting them at dusk in the middle of the road, to watch with relish the bewilderment of motorists on approaching these apparitions. As a student at the ancient and honoured al Azhar, which for a thousand years has been the fountain head of orthodox Islam, this young man suppressed his desire for artistic creation, though still aware of it within him. Then one day, fate brought him to the Institute.

For his first attempt at sculpture he brought in a large stone he had found lying in the road and set about it, soon discovering, however, that it was unsuitable material. Next he found a piece of petrified tree in the desert. This he attacked with an axe, producing a remarkably original composition called the "Emancipation of Women".

Professor R. Peers, then Deputy Vice-Chancellor of Nottingham University, visited Egypt and saw the work at the Higher Institute of Education. Professor Peers called it "one of the most interesting educational experiments in the whole of my experience." As a result, he organised an exhibition of these students' works which was held at Nottingham University and entitled "Spontaneity in the Art of Adult Egyptians".

I know of but one instance in our immediate household where the desire to paint creatively showed itself. One of our garden boys aged about fourteen, a lad of character, though not addicted to gardening, would sometimes be found with a scrap of paper and two or three paints, dabbing away at a Mattisse-like composition which wholly engrossed him, to the detriment of his job. This was many years ago, before the discovery of hidden talent was much taken into account, so, alas, this possible genius was discouraged. It is a little disturbing to look back on it from a modern psychological viewpoint, for this boy soon began to get into mischief and was packed off to a reformatory. The story, however, is not all negative, for he joined the reformatory band and derived much outlet, pleasure and benefit from his new musical form of expression. But were we responsible to Egypt for losing her a genius? Who knows? I find myself wondering sometimes.

10

EXPEDITIONS

As the years passed and we left childhood behind, our expeditions became more enterprising. In 1931 four of us set out one day in two cars to visit the desert monasteries of al Natrun, north-west of Cairo. The Cairo-Alexandria desert road now runs not far from these monasteries and it is a comparatively easy task to reach them, but in those days it was an undertaking. Our cars stuck frequently in the sand, but by dint of pushing and pulling and struggling on, we came in sight of our destination after having had to bivouac in the desert for only one night. "Bivouac" is rather a euphemistic term. All we did was to scoop a hollow in the sand for a hip, a hollow for a shoulder, wrap up well, and lie down. The desert at night is friendly, with usually a myriad stars to watch; though I remember it once so dark that I could hear the beat of wings close overhead as migratory birds sped by, but could see nothing. It is only at dusk, as nightfall gathers, that the desert is strangely impersonal and frightening. The warm brown flints turn elephant grey, and the yellows sink to a gloomy beige. It is beautiful still, but has something of Dr. Jekyll compared to the Mr. Hyde of dawn and morning, afternoon or night.

We did the last bit on foot, as both cars had stuck, so we approached the first monastery in absolute silence. And the silence of the desert can be absolute. The only live things in view were a few swallows which circled round our heads, swooping back and back again in great curiosity. They sometimes glided by only a foot from our faces.

On arrival we clanged the great bell in a whitewashed tower above us and waited. Eventually a young bearded monk opened a postern gate and welcomed us in. These religious establishments were founded in the early centuries of Christianity and have been inhabited by Egyptian Christian monks ever since.

Here they live frugally, aloof from the world as they study and pray, in their white, fortress-like monasteries. Robert Curzon, in his book on the monasteries of the Levant, writes of this place in the 1830s. Its life has changed little since then.

Another favourite spot of ours, very easy of access, was a Moslem monastery inhabited by Dervish monks of the Turkish Bektashi order. They live on a terrace of the Mokatam hills behind Cairo. There is but a handful of these monks left now, as their mother establishment no longer exists. They are fair-skinned for they are of Albanian stock, and they wear tall white felt caps on their heads, the sign of the order.

Running deeply into the Mokatams behind the monastery is a lofty tunnel, a stone quarry of dynasties ago. An old holy man is buried right at the end of this huge cavern. His bones had lain peacefully there many years before the monks settled around him. As is the case so often in the East, they chose for their home a place already hallowed; like St. Catherine's bevy of angels who selected Moses' mountain, so these old monks chose the tomb of this long-revered elder.

The poor women of Cairo visit this place frequently. They can be seen rolling over and over down the stone floor of the quarry where the saint is buried. This performance is supposed to make them bear numerous and healthy children. It is meant to be accompanied by prayer and devotions; this may be so, but it is usually accompanied by much giggling as well from the peasant girls who try it.

Here, literally in the heart of the hills, it is dark and beautifully cool in the hot months. The sun is almost blinding as it

beats off the white rock-side of the Mokatam when one
emerges into full daylight. A few yards away is the monks'
kitchen. On feast days huge cauldrons of soup are cooked for
distribution to the needy. On the walls hang an odd mixture
of cooking utensils interspersed with trophies of war and
trophies of the chase; for of old they were a hunting and
fighting order. Red cats, black cats, white cats, tabby cats and
cats in which all hues merge wander round these premises
with that proprietary air universally acquired by cats. The
monks have made a charming garden along the cliff edges to
left and right of the cave. It is a garden in the Eastern style,
with a trellised grape vine overarching a long path. The slats
of the pergola make a criss-cross pattern on the dust below.
Citrus fruit grow here and little crops of green vegetables,
with tufts of verbena-scented geranium straggling easily over
the edge of the beds. In one of the caves behind, well out of
the sun and placed to catch the north breeze, the monks have
planted some trails of ivy which must be about the only ivy in
Egypt. There is a magnificent deep red bougainvillea which, in
its flowering season, splashes across the limestone cliff. And
beyond is a pool of water. It is shallow and long and is lined
with blue tiles. Round the edge is a little border of marjoram,
the sweet scent of which is drawn out by the sun. The monks
are happy for one to sit in this peace-giving spot where the
rumble of the city is just discernible, but far away and below.
It is one of the best places from which to watch the setting
sun, for every speck of dust over the city catches and reflects
the colours as they change. Though beautiful at any time, by
moonlight it has enchantment. It is then that the sound of
running water as it curls round the base of the cypress trees
seems to carry with it something of paradise. Above, against
the sky line, is the ramp built by Napoleon up to the
Mokatam heights.

The Arabs have a legend about the Mokatams. After the
Creation, as God reviewed His work, the hills and mountains
came one by one to dedicate to Him their streams, trees and

flowers. But the Mokatams came empty-handed, having nothing to offer save their bare rocks and crags. God, however, was pleased with their attitude of worship and praise in spite of poverty. As a reward He said that He would give them the greatest riches of all—the bones of His saints.

There must have been quite a rush on the part of aspiring saints after this pronouncement, for the hole-like dwellings and tombs of past hermits and pious men can still be clearly seen in the cliff sides.

In Egypt, death and life often mingle in a natural stream. It is a common sight to see whole families winding their way to the cemeteries on Fridays (the Moslem holiday) to spend the day round the graves. It is not always in sadness that they go; palm branches and flowers sometimes accompany them and a sort of companionable picnic is had, with babies rolling about in the sun and small children playing tag round the headstones. Yet all is consciously in the presence of the departed. From childhood we had been used to seeing the simple funerals of the people go by. An open hearse is used, draped with a shawl. The body is buried wrapped in this shawl without a coffin. Hired women mourners would sometimes follow, beating their breasts and tearing their hair, their faces often daubed with a blue dye. Their professional hysterical grief was odd compared to the philosophic and dignified expressions of the true mourners following the body, on foot. Some of the Ancient Egyptian wall paintings on the Luxor tombs show the same difference between the true and the hired mourners. These women have now been banned from the streets of Cairo. It is many years since they have been seen.

In our Sussex home, we had an oak backless bench, or so it seemed to the casual observer, but in reality it was the form on which the coffin was placed in church during the service, in village funerals generations ago. It was drawn up to our long refectory table and on it sat a row of small children (my sister is now the mother of seven) eating their tea in the silence of concentration. Their bright eyes, just visible over a mug or a slab of bread and jam, were very much alive. This is the only familiar English sight which, for my mind, links life and death together in a single natural composition, such as is frequently seen in Egypt.

The performances of holy men known as dancing dervishes are now extinct in Cairo, but we visited them once soon after I left school. As most people know, their dance is not the breathtaking whirlwind sometimes imagined. It mostly consists of sedate gyrations to the accompaniment of a reed pipe and drum. The full skirts of the dancers flow out round about them in the most decorative manner. From the balcony where we sat each dress looked like the calyx of some large lily. The exhaustion and faint from which the dancers sometimes collapse result from the length of time they keep this stately movement going, not from the frenzy with which they perform it.

When we returned home that afternoon we thought we would try a few such gyrations ourselves. Round and round we spun on the garden balcony with far greater energy than the dervishes displayed, so consequently in a very few minutes we were in a mist of giddiness. "Isn't it odd?" I remember saying to my sister as we were still swinging round, "I get the impression of a figure standing close by watching us, there's no one there I'm sure. It's only a sort of mirage caused from being so dizzy."

When we did stop, however, the mirage slowly became less of a blur and more of a person. There stood an aghast young man who, being newly appointed to the Residency staff, was paying his first call on my parents. This extraordinary sight was his first encounter with the family. I do not know which of us was most embarrassed. He was, I think, for his powers of diplomacy were given a hard test. He is now an ambassador, so past the reach of such strange receptions, but I expect he remembers it as clearly as I do.

Alexandria and the expeditions which can be taken from there are of a different nature from the rest of Egypt. To extract historic charm from Alexandria, a rather detailed knowledge of her past is essential, and then it is a help to give that knowledge the free rein of imagination, for little is apparent to tell of what has been. Stand on the modern Corniche road by the eastern harbour; fling an arm out (south, east or west will do, for no one can be sure), and say: "Here stood the great University, Museum and Library." Walking down the Boulevard Saad Zaghloul, you could say: "Here stalked Cyril, Bishop of Alexandria, as he fumed against Nestorius, the zeal of their divergent views creating a breach in the Christian Church which has lasted hundreds of years." Pass by the gay public gardens of Nouzha and muse on the poet Callimachus who lived in this vicinity. The highly imaginative, armed with a Shakespeare, can even reconstruct the loves of Cleopatra and the black ending of the house of Ptolemy.

One site is certain, however. On the promontory dividing the western from the eastern harbour stands an old square fort, originally built by a Mameluke Sultan in the fifteenth century. On this spot stood the Pharos, a wonder of the world. The great beams of this lighthouse shone far over the Mediterranean, fed by a constant, giant bonfire within—an awe-inspiring sight of which but the foundations are left. Ibn Batuta, the loquacious traveller from Tangiers, passing this way in the fourteenth century described it then as fast disappearing.

The place to study the beaux arts of past Alexandrians is the fine Graeco-Roman Museum. It is not large enough to produce the suffocating effect brought on by the contemplation of some museums, nor small enough to be insignificant. It has a courtyard in which shrubs and creepers rub shoulders with Ptolemaic deities. The Jovian Osiris who sports a basket effect on his head combines so well with canna and hibiscus. And the bulk of the garlanded sarcophagi make poignant the light leaves moving in the breeze, throwing their thin, waving shadow on the marble. Further, this Museum possesses some thoughtful, quiet guardians whose philosophic murmurings are a pleasure to hear. "Behold this," said one to me, pointing to a mummified crocodile, "they worshipped it of old. Poor people, they knew not their Maker." In the next room, apropos of what I forget, a guardian told me how, in the days of his youth, fishermen sometimes caught a porpoise off Alexandria. Its body was taken round the streets on a hand-cart, and oil from it was sold in little glasses tastefully displayed round the centre piece. "Very beneficial for pains in the bones," he said, but he had not seen such a thing in Alexandria these forty years.

We would often motor westward from Alexandria into the desert which leads to al Alamein, with friends and relations, taking the road out of the town past the docks. There is now a better road avoiding the crowded town area. King Cotton reigns nearly supreme here, though he does share his kingdom with the humble onion, one of Egypt's largest exports, after cotton. The warehouses are stocked high with great rectangular cotton bales, waiting to be shipped to the world. The clatter and shouting is terrific as the Alexandrian commercial carts rattle over the cobbles, the trams clang along their network of lines, and the human element everywhere has something that must be said very loudly and often, in all directions. The particular cart met here is low and narrow, constructed for piling high the baled cotton.

Soon one is in a semi-desert area with the sea visible behind white sand dunes. Along this stretch westwards, the Ministry of Agriculture has been making some interesting experiments. Fig trees, olives, and vines have been planted with success. There is nothing quite like the smell of fig tree leaves warmed by the sun, it is delicate and haunting. In Graeco-Roman times this summer scent must have delighted many a sensitive nostril for the coast was then quite thickly populated; much grain was grown too.

Some forty miles west of Alexandria you can see, standing on a desert rise above the coast, a miniature Pharos of

Ptolemaic times. Beside it are the gaunt walls of a temple. This is all that is left of Taposiris Magna, the gay city so beautifully situated of old between the Mediterranean and the shimmering lake of . This ruinous spot is now called Abu Sir, in which words some scholars profess to hear the last, sad echo of the name Taposiris.

Lake Mareotis is still water-filled to the east, where thin-legged fishermen push their craft through tall reeds, and terns with scimitar wings fly above them, fishing in their own more skilful fashion. Further west is a great stretch of saline deposit, slushy in winter, but with the evaporation of summer it shows as shining acres of ice. The salt has an aspect unbelievably like snow and frozen water on a sparkling frosty day. At other seasons it is as red as blood from a small weed of that colour which flourishes therein. The western end of Lake Mareotis is now a dry depression in the desert.

The whole of this area is ghostly, but peopled with gay ghosts. Ptolemaic and Roman Alexandria had their white villas everywhere, surrounded by the vines which gave the famous wine. The lake was busy with trading craft and pleasure vessels. Noise of commerce and chatter of tongues must have rung round the coasts, now so still and silent.

Most of these Graeco-Roman villas were built over large artificial cisterns into which the periodic rainfall was collected by their owners, for water has always been the difficulty along this stretch of coast. When my wise, and original-minded father built our Sussex house, which is also in a rather dry area, he insisted on first building a large cistern in Graeco-Roman fashion and, over this, erecting the house. Some friends and advisers shook their heads, but it has been a great success for the last thirty years and the collected rainwater is invaluable for many purposes.

Farther into the desert south-west of Abu Sir is the ruined church and monastic precincts of Abu Menas. Menas was an Egyptian soldier, a devout and courageous Christian who while serving Rome in Cappadocia was martyred for his faith.

Some fellow soldiers brought his ashes back to Egypt; but when the camel on which they were carried was passing this spot, it stopped and refused to go further, from which Menas' friends deduced that his spirit was choosing this as his burial place. It was only some time afterwards that the buried Menas was discovered to have holy powers. A shepherd boy noticed that a sick sheep walking over the grave was healed. In no time it became a place of pilgrimage from far and near, for rich and poor, many of whom seem to have been truly healed of their ills.

Everyone took away a little earthenware bottle with the figure of Menas between two camels stamped upon it. These objects have been dug up in far-flung places of Europe as well as in the Middle East showing the wide popularity of the Egyptian soldier-saint.

A few Bedwin goats now nibble the scrub among the ruins, and lizards dart under the acanthus capitals erected in honour of Menas by the Emperor Arcadius.

It is presumed by many that the rainfall in Roman times was here greater than it is now. But cultivation is said to bring rain with it, and vice versa, so if the Egyptian government's agricultural efforts and those of private enterprise, can succeed in breaking the vicious circle, perhaps this land will return to prosperity.

The present Bedwin tribes who roam this area have a precarious existence. Body and soul are kept together by the harvest of a desultory, scattered barley crop sown, apparently, at random in the dips and hollows of the desert, and depending for its fruition on the winter rains which sometimes fall and sometimes do not. Yet, these Bedwin are a fine looking race on the whole; the women, upstanding and open-faced, move with great grace. Their tribal mark, two indigo blue lines from the bottom lip down the centre of the chin, give them a distinguished look. Their dark blue or black robes are usually bound tightly round the hips with a sash of crimson cotton. The men do not wear the kuffiya, which is the headgear of the eastern desert Bedwin. These men wear small skull caps and, cast round them as a coat, a white, hand-woven length of woollen material interestingly reminiscent of a Roman toga. This is thrown over one shoulder with great style.

These Bedwin, owning practically no instruments, have recourse to the most primitive methods of harvesting. In a good year the barley is just clawed up in handfuls, roots and all, which come easily out of the sandy soil, or rather soily sand, which is a more accurate description of the substance in which it grows. At this time there is much merry-making. Camels and baby camels, donkeys and baby donkeys, career round the threshing floor or watch the scene, peacefully content according to their age and generation, knowing that food for another year is assured for their masters and for themselves.

If the spring rains have fallen well, early in the year, this desert is a multi-coloured mass of wild flowers, like cloisonné enamel: white stars of Bethlehem, yellow marigolds, blue burrage, and tall waving asphodel, with small scarlet poppies running in and out of everywhere. This does not stay long for the sun scorches it, but while it lasts it is a paradise. In a year of little or no rain, it is a different story—no flowers, no barley, and saddened, wandering Bedwin with gaunt faces. The Egyptian government have come to their aid on such occasions with gifts of seed barley for the next year and some for food in the current year.

The little desert town of Amria lies to the south of the coast road, and here an interesting experiment was initiated in the lean years after the first world war when the Bedwin of this region faced real want. The English Governor of the province and an Englishwoman took the initiative. It was through the Bedwin women that they worked. They gathered them into Amria where simple weaving looms had been set up and here the women were helped to produce attractive rugs from the homespun wool of their own flocks. Indigo was the only dye used, and the rest was all shades from white and beige to deep brown, in fact every tone that the co-operating goats, sheep and camels could produce. These rugs sold well and many of them found their way to homes in England.

After several hours motoring through this country we would draw up near some stretch of the seaboard where the ground was firm enough to carry the car. Choosing this ground needed some experience and skill. Here we pitched our little tents and unpacked the stores. Forethought had to go into these expeditions, for every drop of drinking water and crumb of food, all extra petrol and equipment, in short, everything, had to be brought with us. So the unpacking process was done with a certain silent concentration. When all was checked as present, we relaxed.

In a few minutes, we were racing over the world's whitest sand, into the world's bluest sea. It is more than blue, for the white sand shining through the water produces kingfisher hues of translucent sapphire, turquoise and jade green. This is actually reflected off the sea on to the white sail of any passing vessel and on to the white wings of seagulls gliding above it.

This coast is a wonderful place for bird-watching when the migrants arrive and leave. A sudden flash of blue against the tawny desert is the roller bird on the wing. Golden orioles pass by, stopping in the evenings to eat the fruit of a mulberry tree where such can be found. The little local owls are fearless characters. In broad daylight they sit on a prominent stone and, with amber eyes flashing, shriek with rage at any intruder, man or beast.

The oldest consecutively inhabited building in the world is St. Catherine's Monastery in the peninsula of Sinai. This was our goal for another expedition as a group of us set out one spring morning in 1936.

The Suez Canal was our first obstacle. "Patience," says an Arab proverb, "is the key to all doors." We rattled various other modern, and as we thought, more efficient keys, but to no avail. At last we were reduced to the time-honoured master key, and patience worked its potent way with frontier official and ferry service. The Rubicon was over.

Here is the real Sinai desert through which the drug traffickers often try to import their evil wares. Exciting tales of fighting the drug traffic are legion. The ancient desert art of tracking plays a prominent part in many cases. A true tracker can tell what type of camel has passed, the rate at which it went, how heavily loaded, and other relevant points, by variations in marks on the ground almost imperceptible and quite beyond diagnosis by a European.

Some years ago an aged sheikh was slowly crossing Sinai by camel on his way to hospital. A Bedwin has to be more than slightly ill before he will consent to be taken to hospital. As this small caravan was wending its way across the desert, it fell in with a company of frontier force who were in pursuit of drug traffickers. They had lost the tracks and feared that their quarry might escape. The old sheikh was a skilled tracker. Here was just the piece of excitement needed to revive him, so he thought, for drug traffickers at bay are often desperate. He insisted on joining forces with the search party and off he led them at top speed. The gallant old man kept it up for hour after hour and only when the criminals were almost rounded up did he let himself continue his journey to hospital.

We, however, ran into no such adventures. Our cars turned south and we raced along the canal; we then followed the Gulf of Suez coast, though we were a good way inland of it. Our first halt was Marah, a small oasis of palms and one or two mud-brick huts. "And when they came to Marah they could not drink of the waters of Marah for they were bitter. . . . And the people murmured against Moses saying, 'What shall we drink?' And he cried unto the Lord and the Lord showed him a tree which when he had cast into the waters, the waters were made sweet." We did not put the validity of Moses' experiment to the test, thinking it might be unfair after so long a passage of years; and though they might have been sweet, they were certainly green.

Later in the day we reached the only spot on the whole route which could be called a settlement. This was Abu Zeneima, where the presence of man is to be accounted for by the presence of manganese. Here lived a handful of people, isolated to a degree, the desert behind them, the sea ahead.

In the evening two of us strolled along the beach barefoot; slowly on and on, through water when the small waves washed round our ankles, and on the firm wet sand when they retreated. The sea was the colour of heather shot with powder blue and gold, and the sky was powder blue and gold shot with heather. It may be surprising to some that in a wholly desert journey, colour should play so prominent a part.

Our next day led us inland, climbing slowly all the time, hour after hour, so that it was hardly perceptible; but by nightfall, with our goal reached, we had five thousand feet below us. As we proceeded, the rocks and crags grew ever wilder and the confusion of colour more tumultuous, purple, crimson, yellow, mauve and fawn. Here was no road and often no track. We wound up in and out of the valleys and gulleys slowly nearing our destination. And all the time this barren wilderness was peopled with figures—in the imagination, it is true, but their memory made real their presence. Suddenly we came upon a thick belt of scrubby palm in a narrow valley. This is the oasis of Pharan. There is not much to see now, but in the adventurous childhood of Christianity it was the centre of a bishopric. Then, but a mental turn of the page was needed to see the tribes of Israel plodding onwards, their little brown and black goats shuffling along through their own cloud of dust, as the Bedwin goats do today, stopping to sample some desiccated leaf, then tripping on to catch up with the crowd. Moses, the man of God, passed on with his weight of responsibility, a job as fraught with difficulties as any ever undertaken.

Next comes the valley of the turquoises. The Ancient Egyptians mined these rocks for the semi-precious stone. Several other intermittent attempts have been made through the ages, but not successfully. Then there is the Wadi Makatab, the valley of the writings, with many strange inscriptions and drawings on its rocks. There are learned professors who consider that the origin of our alphabet is to be found among these Sinaitic scripts. What of the present inhabitants of this region? A solitary Bedwin strides by, out of the blue and apparently into the blue with a steady, long and swinging gait. Then we pass near a spot where an American astronomer had lived with his wife and little son for several years, high up on a barren peak, pursuing the cause of science. At the head of one of the valleys is a garden and spring cultivated by a Greek priest sent from the monastery many miles away. But otherwise there was no one at all.

As day closed, we wound upwards expectantly, for the monastery was not far off. But we were not destined to arrive without trouble. In the evening light it was difficult to pick out the best course up the wadi bed. We thought we were on hard ground, but suddenly there came that sensation known only too well to desert drivers. We were in sand—a sinking feeling indeed. Out we clambered and worked hard to free the car, for none of us wished to be stranded for the night in that cold, darkening desolation. At least, it was most desolate when we first stuck; but before long, some half dozen Bedwin imps materialised from nowhere and danced round in a high state of excitement caused by our mere presence. In the failing light they appeared like the dancing ghosts of little grey monkeys.

Our combined efforts comparatively soon met with success. As we put our shoulders to the back wheels, the car lurched forward again. Anyone who has ever pushed a heavy vehicle stuck in sand, knows how, when the wheels grip once more, the sand spurts up behind, covering one's face and eyes and cascading down one's neck. It is a welcome feeling, none the less. On this occasion the sand is not pale yellow like the open desert, but a wonderful purple-red, worn by the wind from the rocks around. A colour like the splash of wine.

These tracks, difficult at all seasons, are impassable after heavy rain or in some winter weathers. The high passes are often blocked with snow. Snowdrifts, and mountains over eight thousand feet high, are not usually connected with Egypt. But this is Egyptian territory and they are none the less facts.

Quite shortly we turned to the left up a narrowing wadi, and there ahead of us were the fortress-like grey walls and spear-pointed cypresses of St. Catherine's. But we were not there yet. A steep narrow ramp with a drop to one side had to be negotiated, and our car jibbed at this. Twice we tried, and twice rolled back again to the bottom. Most of the passengers were by now so weary that they ceased to care very much, thinking that if they must die, at the foot of a monastery and at the end of a pilgrimage was quite a good choice. However, the third attempt was successful and landed us safely at the great entrance door itself, and we clanged the old bell high up on the wall.

How many adoring eyes of Russian pilgrim peasants have glowed with zeal in tired, drawn faces, as they first saw this holy spot?

In the sixth century A.D. the Emperor Justinian founded this monastery in honour of St. Catherine of Alexandria. She was the young martyr who, tradition asserts, stood up so bravely to the Emperor Maximinus, challenging him to give up the worship of strange gods. Pagan philosophers were sent to reason with her but retired in disorder. Some historians say they were converted. The Emperor's wife was also sent, but she stayed and was certainly converted. Maximinus then ordered Catherine to be strapped to the wheel, however this instrument of torture collapsed at her touch. But execution proved fatal. A bevy of angels removed her body, wafted it eastwards through the air, and deposited it carefully on this mountain top in Sinai.

How strange is the way in which things, symbolising old beliefs from one side of the world, become woven round other objects, and push their way across sea and land to quite different parts of the world. The connecting link often withers and is forgotten. What little boy, gazing in awe at his Catherine wheel as it illuminates his garden in Hampstead or Clapham on November 5th, has in mind Saint Catherine of Alexandria and her heroic stand for what she felt to be right?

There were then only about twenty monks in the monastery, some of them uncouth, shepherd-boy types from the Greek islands and Cyprus, some more cultivated, soft-voiced men from Athens and the mainland. Welcoming us, they led us through the thick-walled passages under low heavy archways, round buttresses and past nail-studded, ancient doors, till we emerged on to a veranda running round an internal courtyard. Our whitewashed rooms with iron bedsteads gave off this veranda.

We were tired and breathless from the unaccustomed height. After a meal, the product of a culinary-minded monk, we fell asleep. All was oblivion, till sometime when the morning was stirring in the air, though it was still dark, a strange clanging noise rang through the place. A monk was beating a short wooden plank which acted as a bell. It was of special wood and, when forcefully hit, emitted this curious soft but all-penetrating call. The monks trooped down to the church. We, too, attended a service later on in the day. The Greeks in their chimney-pot hats, black robes, and long hair, sang the beautiful old chants and swung incense holders. The gilt mosaic and carved capitals looked down on it all reverently.

In a miniature chapel behind the altar is the spot where, tradition says, grew the burning bush seen and wondered at by Moses. "Put off thy shoes from off thy feet, for the place whereon thou standest is holy ground." This was the commandment then and it remains the commandment today. We slipped off our shoes and silently went in.

Not far from the church stands a little whitewashed mosque. The actual construction is fairly modern, but many traditions gather round it. Some say that the prophet Mahomed himself visited the monastery and requested that a mosque should be built within the walls for the use of the Moslem servants of the monks.

These monastery servants, hewers of wood and drawers of water, are a curious strain. They are dark-eyed, sallow-skinned men, a gentler looking breed than the hawk-eyed Bedwin without in the wilderness. They are said to be direct descendants of some people sent here centuries and centuries ago, from Wallachia, a province in south-east Europe, now part of Roumania. These Sinai Wallachians are called Jebellia. They speak Arabic and profess to be Moslems, but the real Bedwin does not own them.

The refectory of St. Catherine's is one of the most remarkable places. The long wooden table is carved at intervals with the coats of arms of crusaders who visited this spot during the wars. Beyond the refectory is the library and treasure house. Anyone, with the story of the Codex Sinaiaticus foremost in his mind, expecting an atmosphere of "treasure" will be disappointed. It is an unromantic room with yellow pitch-pine cupboards more suitable for housing the duller forms of school books than anything else. But do not be put off—the treasure is there nevertheless. One by one, rare objects will be brought out and quietly unwrapped, jewelled Bibles, illustrated manuscripts, beautiful vellum and rich ikons, many of them lavish gifts of long-dead Czars and Czarinas.

The monks are almost entirely self-supporting, though supplies are occasionally brought up from the coast, several days' camel journey away. They show you, with pride, how they even make their own tallow candles for the church. In a dark recess of the battlements you can see rows of them hanging up to dry. A curious sight.

Though peace now reigns in the surrounding desert, for centuries past the monks have led a restive life, either just pestered or violently attacked by marauding Bedwins. You can still see a strange contraption, a sort of windlass, by which visitors were hauled up into the monastery in a basket from below, as being a safer means of entry for those within than the opening and the shutting of a door, however strong. It is used to this day for the occasional lowering of bread to the Bedwin if they are known by the monks to be in need of it.

Outside this monastic fortress, though within the main walls, lies a delightful garden. On all sides the high red mountains tower upwards, but here with water running in and out, is the dark green of cypresses, the pastel of olives, and the green, so luminously bright that it almost sings, of almond trees in spring foliage. Wandering in this enchanted spot, the unsuspecting visitor comes on an innocent-looking white house. If he peers through the windows he may get a shock; for what he will see is rows and rows of human bones neatly arranged, skulls together, legs together, arms together. These are the mortal remains of past brethren from the monastery. Possible burying places are scarce in the hard, red rock, so what is available is used over and over again. When the bones are dry, which does not take long, as no coffin is used, they are dug up and stored in this weird little house. What happens if the monks do not die at convenient and regular intervals, is not related. If the visitor ventures within, he will see an even stranger sight. Just inside the door is a skeleton dressed in monk's clothes; with a rosary hanging from his bony fingers, he sits on a chair guarding the bones of his fellows. He is a certain St. Stephen who is supposed to have sat here for the last thirteen hundred years. The living monks are on most natural, almost jovial terms with these remains. They know many of them by name and smile in a friendly way at the old skeleton porter.

Nearly three hours' hard climbing the next day took us to the topmost peak of Jebal Musa (Mount Moses). A young Greek monk, one Stavro by name, tucked up his skirt and set the pace, while a nimble little Bedwin boy darted about us like a coney in the rocks. Even he, however, steadied down as we neared the top; all breathed slowly and deeply for we were now well over seven thousand feet above sea level. The presence of generations of pilgrims trudging up the mountainside, their last effort on a journey of effort, was with us at every step; and with us, too, was that other majestic lonely figure who had talked to God, face to face, "as a man speaketh unto his friend."

At the top we looked out over leagues of rugged, red mountains, as desolate as the mountains of the moon, vast and endless. Suddenly at our feet out scampered a little mouse, gave us a shiny-eyed wink and bore off a fallen crumb of our picnic cheese. He sat upon his small hindquarters and ate it with relish. There he was, a few square inches of life, in this gigantic barren scene, yet he was completely master of the situation. On the way downwards, we spotted that unique bird, the Sinai rose finch. Its beautiful pink feathers are just the colour of the rocks and provide a perfect camouflage. Our thoughts on the wonderful protective devices of nature were shattered a few yards down. There was a lizard basking on a particularly pomegranate-red piece of rock and its whole body was a streak of the brightest Prussian blue ever seen outside a paint box.

Before our party left the following day, the Abbot presented us all with reproductions from an interesting old engraving possibly of the sixteenth or seventeenth century, showing the monastery as it then was, which was strikingly like it is today except for the angels and saints depicted hovering round the mountaintops, and the Bedwin attacking the monastery from the desert. Each saint is named in Greek, and there is a Russian inscription below the picture.

At last we departed with many warm farewells. Our two cars slithered over the loose stones down the ramp. It was less dangerous than the twilight approach, but we were still a bit apprehensive, anyhow, sufficiently so to jump nearly out of our skins when, having gone about two hundred yards, a resounding explosion behind us shook the whole valley and bounded and echoed off the rocks. This startling report was but a final expression of farewell from the monks who had fired off, in our honour, an ancient piece of cannon from the walls.

The Rowlatts' boat, the *Ablah*, on the Nile

11

A REMARKABLE LIFE

No normal people living in Cairo, with moderate advantages at their command, need blame their surroundings for becoming mentally stagnant. For besides all the countless things to see, there is a wide range of lectures organised by cultural societies and educational establishments, and they are often free.

A lecturer who deeply impressed me has had what must be one of the most amazing life histories of any modern Egyptian. It shows something of the possibilities latent in the Egyptian character, and its power of overcoming unpropitious circumstances.

Dr. Taha Hussein was born some sixty-three years ago in a little mud house near a small town in Upper Egypt. One of the first things he can remember, so he says, is finding his way to the fence of dried maize stalks surrounding his home. Putting out his hands, he would feel this fence up and down in a reassuring way. It was the end of the known world to him and he used his hands on it, for his hands were his eyes.

He remembers, too, being called in from the compound by his elder sister to go to bed, and if he did not come she would pick him up by his little cotton galabia and remove him bodily. She would deposit him gently on the beaten mud floor by the stove where all the family slept. Before he settled down, his mother came night by night and put drops of a sort into his poor eyes; an unavailing hope.

He was the seventh of thirteen children, all loved and cherished by their parents. The death of an eighteen-year-old son from the 1902 cholera epidemic, and then of a three-year-old sister, were sudden blows, the sadness of which haunted their parents for ever.

When Taha was a bit older, he started going to the village school, on his brother's back at first, for he was too weak and unsteady for the walk. Here he was placed on the ground where he often played silently in the corner with the pile of shoes shed by the scholars as they entered the school, before they squatted down to hear and recite their lessons.

The old sheikh who was the master, and his one assistant, taught the children the elements of the three R's and he taught some of them to memorise the whole Kuran. This feat seems wonderful to Western minds, but in the East it is a fairly common accomplishment among those who go in for learning in the old style. The small boy was now set this task by hearing the chapters read aloud and repeating them verse by verse.

The boy's father had instructed the old schoolmaster to bring him his son for a test when he knew the Kuran by heart. But Taha, like many boys in any land, when once he felt he knew his work, ceased to take much interest in it, and in carefree fashion told his master each day what chapters he had gone over when, in point of fact, he had done no such thing but had idly sat listening to the others or following his own train of thought. Fate, however, overcame him in a way that fate has on these occasions.

"Now we will go and visit your father," said the old man one day with no warning. As they entered the house the master exchanged the traditional greetings with the father. Then refreshments were called for—a whole mug of melted sugar for the schoolmaster, which he sank in one gulp. Slowly and formally they arrived at the point. Did the child know the Kuran yet? Well, let him recite chapter so-and-so. The boy opened his mouth, said the first few words, hesitated, said them over again, stammered, and stopped. His lenient father tried him with another chapter and another, but always with the same result, until it became clear that he was quite unable to manage what was to be his passing-out examination.

The boy's father was tolerant with his son, but blamed the old man. The schoolmaster swore many solemn oaths that he had actually heard his pupil recite the whole Kuran, frequently and recently, wherein he lied. So there was nothing for it but to return to his studies until such time as he could really satisfy his father, and the old schoolmaster was encouraged to this end by the gift of a new gown and shoes.

From his babyhood onwards, Taha Hussein had imbibed a wealth of folklore and country tales. He would listen entranced to the village storytellers and their legends of the Arab heroes of old.

He learnt from the women, too, curious stories of magic and wonder, of djino and spirits who came alive at night.

A canal flowed through the village and he soon learnt how a huge fish lived in it, and in the stomach of this fabulous fish was a magic ring, in fact the very ring worn by King Solomon himself. All the village children knew that if this fish swallowed one of them and he was able to survive the operation, he would then be master of the ring and consequently master of the slave who could appear at a bidding and grant the heart's desire. It was a matter of discussion among them whether they would have the courage to face this experience if the big fish materialised one day, and looked as if he actually was about to swallow them. Then at night, as he lay on the ground, the small boy had to pull his coverlet right over his head, for only then would he have full protection, so it seemed to him, from the evil spirits who roamed abroad. He was often wakeful and lay listening to the village sounds, the last dog baying at the moon, the first cock crowing, or the night wind in the palms. He was familiar with these sounds and knew much of their meaning, though visually they were a blank to him. But the sounds from which he hid under the coverlet were the little squeaks and rattles about the house, from wood and iron and pots and pans—all things inanimate and harmless by day but baleful spirits at night. So Egypt's future Minister of Education drew his head right under cover and prayed to the Almighty for protection—a prayer that was surely heard.

Some years later, when he was rather older, there was a bustle and upheaval. The family were moving house. This involved a train journey. When the new station was reached, all the babies and bundles were handed out amidst much excitement and fuss, and the family party moved off to their fresh quarters. Not till then did they realise that nobody had helped the blind boy out of the train. In fact, he had been left behind. Other passengers on the train had come to his assistance and he was put in charge of the station master at the next stop, whence a harassed family retrieved him. The humiliation of this incident cut deep into his heart.

The next step in his life was an important one. At the age of thirteen he joined his elder brother at the Cairo University of al Azhar. Al Azhar was founded in the tenth century for the study of the Moslem religion, of jurisprudence in all its branches, and of the Arabic language with its extremely complicated syntax and grammar. From that day to this it has been one of the world's centres of Moslem thought, and has included thousands of students from as far away as China, Abyssinia, Ceylon, Morocco and Indonesia. There have been some alterations recently in the curriculum and in the running of this university mosque, but even now the atmosphere and aspect of the place is medieval.

Inside the colonnaded courtyard the turbaned professors sit each beside a column and their students gather round them for a lecture, cross-legged on the floor, in the same manner in which St. Paul must have sat at the feet of Gamaliel. The students cover a great range of ages, for they can come at about thirteen and stay on for whatever stretch of years they care to remain, taking their degrees when they feel ripe for it.

Until recently none of the faculty received salaries and no student paid for his tuition. All was endowed, and staff and students alike, according to their scholastic seniority, received free loaves of bread from the endowment. Many lived in great poverty, but their needs were few and learning was their chief concern.

Into this establishment came the highly sensitive lad of thirteen, in his new long black coat worn by students, his soft tarboush and white scarf wound round it. As he slipped off his shoes at the entrance, on the hot day of his first appearance, his feet felt the cool stone courtyard and the breeze from the shaded colonnade touched his temples. His heart beat fast in expectation and delight, for he had arrived, so it seemed to him, at the source and fountain-head of all learning and wisdom, with nothing to do but to drink it in. The fact that he was blind daunted him not a bit. It hardly occurred to him that, as far as learning went, it was a disability at all.

Everything he heard he memorised. It became impressed on his amazing memory, and he was able to study it in his head and comment on and discuss the subjects verbally with his professors.

The two brothers lived most humbly in a room up a narrow dirty staircase, in a narrow dirty lane where the smells in summer hung almost tangibly on the air. The blind boy learnt to feel his way along this alley. He grew to know where were the holes and rough patches in the ground, and where the mess of rubbish was most slippery underfoot. He could tell, too, when the café was passed on the left, by the noise of the hubble-bubbles being smoked there.

He and his brother would rise at the sound of the call to the dawn prayer, delivered from a nearby minaret. After saying their own prayers, off they went to the early lecture and stayed in the university mosque till the midday meal, which they prepared for themselves in their room, and for which they were joined by one or two student friends of the elder brother. They squatted round a bowl of beans and pickle most days, or meat and vegetable stew, and their evening meal was the same. An occasional treat was a box of biscuits made by their mother, with much love and care and painstaking saving of cash to buy the ingredients. But at times the lads were so financially reduced that they could purchase nothing but a little black honey into which to dip their free ration of bread.

These meals, however humble, were gay and social affairs for the elder boy and his friends, but the thirteen-year-old student suffered tortures. Not being able to see what he was helping himself to, he frequently spilled his food, and this caused him great humiliation. The more nervous he became the clumsier he was, and the more he felt that his companions despised him; though this was not the case, for his brother was very fond of him. Then there were long hours of loneliness for the lad, when his brother went to the afternoon lecture which he was too junior to attend. He had nothing to do except to sit in the corner of their room huddled and alone, in his own world of darkness.

As time went by, two things happened. A cousin, a young contemporary of his, joined the university, and they did everything together; his days of loneliness and shyness were over. The other thing was that the more he learnt and discussed with his professors, the more disillusioned he became with their outlook on life and their erudition. He would air his views, perhaps arrogantly for one so young, and was told to stop expressing himself thus or go elsewhere. Al Azhar was in need of reforms in the curriculum, and a widening and modernising of outlook (which have since taken place), and some progressive spirits were fighting for it; but the conservative element were in control and were not prepared to take new ideas from a student, young, blind and poor. Had they foreseen what fate had in store for him, they might have thought twice.

But young Taha Hussein, with the new ideas pounding in his head, was in no mood to acquiesce. He wrote a direct article attacking al Azhar and the Rector. This he took to a newspaper for publication, where he was lucky to meet the editor, who found out the whole situation and informed the youth that he would not dream of publishing such a document, for it would in no way help anyone. But from then on the young student saw much of the editor, who had sensed his outstanding qualities, and through this friendship he met men who moved in the fast-developing modern intellectual life of Cairo, as opposed to the conservative stronghold of al Azhar.

In 1908 the Egyptian University at Giza was founded, and this represented the seat of learning for the forward-looking lay world. Taha Hussein now started to attend lectures at this university in the afternoons, while continuing at al Azhar in the mornings. It was a strange two-sided life. He had a foot planted in each, different, intellectual sphere; but his heart was not equally divided. The modern university claimed it almost all.

The time soon came when he left the old behind him and devoted himself to the new, from which university he was to emerge in 1914 the first doctor, and to hold in 1919 the Chair of Arabic Literature in the Faculty of Arts, and later to become Dean of that Faculty. After a brilliant student career at this university, where he learnt much from the European professors as well as from the Egyptians, he won a scholarship to the Sorbonne, for he now had mastery of French as well as of Latin and Greek; and when there he won the Saintour Prize for his Doctorate Thesis.

At the Sorbonne, a young French woman student was asked by the authorities if she would be willing to read his books to him and write to his dictation—for this was still, as it is today, his only means of study. From this purely academic start there developed in both young people a deep affection one for the other. They were married, and the continued self-effacing devotion of his wife has gone far to make possible Taha Hussein's career.

He was made the first Rector of the University at Alexandria, and with his appointment in 1950 as Minister of

Education, his great aim was to carry out the project of free education for all Egyptians.

Dr. Taha Hussein's output of literary work has been tremendous. It includes criticisms, essays, autobiographies, novels and translations from as varied authors as Sophocles, Racine and Paul Valery. And, in addition to his being Doctor Honoris Causa of the Universities of Lyons, Montpelier, and Rome, he has received the honorary degree of Doctor of Letters at Oxford.

One wonders who would have been most surprised, fifty-five years ago, had this occasion been foreseen. Would it have been his mother, or the old schoolmaster who took the minimum of trouble with his quiet but difficult pupil, or would it have been the little blind boy himself who, as he was led home from school through the dusty alleys, often knew full well that he had not even attempted to master his lessons for that day?

12

RETURN AGAIN

DURING the whole of World War II I was in England, and only returned in 1947 after an interval of more than eight years. So much was the same, the scents and sounds and colours extended my five senses to the fullest pitch of pleasure. Even having been continuously ill in the seaplane for twelve hours, and having to be revived on arrival by my father's best brandy, could not spoil this return. The colours of the garden, and the fruit stalls, the translucent shell-pink of the desert in the morning light, this and so much else entertained and gladdened my heart.

I must emphasise that any joy I felt in seeing Egypt again was in no way by comparison with England, war or no war, for I love my own country and derive endless pleasure from her many aspects. All was in addition to England and her people. But there were also sad things to discover—poignant legacies of warfare. Where was the dear old Sudani doorkeeper of a house in the town, whom we all knew and loved? He had been killed one night by a blow on the head from a drunk British soldier, I was sadly told. And then there were the new burial grounds. Row on row, the headstones told of young Englishmen who had given all they had in fighting the enemy which had threatened Egypt; and they now lay on the edge of the desert far from their homes.

It was strange and homely to be talking Arabic again. The words came creakingly to the surface not seemingly through the medium of the mind, but as if they had been deposited all these years somewhere in the pit of the stomach. Poetry, says A. E. Housman, comes from that region of the anatomy, more than from the head; so, as the sound of Arabic has always had, for me, a certain content of feeling, perhaps this phenomenon was not as surprising as it sounds. However, my written Arabic, such as it was, suffered badly from neglect. I tried to decipher an invitation in Arabic, and eventually concluded we were bidden to attend night watchmen's sports, improbable though it seemed. But on seeking expert advice I was told it was the notice of a Princess's funeral.

It was not long before old friends and servants gathered in from here and there with a great welcome. Those well known to be rascals extended as heartfelt a greeting as the others. One such happened to be standing up in the back of a lorry passing our house when he saw me in the road. I did not recognise him at first, but noticed that he was leaning through the partition dividing him from the driver, and belabouring this unfortunate being with blows and cries to stop. The brakes screeched on, down he jumped and, kissing the tip of my fingers, showered blessings upon me.

There were also some rather quaint scenes with old servants of other families whom we had known since childhood, but who were now employed by different unknown people. It happened thus with a certain chauffeur standing beside his car, who rushed forward to welcome me and catch me up on the news of the last eight years, while his astonished employer sat in the car and waited.

For the first few days I asked nothing more than just to wander about the house, garden and vicinities. Unnecessary activity, restlessness and tension melted away, and I found myself strolling round with an idiotic but deeply contented expression on my face, gazing at the old corners—a bit of wall, an ancient tree, or a hole where lizards had forever lived. Almost every square yard was peopled with the past, with friends and family and a thin, restless child that had been myself.

In a certain china shop in South Audley Street is a door which opens as you approach it. Our house and garden seemed like that. Each bit had its invisible button and, as I stood on it, a door opened and showed me little framed scenes which took place on that spot, fifteen, twenty-five, thirty-five years ago, dipped in the dye of pleasure, fear, great joy, or deep sadness.

Down by the sea at Ramleh it was the same. I took the first opportunity of slipping away to the well-known bay of our childhood. To the outward eye it was sadly changed. Much was encased in concrete terraces with row on row of bathing cabins. But the familiar was there too, the feel of the sea anemones, the sound of the waves on a certain stretch of beach, the instinctive knowledge of which rocks were slippery and which were safe, which pools were full of fish and which of shrimps. I wandered peacefully around accompanied this time by the shades of myself aged eight, my father aged eight, and my grandmother aged eight, all on the same pursuits in the same place, feeling the same reactions and emotions.

Around the little Ramleh lanes the discovery of a new baker's shop, or the disappearance of an old pepper tree, somehow made more vivid the unabatable march of time than the contemplation of such things as the relics of Tutankhamen ever produced. I felt old and impersonal as I wandered round, far older than the oldest person I saw, not myself alone but a representation of five generations in one.

Back in Cairo there were some wonderful everyday mornings in the house to savour. One day two enormous cupboards were to be removed from one room to another. A gardener was sent out and told not to return till he had flung his net round two wayside porters and brought them back. In no time he returned with a brace of grinning, ragged characters, said to have been known by him from childhood.

Then the fun began. Aided by a rope, two garden boys, and three house servants, they started to shift the things, with much grunting and groaning, exclamations, and frequent calling on the Almighty. At one moment, the detachable fancy top of one cupboard caught in the doorway—"Take off her hat," shouted one—"*sheel barneetaha*" "take off her hat"— the others took up the cry.

A railway journey almost anywhere in Egypt is a good opportunity of making friends. I remember a journey from Cairo to Upper Egypt that I took about this time. It was a day train, second class, which meant that my companions were Egyptians of all sorts. The company was so removed from anything European, leave alone Anglo-Saxon, that I was not quite sure what reception I would get. But far from animosity, I met the well-known kindness of old; almost embarrassingly pressing at times.

Naturally, your own behaviour affects the reception you get; and without a little Arabic the style would be cramped. But I believe that anyone with a minimum of words and even the flicker of a smile would be accepted as one of the family immediately. You are pressed to share the food and drink. Monkey nuts and lettuce form a large portion of the former, so that by the end of the journey the party is happily sitting ankle-deep in nutshells and the outer leaves of the huge Egyptian cos lettuce. The drink is usually water, in an earthenware jug which is passed round to everyone, though it is just as well politely to refrain from this communal jug from which the water is drunk without the intermediary of cups. You will be expected to answer all manner of personal questions as to your age; whether you are married; if not, why not; number of children, and so forth.

If you have a minor ailment—a cut finger or a cough—endless home-made prescriptions will be showered upon you for its cure. It is an all-day journey, and the families, bundles, and animals push in and out at numerous small stations. They often urge you as they leave to break your journey and stay with them for a few days.

It is not only chatty families of women and children who show such friendliness. There comes to my mind a lonely old shepherd in a palm grove. My father and I had left our car and strolled over to have our picnic in the shade of the palms. We did not notice anyone nearby until this old man came silently over and squatted down beside us, with only a word of salaam by way of conversation. He unwrapped his coloured handkerchief and produced his lunch too, bread, tomatoes, and white cheese. He simply took it for granted that if three human beings were eating in a palm grove simultaneously, they would naturally do so in company.

Most railway journeys are full of incident, but the height of it all is apt to come at the time of the return of the Pilgrimage from Mecca. The stations are then thick with every type of aged holy pilgrim. Men and women are welcomed with the peculiarly Arab tongue trilling of the women, hand-clapping and dancing. In and out of this, the harassed station staff try to get the pilgrims who are only changing trains sorted from those whose destination has been reached. Holy ladies, all dressed in white, dash up and down, with any religious calm they may have acquired in Mecca scattered to the four winds.

Old men with long white beards and distracted eyes are pushed in and pulled out of trains, while relatives appeal to the skies, to the government, to anyone, to stop the train as the Pilgrim Mohamed has been lost, and has anyone seen him? Seventy out of every hundred male passengers would be called Mohamed so the chance of a helpful answer is remote. Other families rush up and down asking all and sundry where the Lady Pilgrim Fatima can be found. She too is lost.

In the middle of such a scene one year I saw an old peasant with a wooden leg trying to sell his oranges. But somehow, in spite of his efforts and his stumping up and down the platform, he appeared to sell none. It seemed to me, as I watched him, that all of the pathos in the universe was concentrated for that moment in the one old man. What passing figures, for no deep reason, can suddenly wrench one's heart!

Among the new friends who strolled across my path that year, one did so literally. He was six or seven years old, non-existent when I was last in Egypt. He told me that he worked for the neighbouring hospital. On being questioned further, he vouchsafed the information that, actually, it was he who was the night watchman. His air of intrepid *savoir faire* would have made this nearly believable had not I known that his father held that post.

I had an amusing conversation one day with another individual from the domestic staff of the same hospital, Mahmoud by name. He had been one of the late King Fouad's personal ironing men, and had once been all set to visit England with his royal master. In company with others, he had received a fortnight's instruction on how to behave in England, which included such points as eating everything with knife, spoon or fork and always using a handkerchief. This was all explained to me in action, with graphic visual aids on how not to deal with your nose when in England. But then, when it had come to the point of departure, it seems that his wife was so certain that he would not survive the perils of the sea that he began to believe it too, and cried off the whole adventure.

My first amble through the old parts of Cairo was filled with scenes to listen to and watch. I pushed my way along slowly between a barrow of bright pink sweetmeats, their vendor shouting out the beauty of his wares, and a donkey laden with vast watermelons in a rope pannier on either side. The top watermelon was placed in evidence in the centre of the donkey's back, and was cut open to show the succulence of its pink interior. The sweetmeat seller kept the flies off his barrow with a palm-leaf whisk. Had it been a feast day, delectable dolls, all made of sugar, would have stood round the edge of the barrow. The vendor would have told the passing children about them in a voice that could have filled the Albert Hall, though his prospective buyers might have been but six inches away.

A smell of spices wafted down one narrow way only a few feet wide. Following my nose, I came to a young man pounding cinnamon in a large mortar fixed in the ground, using every muscle of his back in wielding the heavy pestle. He did not stop his work as I passed, but smiled and nodded.

A little farther down was the bazaar of the tailors. They sat cross-legged in their little open shops, stitching away at beautiful coloured clothes worn by the sheikhs at the neighbouring al Azhar University. I wandered on to where the specifically Egyptian patchwork decoration is made to line the inside of the huge marquees and tents put up for receptions at funerals, weddings, or circumcisions. Women and small children passed in and out of the throng. There was a great sense of freedom; people were quite at liberty to spend a quarter of an hour in the middle of the road, catching up on family news with a cousin met by chance, or to tear along on a bicycle at the speed of the wind, missing all comers by a hair's breadth; nobody minded much.

The women carried their babies on their shoulders, where they perched themselves with great adroitness. I saw a baby of only a few months old, sound asleep there with its head resting on top of its mother's head, while she entered into a great barter over buying a couple of tomatoes, both arms gesticulating freely.

The names of these streets and quarters stirred in my mind the history they had witnessed. Al Gamalia, with its smell of soap, from where we always bought our kitchen variety, is called after Badr al Gamali, the eleventh century Armenian general who fortified Cairo for the Fatimites, building the three magnificent gateways which still span the thoroughfares close by.

In the Ghuria quarter is the decorative mosque of the Mameluke Sultan al Ghuri who had fallen fighting the Turkish invasion of 1517. As I passed, men and boys at their studies slipped quietly in and out, pausing only to put on or off their shoes by the threshold. Some narrow streets now witness to past glory only by their names. Sharia Bein al Kasrein, "the street between the two palaces", alludes to

Fatimite riches of which not a trace remains. But in the Suk al Nahasseen, the copper workers' market, the clang of copper beaten into bowls and ewers still mixes with the clatter of life around and, it must be said, with the hoot of bus horns and the blare of wireless.

Yes, gramophones, radio, cinemas, all are there but the ordinary working families do not yet seem blasé about their entertainments. The performing monkey dances to the tambourine as gaily as he did in my childhood. At midday he and his master settle comfortably in a shady corner of the road, undo their parcel of lunch which they share (fair do's all round—the monkey sees to that), and then they have a snooze till it is time to wander on for the matinée performance in the next street. Sometimes a wedding or a circumcision procession passes by. In carriages or carts some twelve to twenty children per vehicle will be piled high, singing, shouting, or even dancing if they can possibly do so without falling off.

Standing on the old city wall of Badr al Gamali's I have watched below me the gay sight of enthusiastic customers aged from about eighteen months to eighteen years old, clambering on to the most antique of roundabouts made of wood, where it was not patched with petrol tins. Being innocent of any mechanism it was pushed into motion by one or two individuals, galabia in mouth, who ran round with it till the sweat poured off their faces. But they still had breath enough to join in the cheers of their clients when the contraption reached the speed of about six miles an hour.

The juggler-cum-strong-man-cum-trickster can also be seen in these parts. He performs with a great sense of drama. The coup is worked up to slowly, tension mounts, his audience lean forward. But no—just before the huge bang or the great leap he hesitates and stops. Something needs adjusting, or the smaller children have crept in too near and have to be pushed back into place. The *détente* has broken the atmosphere so it has to be worked up again—fatal, if you happen to be in a hurry; but luckily none of the pit, stalls or dress circle seem to be, and I, who am only watching from the wings, will just have to be late.

The capacity of the common people for simple enjoyment is best seen on a public holiday. There is a great feast held yearly in honour of Abraham's willingness to sacrifice his son at God's command. The old story in the Kuran closely resembles our Biblical tale, but with one major difference. Whereas we are taught that Isaac was the intended sacrifice, Arab tradition says it was Ishmael, Hagar's son, who filled that rôle. The feast comes at the end of the annual pilgrimage to Mecca when pilgrims sacrifice a sheep or like animal, in commemoration of Abraham's obedience and God's deliverance.

For the upper class Egyptian it is a welcome break from work, a chance to drive into the country, to visit friends or to play games at the beautiful Gezira Sporting Club. But, as on our Bank Holidays, to see the full impact of it one should mix with the populace. If you stroll in the poorer quarters and narrower streets on the eve of the feast you will see sheep tethered outside many a little home. Not being caught in a thicket like its Biblical counterpart, it is free to nibble its last meal in peace, devoid of apprehension. Though its origin is in the idea of sacrifice, these sheep also provide a hearty meal for the households which have saved enough money to buy them. Some of the very poor also get a good mutton meal, for sheep are often provided for them by the more well-to-do.

If you move from contemplating the sheep in the alleys to where the little shops begin, you will find that the ones selling sweets and toys are crowded to capacity. With mothers and children? No; the shopping crowd consists wholly of fathers. Each tuppenny whistle is picked up by a father, blown, and solemnly replaced. Each father moves on six inches, blows the next whistle on the counter, while the father behind him stops to sample the still damp one just rejected. After much serious thought the suitable whistles are chosen, which, with sweets, balloons, and little handbags of coloured plastic for the girls, make up the usual presents for the ordinary working man's children.

The first day of the feast is greeted at sunrise by rounds of cannon fire. This is immediately followed by a dawn chorus of all the whistles bought by devoted fathers the previous evening. Each whistle is now firmly in the mouth of their offspring who have a remarkable capacity of permanently exhaling without pausing to inhale. Through this holiday hubbub floats the muezzin's call to prayer, always serene and beautiful even through the microphone of modern times.

Soon family crowds begin to gather in favourite public gardens and open squares. In Cairo today the place *par excellence* for holiday jaunts is the new Corniche road constructed for a long stretch along the right bank of the Nile. This is a godsend to the people for here the air is fresh, there are grass plots, some trees for shade, and occasional benches to sit on. From now till the evening more and more families gather till, by late afternoon, the full splendour of the holiday strikes the eye. Every child has on new clothes of startling hue, and children are as the leaves of Vallombrosa for number.

A proud father strolls up and down with his three little daughters who are in scarlet satinette from top to toe, and two small boys, more sombre in green striped galabias. They are soon joined by four cousins whose choice for this year is magenta. The youngest magenta wearer is under two and, considering that the last frill of her much frilled dress reaches to the ground, she manages it with great agility, for though the older members of the family may be only strolling, she has to keep up a jog trot or be left behind.

The Egyptians' love of their children is evident on these occasions. The fathers and elder brothers take just as much care of the small ones as do the mothers and sisters. It is often a father who stoops to take a stone out of a child's sandal or a brother who notices that someone in yellow with purple spots is asleep on the grass, so will have to be carried now that the family has decided to be on the move again. Considering the numbers of babies and children to every ten square yards there is surprisingly little crying. Occasionally a new handbag is enthusiastically swung round as if it were a sling, by its owner (dress royal blue, hair ribbon yellow), thereby hitting another child in the face (blouse mauve, shorts emerald). But even so, the howling is short-lived.

In and out of the family parties, boys on bicycles weave at speed; their machines, hired by the hour, are specially decorated for the feast. Other children pile into ancient horse-drawn victorias; four on the seat, four on the folded hood, four on the knife board, two on each step, two on the box and two on the coachman's feet. More than this is considered almost a squash. The old horse who clip-clops up and down the road does not think much of the feast, in spite of sporting a blue bead necklace, a bunch of pheasant feathers on top of his head, and some paper flowers in the small of his back.

A girl on a bicycle is almost never seen, but girls are well to the fore in the carriage drives. Any age from six to sixteen can be seen in some elevated position on the pile, clapping her hands in rhythm and leading her brothers in song. From time to time a smart gig flashes past, drawn by a trotting Arab. The owner, a prosperous farmer or merchant in new flowing robes, holds the reins and keeps one foot permanently on a tinkling bell to announce his passage.

As evening falls, horse- or donkey-drawn carts go rattling by, stacked with families who have elected to spend some of the feast, often including a night, camping round the graves of their defunct relations. And here they now are, jogging home from the cemetery. A traditional form of wooden chest, with seat above it, accompanies them on the cart; their wraps, paraffin stove and other necessities are within. They look sleepy, perched squatting on the cart, but they have had just as gay a time as the others, and the presence of the dead has in no way inhibited the full play of whistles and balloons. To them it is just a way of passing a holiday in rather a wider family circle than is possible if limited to the living. In fact the children may have had all the fun of the fair, for ramshackle swing-boats and hand manoeuvred roundabouts are often erected near the cemeteries to cater for the festive needs of the visitors, you cannot call them mourners. These customs and the lodges built round the family tombs are strangely reminiscent of the Ancient Egyptian cult of the dead.

The crowds on the modern Corniche are not without their entertainment either. The time honoured performing monkey appears on the scene and a great concourse of children gather; it thins a bit just before the antics end and the tambourine is handed round for halfpence, but enough fathers and uncles remain to make it a sound financial proposition. The monkey salaams each donor and they disperse.

A great attraction for those gathered by the Nile is a row in a dinghy or seat in a sailing boat to the opposite bank and back. The local *Skylark* ploughs back and forth all day loaded to the gunwales, alive with shrieks of merriment, and simulated fear from the girls which adds much to the fun. The small boys who have hired a row-boat for half an hour unattended, have more reason to fear, but perhaps luckily they seem unaware of it. A thin-armed ten-year-old manfully pulls an oar with uncertain rhythm, while his friend of similar stature pulls another oar to another timing. There is a stiff breeze and a considerable current, but somehow or other they eventually make the bank again.

A little boat moored to the side has laid in a stock of Pepsi Cola, bottled lemonade and like drinks which are in great demand. The rigging is decorated in the "dressed over all" style, but instead of flag signals, bottles of these coloured drinks are slung on a rope and looped aloft.

It is long after dark and the neon lights outline Kast al Nil bridge before the rather exhausted children are gathered up and the great trek home on foot begins. It is prefaced by some piercing calls for children not accounted for in the family round-up; "Ya binti ya Leila"—"Oh my daughter, my Leila," "Enta ya walad ya Yusef"—"Oh you, the boy Joseph!" If high pitched enough, these yells bring the children scampering back from somewhere. The babies are slung up on their mothers' shoulders and the party moves off.

One young man of about two shuffles homeward holding on to his mother's black wrap for support. He has to shuffle because unfortunately the vital elastic of his sky-blue pants has burst and they are round his ankles. He keeps up the requisite pace so does not think it worth drawing his mother's attention to the state of affairs. Anyhow, it seems to him pleasantly cool to proceed thus, bare from the waist down, though rather over-clothed around the feet.

Lastly, there appears a crowd of young peasants. One has the darabouka, a hand-drum of skin stretched over pottery which he plays deftly with his fingers. Several of his companions leap and twirl in elegant dance, as they circle above their heads the heavy stick carried by all country folk. One shouts across to his friend as he dances: "Ya Ibrahim," he calls. Hearing that name, honoured by three great faiths of the world, one's mind goes back to the reason for all this jollity. "And the angel of the Lord called unto him out of heaven and said, Abraham, Abraham: and he said, Here am I. And He said, Lay not thy hand upon the lad neither do thou anything to him for now I know that thou fearest God, seeing that thou hast not withheld thy son, thine only son from Me."

Between modern Cairo with its boulevards, Parisian shops, great offices and flats, and the fashionable Gezira gardens, villas and Sporting Club, runs one of the oldest highways in the world, brown and broad. It is not crowded thickly like the alleys of the old Arab city or the streets of twentieth century Cairo. But its traffic is full of character with a life of its own which I never tire of watching. "When a man is tired of London he is tired of life," said the great Doctor, with which, being a London lover, I heartily agree; but I would add the Nile to that category. London has the advantage that you can savour it as you bustle about doing whatever it is you have to do, getting wherever it is you have to get. But for the Nile you have to be ready to down tools and watch either from the banks or from some craft on its surface. I do not know the upper reaches of the river, the hippos, the crocodiles and the sud, but I do know the homely lower Nile flowing through towns and fields.

Gezira is joined to the mainland east and west by four bridges. Two of these open at regular intervals to let the river-craft through. The main boat is a ghiassa which has a huge sweeping lateen sail with sometimes a small auxiliary sail near the prow which the boatmen call the garia, or slave-girl. A lad-climbs up the sky-high mast to furl the main sail, clinging to it with his toes while he uses his arms on the canvas. Depending on the wind, the sails are fully or half-furled as the boats glide through the swung-open bridge.

The craft gather up and down stream from the bridge several hours before the opening, quietly waiting for the time; but there is nothing quiet about the actual passage through, once it begins. The boatmen tear up and down from prow to stern keeping the craft clear of each other, sometimes with punt poles and sometimes by bracing their backs against part of their own ship and pushing off the neighbouring one with sheer pressure from their feet. All is accompanied by cries and hulloos, advice and vituperation. But considering the amount of boats in a confined space and the strength of the current, the whole performance is most skilfully done.

The cargo is often stone from quarries up the river which weighs down the boat to the gunwales; or they carry earth-enware water jugs, each shape with its name and use, from the huge zirr with its pointed base, ballas which the women carry on their heads in the evening and dip into the river for the family water supply, to the little qulla from which the water is actually drunk. These are mostly made in Upper Egypt and brought down for sale in the Delta. The knowledgeable can tell where the pots have come from by the colour of the earthenware—a greeny tint from Kena and Sohag and sooty grey from places where the potters blacken the ware by smoke-producing substance after firing. The lightest but most voluminous of cargoes is *tibn*. This is just chopped straw used as fodder for beasts of burden. It is piled so high in the vessel that the heap has to be architected with an inward sloping batten and then often covered with a coarse rope like a giant's hairnet, to keep it in place. They even resort to sticking planks out from either side of the boat and piling the stuff on this too; though hanging perilously over the water, it seems to come to no harm. One of our earliest forms of joke (it dated from my mother's childhood), was a riddle: "Why are the *tibn* boats piled up like that?" "To prevent them *tibn* over, of course." A pun that can only be justified by the fact that it amused the under-eights. This sort of freight gives the sailors very little living space, literally a yard or two. But their needs seem few. Flour for their bread hangs in a sack half up the mast to prevent the rats getting at it. They are a cheerful lot, singing snatches of song as they lean their full weight on the huge wooden beam of a tiller. They are hardy too, for the sun scorches down in summer, and the winter winds would penetrate a fur coat, leave alone the cotton clothes they mostly wear.

Close to Cairo's busiest streets, within hailing distance of the trams and the limousines, little fishing boats go out in the mornings. They are row-boats with sharp pointed bows, and are family affairs manned by Pa, Ma, and the children. Auntie, Uncle, and the cousins are often in another boat. Between them a net is laid and painstakingly gathered in. The women and girls do their full share at the oars or with the net. I used to watch a little girl of about twelve in a gay mauve dress at work with her parents, enjoying every moment, by the look of her. The small fish are sold close by. Some go to make fasikh, a salted fishy substance with a smell all its own for pungency.

There are steam barges too on the Nile, that carry down great bales of cotton to be spun in the factories near Alexandria or to be shipped to Liverpool and the West. Some of it is the finest cotton in the world. These barges come upstream again with cargoes of all sorts, often with machinery, pumps, cars, tractors, and all that modern Egyptian agriculture needs. These barges are less picturesque than the sailing ships, and have nothing to compare with the sweep of the great masts, but they make up for it by a sort of fussy liveliness. Their crew have more room, and often express their personalities by growing something green in a petrol tin. These tins are then white-washed, as a sort of insurance, I always think—if the plants do not flourish well, at least the tins will look gay.

The skippers are apt to bring these barges up to the wharves with a wild sweep and rush, a scatter of foam, and much shrill hooting; I watched one such arrive with an extra dash and swirl and yet with great skill. On looking more closely, I was astonished to see a woman at the helm.

After the craft and the people, the birds take place of honour on the Nile. The white herons fly in parties up or down stream to their roosting places at sundown or at sunrise; but at any time of the day there seem to be a few on their way hither and thither, in companies of four or eight. They fly close to the water usually, but never have I seen them go under the bridges, though there would be plenty of room. No, up they have to come with effort, into the wind if there is one, over the bridge, and down again the other side. Why, I wonder? Is it in protest against such innovations across their river? The Pharaohs built no bridges. They had more consideration. Some of the bird life of Egypt is very ancient, and is beautifully depicted on tomb walls. About ninety different sorts are identifiable in Ancient Egypt from their descendants known in Egypt of today. The kites (newcomers by comparison with others) scavenge much off the face of the Nile. They take the most lovely swoops and remove the most revolting offal from the water, hardly damping a claw in the process. Out of the towns the mud edges of the river are full of bird life, from the miniature ringed plovers to great grey herons fishing in solemn solitude.

Once, on a Nile steamer in Upper Egypt I awoke early. The dawn had painted all the scene shell pink. On a shell pink island in the shell pink water was a flock of pelican. I can hardly use the words 'shell pink' again, but actually that was the colour of their wings as they held them up to catch the morning sun. These birds are not seen further north on the river banks, but sometimes they fly high up in the sky over Cairo, specks only discernible by keen eyes, but they, no doubt, high though they are, steer their course by the shimmer of Nile below them.

How rough and wild the Nile can sometimes be when a khamseen wind whips it up to tawny waves, lion-like in colour and in fury! The sun is then obliterated by fine dust which gets into one's very teeth, and harsher sand that drives with cutting force against one's face. But more often the river is still the servant of Egypt, not her master. On such an evening we came home from visiting the twelfth dynasty tombs at Beni Hassan. We had ridden through green clover fields as the sun lowered, on donkeys with just a piece of sacking for saddle. It can be a comfortable clip-clop when you are used to it, sitting well back with feet out for balance. As the sun touched the horizon, we climbed into an old boat to ferry slowly across the Nile. It took some time, for there was not much wind. The scent of beans in flower was carried to us by a light mist. Every hue of the sunset was reflected in the water. The old man crouching by the tiller sang a meandering song, well tuned to the evening and the mood. It was dark when we reached the further bank. Nothing particular had happened on that journey, but it had become easier to understand why the Nile had been the focus of emotion for so many men and women for so many thousand years, in life and in death.

Death came to my father, Frederick Terry Rowlatt, the last of Amelia's sons, in March, 1950. He had always hoped to die in Egypt and this wish was granted. It would have been a satisfaction to his grandmother, Sarah Terry, who always so hoped to return to Egypt herself, to know that the grandson who bore her name lived and died peacefully there, loved and respected by Egyptians high and low, rich and poor.

During his last illness, in addition to his friends' inquiries, some apparent strangers, unknown and humble workers, used to stop me and ask after him. At his death, families of past servants came continually to express their sorrow, some from quite far away, many in tears. It was the end of an era.

"He gave his heart to the country of his adoption," wrote a correspondent in *The Times* at his death. "In the bank long after he had ceased to be Governor, he was referred to by humbler members of the staff as 'our father'." The Arabic radio programme spoke of him; and an editorial in the *Egyptian Gazette* described him as "a man of whom both Britain and Egypt could be proud." His mother and father would have wished for no better epitaph for their son. Among the many Egyptians at my father's funeral was our old retired gardener whose son was then our head gardener. As the coffin passed down the aisle of the Anglican Cathedral, he stood erect in his pew, a dignified though toothless figure, and gave a military salute which would have done credit to a guardsman,

My father's brother, Charles, had died in England a few months earlier. Charles in England, and Frederick in Cairo, kept up a regular correspondence. The family enthusiasm for sending Egyptian vegetable seeds all round the world, in which they had indulged for over a hundred years, was still going strong. In one of Charles's last letters to his brother, when they were both old men, he writes: "Would it be giving you any trouble, bother or difficulty to send along a small tin of Eruca Sativa, better known as gargir. . . . Perhaps it would be possible to send it by air mail; even some loose seeds in an envelope would be welcome."

Six weeks later he writes: "I enclose three leaves of gargir to show you how it likes the climate." He had also asked for a piece of Arab bread, to remind him of the old days. "The bit of Arab bread pleased me much and was quite edible.... I feel that I think of the past times in Egypt too much. I wish I had the desert to walk in, as you have, and find therein as you do the peace of mind that modern conditions of rush, vulgarity and bad manners tend to eliminate."

Although with the death of Frederick Rowlatt all official connection with Egypt ceased for our immediate family, yet more than a century of life there does not die quickly in the veins.

Unloading tibn at the wharf near Old Cairo

13

SOMETHING NEW

THE next time I visited Egypt was in January, 1954, eighteen months after the start of the Revolution. As the aeroplane landed gently on the runway in the desert, and the passenger after so effortless a journey had but to step forth from his armchair on to Egyptian soil, I could not help contrasting the journey with some of our family trips in the past, back and forth between English and Egyptian homes. Those drawn-out adventurous travels of Sarah and Sidney Terry's, or the Victorian bustle and fuss of my grandparents' days; a Fan-Tag they then called it. "There was not a Fan-Tag when they started on Thursday week," runs a letter of 1885, "but Fred says there was one when they left Paris, and Pa thought they would miss the train and poor Ma had to hurry into the omnibus eating and hugging a bottle of wine which alas slipped through her arms on to the platform and smashed, leaving a stream of red fluid."

The Fan-Tags had not diminished much in my own youth. Especially on the day when two of us, both under four, wandered round the pile of waiting trunks just before the start, tearing strips off all the newly applied gummy labels that we could reach. They were the old-fashioned type covered with information about what was needed in cabins, what for the hold, and so forth. We found that we could just loosen the corners with our fingers, and then, of course, to tear them into curling ribbons of paper was irresistible.

Nannies, governesses, French maids, deck chairs, sewing machines and babies' baths all featured among the personnel and paraphernalia of these journeys. Bank messengers flitted round the scene, lifting the children out of carriages, into trains, over luggage and through barriers. One old Bank servant nearly lost the friendship I had felt for him during my early years of life by insisting on lifting me around for quite a year after I was able to lift myself. But he realised the error of his ways and we were friends once more before the situation had become critical. His son, now an old man himself, sits in honourable leisure in the Bank, outside the Governor's office. Musing thus I walked over to the Custom House and airfield offices. Pictures of the past soon faded from my mind as I prepared to deal with the present.

Almost at once I realised that there was indeed something new about the place. Quietly and efficiently our passports were dealt with. There was a notice up saying, "Welcome to Egypt", and another asking us to give no tips. I rather wonderingly complied with the latter and to my surprise was not asked for a tip from the porter. That was food for thought.

A few days later when strolling near the Muski I hesitated for a moment while debating where to go next. A quiet spoken policeman stepped forward and asked in perfect English if he could help me. I thanked him, explaining the position and he moved on. This was my first encounter with the newly formed body of men called Tourist Police whose main function is to see that visitors are not pestered for baksheesh or cheated. I saw more of them later on and saw how they did their work unobtrusively and well. But I also found that in some cases the anti-baksheesh spirit was spreading without compulsion. More than once I had a tip politely refused when there was no question of authoritative disapproval.

One cannot write about the everyday Egyptian without mentioning the vexed question of baksheesh for it has unfortunately been very frequently expected and demanded too. Yet

I do believe that the true nature of the poorer Egyptian is largely made up of the giving nature as opposed to the getting, and that the baksheesh habit, long established though it is, has to a certain extent come in the wake of irresponsible visitors. Lucie Duff Gordon, writing in Egypt about eighty-five years ago, said the same thing. When well off the beaten track, she found there was no demand for baksheesh at every turn. I too have happy memories of country people and town people whose characteristics have been just the opposite. There was a baker, for instance, with a little oven in a side street of Cairo below the Citadel. We stopped in our walk to watch him baking his flat round loaves. He was a jovial individual wearing a sackcloth apron and endowed by nature with a round shining face. Without stopping his work he would crack jokes and banter with any passer-by as he wielded his long-handled wooden shovel on which each loaf was put into the oven. He took no notice of us, till as we moved to leave he called out: "Here—wait a minute. You can't go without your loaf. You watched it being baked—of course it's yours." He threw it across to us, insisting that we took it as a present.

My mind also turns to an old peasant plodding along a Delta road north of Cairo in clean white turban and blue galabia. The sun was hot in spite of the eucalyptus trees lining the road, and the way was long, so we stopped the car and offered him a lift which he gladly accepted. As we pushed up to make room for him in the car he explained how he was visiting his son who had a job in town. Before getting out close to his destination he undid the basket he was carrying and pressed upon us handfuls of ripe apricots from those he was taking to his son. Nor would he listen to our protesting that his boy should have them and not us. It was a payment for the lift he said, and was obviously happy when we accepted them in that spirit with thanks.

Unfortunately the members of the population who pester for baksheesh have often made themselves felt more than their pleasanter neighbours. Most visitors, alas, only come across the desperately persistent seller of souvenirs. I feel for him; he has mouths to feed and a living to make. But his importunities can try one high. One way to end his petitioning is to address him in the language of his own people and in their manner: "Listen, son of my paternal uncle. I do not wish for scarabs from the tomb of Tutankhamen. I myself have twenty in a cupboard at home which I too am desirous of selling at fifteen piastres each." Such a speech, in which it is of course mutually recognised that accuracy plays no part, will gain its end and in some strange way create a bond, whereas rudeness is ineffective or worse. A beggar too will nearly always accept the two words "*Al Allah*" which commend him to God. If it is kindly meant and given, he leaves with no remuneration and no ill-will. Such conversations being beyond the linguistic reach of most visitors the Tourist Police fill a very needed rôle.

Having also old friends among guides and souvenir sellers of the other school of thought, I could not but be amused to hear their side of the question. "If I was on top of the Great Pyramid," said one rascal, "and I did a deal with a visitor, one of the Tourist Police would see me through a telescope and would be waiting for me when I came down—what a life!"

Although large organised tours are on the increase again, it is not easy for such a man now that the really wealthy tourist is *rara avis*. One hopes that part of his compensation may come from the added interest being taken by the Egyptian public in visiting and studying their own antiquities. Quite humble families now visit the museums too, and take an interest in what they see there. It is not only the men who go, but whole family parties, children, babies, grandmothers, uncles, etc. I do not think that the visiting peasant or his town brother take a markedly intellectual interest but they view the exhibits with obvious admiration, awe and enjoyment. I watched an old street vendor type of man going the rounds of the Tutankhamen treasures. The policeman who is always on guard there was explaining it to him in his own way, addressing the old man affectionately as "my uncle."

It was during this visit of 1954 that I saw one of the Mena camel-men who used to accompany us every Saturday afternoon so long ago when I was a small child. We talked about past days and then he took it upon himself to describe to me the details of the recent discovery of the famous solar boats near the Great Pyramid. This was not in any attempt to play the dragoman to his own benefit but just through interest in the subject. Actually very little of the discovery had been made public at that point so he had to draw heavily on his imagination. I took with a large pinch of salt his description of the silken hangings discovered on the walls of the underground rock recess surrounding the boats.

One thing that struck me much that year, was the way in which the public gardens in and around Cairo seemed to be more appreciated than ever by the populace. They were especially full of family parties of picnickers and young people playing games. The games idea has taken hold of the nation to a marked degree. And following sports on a large scale is now a favourite pastime of the man in the street. Football matches are watched by every sort of male, from street urchins to high dignitaries of the Government. Their enthusiasm is most vociferous and they take their seats hours beforehand. At the same time, most waste bits of ground in the town have a small boys' football match in progress winter or summer, though the ball may be nothing more than a bundle of rags tied in ball formation and the players barefooted.

The time of conscript army training has given many young Egyptians a good chance of showing any exceptional athletic ability that they may have. Football and hockey players of great prowess have been thus discovered. And more than one of Egypt's remarkable cross-Channel swimmers have had their preliminary training in the army swimming baths. It is a sport to which they seem naturally addicted. The small boys who dive off the Nile boats to cool themselves in summer, swim against the strong brown current with amazing strength.

I recently watched this same sport demonstrated to perfection by quite a different type of Egyptian. The exponents were well-to-do girls from a select school, aged between about ten and seventeen. Their forbears would have been startled, for the female population were not encouraged to such feats until comparatively lately. As I sat there admiring them, a memory of Egyptian bathing belles of a generation ago came into my mind—a very different picture.

It was at Helwan where we were occasionally sent as children to recover from chicken pox or some like affliction. The place is well known for its sulphur springs which are most beneficial for some rheumatic conditions. As well as the proper thermal baths there used to be an open air swimming pool of thick sulphurous liquid, where for a piastre or two anyone could have a bathe. A visit here on the day reserved for women and children was a great treat. Our fellow bathers were usually two or three Egyptian women of the people, who wore as bathing dresses their ordinary ankle-length day dresses. How they giggled and laughed as they splashed around! Though none seemed able to swim, not surprisingly in those clothes, yet they enjoyed themselves immensely. When we dived head first into the pea soup they were loud in their cheers and admiration. Admittedly it was rather a venture to dive into these waters. They were full of little vermicelli type of objects—sulphur worms we called them—but I have no idea whether they were animal, vegetable or mineral, nor do I think even Sir Mortimer Wheeler would have hazarded a guess. We liked to horrify our governess, though she was inured to much, by swearing that these objects moved in the liquid. But we were never quite sure if this was because we troubled the waters ourselves or whether they did it of their own volition. Anyhow I regret to say that, what with braving the sulphur worms and being able to swim and dive, we were apt to show off disgracefully to our admiring audience of Egyptian ladies. I could not help remembering this scene as I watched those modern Egyptian girls in their smart bathing dresses demonstrating so unselfconsciously their complete mastery of the water.

The Egyptian woman of today is showing her mastery of more than that however. There is hardly a profession which she and her sisters do not grace. They are doctors, dentists, university lecturers, chemists and journalists. And the keenness with which some of them train for social welfare is inspiring.

One hot morning I knocked on a door in a little town outside Cairo. The knock produced a rattle of keys and the door was opened. It had been locked for it was the entrance to a girls' reformatory, though once inside all thoughts of prison vanished. The girls were housed in what had been a private house. It was austerely furnished but was light and airy. There was nothing repressive in the atmosphere, nor in the children's behaviour. They were aged roughly from ten to fifteen and all had been convicted in the juvenile courts, mostly for theft. Some had bad homes and some had no homes, but this place had now become home to them.

The Egyptian lady in charge was not the type who exudes efficient enthusiasm, pointing out this and that about the place rather more loudly than is necessary and rather more rapidly than one can digest. She was shy and quiet; only with difficulty could I extract information from her. No amount of mere information however could account for the atmosphere of the place. That was bred of human caring.

One of the visiting staff took me into a class where the girls were learning how to tell the time by the clock. An elementary lesson for twelve year olds one might have thought, but most of them had come from quarters where few people had money enough to spend on watches, and anyhow no one had bothered to teach them such things before. It was a pleasantly informal sort of lesson that developed by degrees into a discussion of what this particular class could do to show their appreciation of one of their mistresses who was about to leave for work elsewhere. One child expressed the thought that they should show by some means how sorry they were to lose her, but that it was important that they did not make her feel so sad at going that she arrived at her new post undermined by the general air of grief her leaving had caused. Those were not her exact words but that was the idea, which struck me as quite an advanced one in the realm of human understanding. I knew the particular social worker who did much of their training and knew that such thoughtfulness was typical of her, but it was interesting to see it spontaneously expressed in their own way by these girls who had unconsciously imbibed it from her.

The next suggestion was that we should all go into the playground and they would show me some of the songs and dances they had been inventing. Out they went, noisily and in a rush. The teacher and I were ensconced under an apricot tree in the shade while the class did their turn. We were extremely hot by now for it was summer, added to which it was in the month of Ramadan and some of the older girls were fasting—from their own convictions, there being no ruling for them on the matter. So I expected the performance to wilt slightly as it proceeded. But no sooner was one dance over than the next began. They were simple affairs of handclapping and circling round to the accompaniment of chanted verses on praiseworthy subjects. But they did it wholeheartedly for it was their own creation.

At the end of the visit I asked the superintendent if there was any little thing I could do for the establishment in return for their welcome. She hesitatingly said that there was not enough money this year to buy a certain drink which all Egyptians think is nearly as necessary for celebrating the feast after Ramadan, as we think plum pudding is for Christmas. A comparatively small sum would buy enough for all the girls. I produced this, which was handed over to one of the head girls who is now so trustworthy that she is often sent out on errands involving cash. Off she went in high glee to a neighbouring grocer's shop and back she came with the stuff. It was not the drink proper but the substance out of which the drink was to be made. It is a thick brown paste of pulped apricot, and is bought by surface measurement, as if it were linoleum, to which unprepossessing substance it bears a remarkable likeness. The arrival of this was hailed as the event of the day and it was carefully put away against the coming feast.

Egyptian social welfare done in the spirit I saw there that morning is bringing great good to the country. It is naturally not all of top quality. But the right ideas seem to be gaining ground even if it is uphill work; and in which country is it all on the level?

Although so many careers are now open to the Egyptian girl, training in the arts of homemaking are not forgotten. A friend of mine is headmistress of a large school for girls. Her pupils are the children of educated parents who are mostly in positions of responsibility. These girls can stay on after their general education and take a training in cooking, dressmaking and other aspects of homecraft. I rang up on my arrival in Cairo and my friend, the headmistress, gave me a warm welcome. An American educationalist was visiting the school the next day and would I come too?

On arrival our first call was paid on a class of fourteen-year-olds who were having an English lesson. *The Vicar of Wakefield* was their textbook. They were happy and eager to tell us of what they were learning. The incident of the shagreen spectacle cases particularly took their fancy. But as our time was limited that morning we concentrated on visiting the older girls who were doing the domestic training. To our surprise we found that we were to be treated by them to a regular mid-morning meal, every detail of which had been prepared by themselves. They had cooked the sweetmeats and cakes, embroidered the table napkins, decorated the room, done the flowers and even painted some of the pictures which hung on the walls. When it came to pouring out tea for me much care was taken to do it in the true English style to which they felt I was accustomed. They both acted as hostesses to us and waited upon us with outgoing charm. Some of these young ladies were already engaged to be married, but instead of rushing off from school to a pre-wedding social round they had chosen to stay on here and learn more of the arts of homemaking.

In so many ways and on so many levels I sensed a feeling out for new values and new thinking; and for new ways of expressing those values and thought. The ordinary people are thinking and are eager for knowledge. It is evident in many a daily touch. I asked a taxi driver to take me to a place in a street with an ex-royal name; this led to the following conversation: "All kings and queens are bad," he shouted backwards through the window partition as we sped along, missing people and things by a last minute skilful turn of the wheel. To this I replied that there did happen to be a certain Queen whom we particularly loved and admired. "You mean Elizabeth," he said, "well she's different. She does not do everything herself. She does not bring in new governments and then turn them out again at will. Churchill and the others do that with her, don't they?"

Circumstances played into my hands on this visit to Egypt from the point of view of hearing what the ordinary man in the street was thinking about. It was the first time in Cairo without the old house waiting to be dropped into, and without a car and all the independence of movement which that means. They were lacks which made one sad in many ways, and it needed a definite decision of the will even to approach the old home which is now used as offices by the army. But severe as the losses were, they were also the door to new experiences which brought riches of their own. One good result was the added touch with all and sundry brought about by travelling in public buses for the first time. This bus service is one of the best features of new Egypt.

Here I met a wealth of natural good manners from fellow travellers. It was rare for a young man not to give up his seat if the bus were full, and on one journey I was even offered a seat by an artisan type of young man quietly and politely, not because I was without one but because he thought his seat was a better one than mine. There were exceptions here and there to this rule of good manners. Students wandering in twos and threes in the public gardens or the road, having nothing particular to do at the moment, would sometimes make some personal remarks in Arabic or English of a cheeky nature. When I turned round and faced them, looking I hope, more grieved than angry, and asked in Arabic if that was their idea of good manners, they more than once apologised and went about their business in chastened mood. But the manners of those who were neither bored nor idle were exemplary.

I came across many young men and women, some in humble circumstances, who were eager to improve their knowledge of English. An English friend of mine was coming to Cairo by bus from a neighbouring suburb. On the seat next to her was an ordinary Egyptian policeman. He had a thick book much marked by study, on his knees. After a while he asked politely if she would read some of it to him there and then to help him with the pronunciation. "It is by a very great writer," he added. It was the works of Shakespeare and for the next twenty minutes' bus ride my friend read aloud lines of the Bard of Avon to an appreciative Egyptian policeman. A surprising number of people knew a surprising amount of English compared to several years ago. In most cases they had learnt it in the ordinary free government schools. The waitings lists for schools run by English or Americans on the lines of those countries were full to over-flowing by applications from parents who could afford them. They said plainly that they wished their children to have such an education because of the character building they felt their sons and daughters would get thereby. The responsibility of this trust is obviously large.

Everyone knows of the tragic events of the preceding years, but by 1954 even before the Suez Canal Zone agreement was reached there seemed to me no trace of animosity visible in the behaviour of the people outside the Zone. The reverse seemed truer. I had a short chat with a policeman, for instance, who was at pains to say how much he hoped our countries would be able to work together in accord. "If God wills, it will be so," said he.

I was in Cairo on the morning that the headings of the Canal Zone agreement were settled. Bands of young men paraded the streets here and there bearing banners with suitable mottoes but looking rather uncertain if they were meant to register triumph over an enemy or mutual congratulations between friends. They were quite peaceful though, and the authorities soon told them to go back to their work. One small boy of about ten or eleven, as he saw me pass by, acquired as savage an expression as he could muster, and said, "The English are going!" To which I replied that for the most part we were equally pleased about it, whereupon his face broke into a friendly smile for no deep political reason but because he liked being talked to, I think.

People one knew, newspaper sellers, small shopkeepers and so on, came out of their way to say how pleased they were that agreement had been reached. Further down the street I saw a group of young men talking keenly on the pavement. Ah, thought I, let us pass by and hear what they have to say on the matter. As I approached I found they were in ardent debate about the merits or demerits of a washing machine displayed to view in the shop window near by.

At about this time I found myself attending a gathering in a small Delta town north-west of Cairo. It was a Coptic Catholic festival which included mass, several baptisms, church school entertainments and light refreshments. The baptisms were conducted with ancient ceremonies that linked the naked, howling baby with the very dawn of the Christian church in Egypt, almost within living memory of Christ on earth. As the baby was dipped into a portable tub, the noise of cymbals and old chants formed a background for the zagharit of the women. This is a high pitched trilling made with the tongue and indulged in on festive occasions by Moslem and Christian women alike.

The community being poor had a very practical arrangement of glass doors which when closed divided the altar from the nave. Having shut these after mass, they proceeded briskly to remove some of the pews and clear the scene for the secular part of the ceremonies. Thus one building served two purposes. The women and babies now joined the men and boys; they had sat separately in the transept during the service. Having just seen the ancient ecclesiastical link with the past I was now to feel the present-day link of the human heart which springs from shared experiences. How warm are these links forged by observing small incidents take the same unintentioned turn as similar small incidents take in one's own surroundings! Here were the under-fives piping away at a lengthy rigmarole dealing with the adventures of a cat, which having ended, they instantly began again. Even applause could not stop them. A Coca-Cola bottle opened nearby in preparation for later refreshment brought all their eyes swivelling off centre to half right. Their thoughts plainly surrounded the Coca-Cola but the tale of the cat did not even hesitate—it streamed steadily on. Eventually an elder sister at the back of the audience, bearing it no longer, stood up, waving her arms at them and cried, "*Bas, Bas!*" "Enough, enough!" And then they subsided.

A nine-year-old now took the stage, apparently a placid, wavy-haired child. But suddenly, like a revolver shot, he hurls at the village audience an impassioned speech in classical Arabic. Its theme is love of Egypt, desire to die for her sake, resolution so to do, the devotion she inspires, and so on. His eyes are fiery and intense. Even his small knee caps twitch with the nervous energy and emotion he lets forth. He thumps the table with his fist. The force behind his treble voice would have reached an audience four times the size of the peasants, local police officer and priest there assembled. It was with relief that I noted how instantly, with the last word declaimed, he reverted from flaming patriot to ordinary little boy. But it made one think.

The next item was interesting. Two boys of about eighteen enacted a little play called *False Civilisation*. One, the husband, sits worried and supperless wondering what has kept his wife out so late. In comes his wife (the other lad) decked up European fashion, tight emerald-green coat, two handbags and much jewellery. "She" explains her absence by two hours at the hairdresser, one to recover in at a restaurant, and two hours at the cinema—all absolutely necessary. Some of the Arabic cracks were lost on me but the audience were spellbound, alternately horrified in silence at such behaviour or vociferously amused. Some of it was extremely humorous. Small children gazed open-eyed and open-mouthed. The moral was further stressed by showing the husband arriving late at work next morning, as a result of his home life, and promptly getting the sack.

Just behind the actors, through the light glass door, stood the altar and the Cross. There were Moslems present as well as the Copts. The simple admiring families, young and old, drank it all in.

The normal instruction in government elementary schools is also imbibed with enthusiasm by the pupils. My mind turns to a little girl of about seven encountered in a suburb of Cairo. She was wandering home from school and was waiting for a friend who was late; as neither of us seemed in a hurry we had a chat. On my asking her how she liked school she lifted her eyes to heaven and said with earnest emphasis, "*Madrassa helwa!*" "School is sweet!" Probably her grandmother and possibly her mother were unable to write their names. And yet one is reminded that literacy is not a goal in itself but only a step to goals of varying worth. What sort of an Egypt do all these young people inherit?

It was during a visit in 1948 that I was first aware of a ferment not far below the surface. There were fine plans talked of to alleviate disease, ignorance and poverty. But plans that never leave the paper stage because of vested interests do not, alas, help the poor. Some of these plans did develop further, to the bricks and mortar stage. But it is a useless and very expensive hobby to build first-rate hospitals in outlying districts, if doctors will not staff them because there is no cinema near enough for their wives to go to. A village maternity clinic rather loses its point if the impoverished mother finds that only with a tip in hand does she get attention. A country could as profitably build itself lath and plaster cinema sets of welfare institutions. The truth of this was being realised.

There were also notably unselfish efforts of determined Egyptians, both official and private, who were trying to bring improvements to pass. They were pouring out goodwill and energy into these efforts; but too many were in danger of being bogged down by their inability or unwillingness to pull strings, and the battle to refrain from using bad means to reach seemingly good ends. These people were the first to admit that all effort to help their under-privileged compatriots depended finally on the spirit in which the work was carried out—in fact, that it dominated everything.

Improved standards of living are still desperately needed today. In spite of the charm and fascination of the old quarters of Cairo, the poverty and overcrowding of the people is striking. Water is available at occasional pumps, here and there, but has to be paid for in cash by the tinful. And when a numerous family lives on a few shillings a day, there is little to spare for washing. Sanitation is non-existent in many areas and signs of disease are evident in too many of the passers-by. A terrifying percentage of Egyptians are partly or totally blind and the infant mortality is among the highest in the world.

The huge, complicated problem of drug addiction holds thousands in its grip. In many cases it is intimately connected with illness. The Egyptian peasant falls a prey in vast numbers to the germ bilharzia, which inhabits Nile water where there are insanitary conditions. It is a debilitating disease, rather than a killing one, but its weakening effect can be very marked and many find that the taking of some drug temporarily revives them, though disaster follows later. Under-nourishment, too, plays a part in starting drug habits.

The International Anti-Narcotics Bureau, in co-operation with the Egyptian police, have done wonderful work in stopping the drugs from entering the country, but at one time it was so bad that some unprincipled building firms were partly paying their workmen in drugs instead of money. It was the poor Egyptian who suffered so terribly from this scourge, but in nine cases out of ten, it was a European who traded in the drug and profited by the ill-gotten gains.

There have been encouraging improvements in this vast drug problem, but in some ways the roots of the problem remain. Many poor people, unable to get hashish or the far worse "white" drugs, have found that the liquid resulting from tea leaves being boiled and brewed for hours produces an artificially stimulating condition. This practice is very popular.

These are some of the obvious evils which worried Egyptians of goodwill in those pre-revolution years, as indeed they still do, but there were others which caused anxiety, and frustration, among those who loved their country.

The King's manner of life was an extreme case, and noticeable, owing to his position; but indulgence, dishonesty, and corruption were frighteningly widespread. Their stranglehold was such that had someone then prophesied that the Egyptian body politic would shortly throw up a group of men who would successfully unseat the monarch and challenge what they felt he stood for, such a prophet would have been laughed to scorn.

Yet, as all the world knows, it has happened. Farouk went rapidly and bloodlessly. The present rulers of Egypt are having to face squarely all these internal problems, numerous and onerous.

With my father's death, all official connection with Egypt ceased for his immediate family. England is now our permanent home; and if we go to Egypt for a month or two from time to time we go as visitors. But over a hundred years of human touch and happiness does not die quickly in the heart and mind, in fact it does not die at all if the relationships which produced it are adjusted to meet the altered circumstance. To wish for old times to revive in the form known is at best idle and at worst retrograde. Change there has to be, and change there most certainly should be. But the important thing is surely that these changes should lead to something creative, positive and unifying. And to be of real value, this should be a link born of the spirit and mutually forged by either side through a partnership in which patronage has no place.

The Mahboubahs and Mohameds, the Fatimas and Mahmouds, who for years have felt part of our family, seem to sense this in their own way. Having now no home or official setting in Egypt, my mother and I recently stayed in an hotel in Cairo. Into the hall comes one of our past gardeners. We had left him four years ago, a lanky lad, now he was a married man and a father. He was carrying an armful of flowers for us. We naturally remonstrated with him, knowing full well that they had come from the garden of his present Egyptian employers. "That's all right," he replied, "they know that I am giving them to you." Much of Egypt is like that, ready to give openly as she seeks new ways of thought and action to express the stirrings within her. The attitude of the West to this new budding, and even more important, the way the West itself lives, will play a vital part in determining the quality and colour of the open flower.

ADDENDUM

This article by Mary Rowlatt appeared in Middle East International, July 1974, and is reproduced here with permission.

GOVERNESS TO A PRINCESS

Although the contemporary social history of Arab countries is of great intrinsic value, a further significance can often be added by viewing it against some aspects of their recent past. The substance of this article comes from a now rare book by Ellen Chennells, "Recollections of an Egyptian Princess by her English Governess", published by William Blackwood in 1893.

The copy in my possession was given by the authoress to my grandmother, Amelia Rowlatt, who lived in Egypt in the early eighteen-seventies and knew Miss Chennells. Another personal link comes through my maternal grandfather, J.E. Cornish, who was also in Egypt at that time and was employed by the Khedive Ismail to build some of the sugar factories mentioned in this text.

IN October 1871 Miss Ellen Chennells arrived in Egypt to take up her post with the twelve year-old Princess Zeinab, daughter of the Ortangi Khanem or Middle Lady, one of the Khedive Ismail's three wives. Above and below her in rank were the Buyuk Khanem and the Kutschuk Khanem (the Great Lady and the Little Lady). This child Zeinab was half-sister to the late ex-King Fouad, for he was a younger son of

Ismail's by another member of the harim; consequently Zeinab would have been aunt to the late ex-King Farouk had their lives overlapped.

When Miss Chennells arrived in Cairo she was given quarters in a house on the Shoubra Road, which was then a fashionable avenue of sycamore and acacia trees. She shared this house with Mr. and Mrs. Freeland, their three small children and a Mr. Mitchell. The two gentlemen were tutors to Zeinab's eleven year-old brother, Ibrahim Pasha, for the Khedive planned to send him to Oxford University in course of time. Mr. Mitchell's special duty was to teach the small boy Latin and Greek.

Miss Chennells first saw her pupil on the second day after her arrival. Early in the morning Princess Zeinab was driven out to Shoubra from the Cairo palace in an English carriage with an English groom in attendance. Two white-clad Egyptian "syces", carrying long staves, ran beside the carriage for the whole way. Zeinab was always accompanied by her slave companion, a Circassian girl of about her own age, called Kopses. They shared everything—lessons and amusements, treats and punishments. Young Ibrahim Pasha also had his slave companion, Shefket, an Ethiopian boy with whom he likewise shared his daily routine.

Miss Chennells had not long been attached to the Khedive's household before much talk arose about a proposed trip up the Nile. Zeinab and Ibrahim, Kopses and Shefket were to take part in it together with their educational staff. Uncertainty about the date of departure caused poor Miss Chennells much worry, for she had heard that a few hours notice was usually thought sufficient for any move. "Bearing in mind the periodical cares of the laundry," she wrote, "often made me seriously contemplate the possibility of substituting paper for linen."

She begged the child to warn her the moment she heard anyone mention a possible date. Zeinab duly asked her mother for co-operation on this matter, but the Ortangi

Khanem was much amused at the idea of needing time to prepare for such a trip. Zeinab explained to her governess that wardrobes did not exist but that everything was kept in boxes. Her mother's seventeen attendants each had charge of some special line of clothing and each Princess had her own laundry staff. All these slaves accompanied their mistress on any such progress. "So," as Miss Chennells dryly commented, "there is no accumulation of work."

One morning, in December 1871, Zeinab told her governess that the Nile trip was to start "the day after to-morrow". Miss Chennells went into instant Victorian action. By the day after tomorrow she stood at the ready in every detail. But Zeinab and Kopses turned up for their lessons as on an ordinary morning. The proposed trip was not even mentioned. Similar announcements, with like results, took place more than once in the ensuing weeks.

At last came an official message that all were to be on board that very afternoon—only personal things need be taken, everything else would be found. Miss Chennells was on board by 4 p.m. but discovered, to her dismay, that "there were no arrangements for dinner, no lamps or tablesticks, no bedroom crockery for washing". Back she went to Shoubra, collected some necessities and returned by moonlight.

The holiday fleet consisted of six large steamers and seven "dahabias". The royal party and their immediate attendants, including French maids and an Armenian doctor, all had cabins in the steamers. The English educational staff were chagrined to discover that their sleeping quarters were on a small "dahabia" towed behind the steamer in which the children were accommodated. They could only join their charges in the early morning when the river cortege was still moored to the bank and only return to their quarters when the ships stopped again at night.

The first halt was alongside the village of Badrashain, from where they were to visit Sakara. The Khedive's wives were the first to set forth, driving in two carriages accompanied by several eunuchs. A donkey-riding group followed, consisting of Miss Chennells, the tutors, the four pupils and their special dragoman. It took two hours to reach Sakara on their donkeys, through the palm trees and desert.

Twentieth century tourists know "Mariette's House" at Sakara, where refreshments are now sold, though many have no idea why it is so named. But at the time of this khedivial visit the great French Egyptologist was living in this "roughest of houses", as Miss Chennells called it, as he was excavating close by under Ismail's patronage. On this day Mariette was turned out of his house and it was handed over for the use of the harim. Large tents had been pitched for the rest of the party. Mariette personally conducted the Khedive and his princesses into the underground tombs of the sacred bulls. When they came out the rest of the party went in. The cavernous passage past the sarcophagi was lit by 300 candles held by Egyptian boys standing at attention on either side.

Miss Chennells describes the return journey: "We ran races with each other on our donkeys and there was nothing but laughter and merry voices to be heard. The Princess and her companion cantered gaily on, singing snatches of opera airs and exchanging with voluble tongue those little passages of wit and repartee which make mixed society so attractive to young people." At one point Miss Chennells found both her donkey and her donkey boy somewhat unmanageable. During the races her animal not only won but carried her far beyond the others before it slackened its pace. When at last it was walking along peacefully, she took out her note book to jot down some impressions. The donkey boy then caught up and without warning smote the donkey's rear. The inevitable happened. It bounded forward at a furious rate, scattering Miss Chennells' possessions. She clutched the reins however, and remained mounted. On arrival at the river the donkey boy had the cheek to ask for extra bakshish for the honour of having got the English lady there first. Luckily Mr. Freeland had chosen to walk back; he noticed something gleaming in the dust. It proved to be Miss Chennells' spectacles without which she might never have made notes of this trip, for she was very short sighted.

A day or two later Miss Chennells recounts how she woke as usual at 6 a.m., but decided not to get up immediately. She was still in bed when a message came to say that all the boats would set forth in half an hour, so would she transfer to the Princess' steamer at once. Apparently a female Victorian toilette could not be accomplished in that time, so she was left on the "dahabia" with no chance of breakfast or subsequent meals unless means were found to board the steamer. One of the crew offered her a little muddy water. "Had we known to what we should be exposed," she wrote, "we would have brought with us some preserved meat in tins, some Huntley & Palmers biscuits, tea, coffee and sugar and an Etna for boiling." But all ended well, for the Khedive happened to order a stop at Feshna to inspect some sugar mills.

More sugar factories were inspected that afternoon, this time at Minia. There was a palace here and Ismail decided that the whole party would spend several days at Minia. Royal salutes were fired and two long lines of soldiers held up awnings as walls on either side of the path from the river to the palace so that the harim could make their way in strict privacy. There was a subsidiary palace adjoining the Khedive's which had been built for the boy Ibrahim, and here lessons were to take place.

Miss Chennells taught in English one day and in French the next. The Khedive wished (virtually ordered) that the current set of lessons should consist wholly of Ancient Egyptian history in which Miss Chennells was luckily fairly well versed. Mariette's *Aperçu de 1'histoire d' Egypte* and Sharpe's *History of Egypt* were their text books. After work they joined the boys and their tutors, playing rounders or hide and seek, all together. Both the slave children happened to be more agile than the princely pair. But Miss Chennells remarked that Zeinab was as pleased with their triumphs as if they had been

her own. Of Kopses, the Circassian girl, their governess wrote:
"She has great vivacity and wonderful tact for so young a person; she never obtruded her opinions, but when required she expressed them with a free and independent bearing which to our preconceived ideas was totally inconsistent with slavery. Her manner to us was quite different from her behaviour in the harim. With us she was the free outspoken member of a free community—outspoken that is to say in what concerned exclusively European manners and ideas; in the harim, as I afterwards had full occasion to observe, she was the quiet, dignified Oriental, receiving notice from her superiors with profound respect but without a tinge of servility."

In between lessons and games the little girls demanded story-telling. Miss Chennells told them all the Bible stories relating to Egypt. Zeinab shed tears at the tale of Joseph and was ashamed of this until she saw that her governess too "was subject to the same weakness".

Meanwhile the Nile traffic steamed or sailed up and down the river. One morning Miss Chennells heard a strange humming noise as of many voices approaching. Then a steamer passed towing five huge flat-bottomed barges crowded with men, all forced labour press-ganged from their Upper Egypt villages to work on a stretch of railroad being built by the Khedive lower down the Nile. In contrast were the numerous smart boats, flying the English or American flag, which were privately hired by wealthy visitors doing the fashionable Nile trip.

The royal stay at Minia was abruptly ended after three weeks. At 10 a.m. one morning they were told that the party would be returning to Cairo by special train in a few hours time. The much looked-forward to trip to Luxor and beyond was off. Miss Chennells and the tutors felt that they and the children could have been sent on up the Nile while the Khedive had stayed all that time at Minia. "It is an Englishman's privilege to grumble," wrote Miss Chennells, "and we availed ourselves of this most heartily, between ourselves. Our pupils preserved the most impassable demeanour; it was His Highness' pleasure, and that was enough for them."

Years later, looking back on this month, Miss Chennells said that she felt it had been a happy time for the children, and it meant much to her that it had been so, as two years after this trip Zeinab was enclosed in the harim; at sixteen she married and at eighteen she died. Shefket, the Ethiopian boy, and then young Kopses, also died within the next few years.

In 1879 Ismail was deposed for his mismanagement of the country and his vast personal expenditure. Young Ibrahim, instead of going to Oxford, followed his father into exile and obscurity.

More than fifty years were to pass before Farouk, the last of that line, was also deposed and Egypt was ruled by a true-blooded Egyptian instead of by successive dynasties of Turco-Circassians, as had been the case for some 700 years past.

INDEX